THE ART OF
BUYING ART

THE ART OF BUYING ART

Alan Bamberger

LTB Gordonsart, Inc.
Phoenix, Arizona, U.S.A.

The Art of Buying Art
Alan Bamberger
© 2007 LTB Gordonsart, Inc.

Published in the United States of America by
LTB Gordonsart, Inc.
13201 N. 35th Ave, #B-20
Phoenix, AZ 85029 USA

Order Line:	800-892-4622
Offices:	602-253-6948
Fax:	602-253-2104
Email:	office@gordonsart.com
Internet:	*www.gordonsart.com*

All Gordon's titles, including additional copies of this book, may be ordered directly from the publisher.

ISBN 1-933295-20-1

The paper used in this publication meets the minimum requirements of American National Standard for Information Sciences -Permanence Paper for Printed Library Materials, ANSI Z39.48-1984.

Printed and bound in the United States of America
10 9 8 7 6 5 4 3 2 1

Contents

This introductory overview summarizes The Art of Buying Art method and its goals, and briefly discusses the method's four component parts – define, select, research, and buy.

The fine art marketplace is more complicated than ever. It's full of products that look and sound like original art, but are no more original than newspaper or magazine illustrations. This chapter will explain what makes a work of art original and teach you how to recognize and distinguish originals from reproductions or copies.

Before you can define what you like, you must first set aside any preconceived notions you have about art and approach the marketplace with an open mind. Doing so allows you to explore and discover the vast variety of art that's available for sale, respond to it, and begin to focus in on your preferences.

Learn how to describe your favorite art in terms that allow dealers and other fine arts professionals to pinpoint your tastes, work within your budget, and present you with the best pieces for viewing and possible purchase.

The art world is full of opinions about how to buy, who's hot, who's not, what to buy, where to buy it, and how much to pay. This chapter will help you to understand, digest, analyze, and act on what art people tell you.

Shopping for art is like shopping for any other product. No matter what type of art interests you, you can find it for sale at more than one venue. Learn how to locate and compare the various establishments that sell your favorite art.

Art dealers and art galleries are a fact of the art business. Finding the best art means learning to interact, communicate, and negotiate with the people who sell it. Get pointers on art dealer etiquette, how to spot the best dealers, who to trust, and who to watch out for.

Art galleries can be intimidating places for the uninitiated. This chapter will help reduce your art gallery anxieties by describing and explaining the physical characteristics of art gallery interiors. You'll also learn to make qualitative assessments based on what you see at particular galleries.

The best customers get the best art. Learn how to favorably position yourself in the art market hierarchy.

Buying directly from artists is very different than buying from dealers. Learn what those differences are and how to proceed when the artist is also the dealer.

Buying art with a keyboard and mouse is the new frontier of collecting. Learn basic facts about how online art buying works, how it differs from buying art in traditional ways, and how to progress from looking at art for sale to locating art you like and considering specific pieces for possible purchase.

This chapter summarizes common art-buying mistakes and explains how to avoid making them.

Knowing how to locate and evaluate information about art and artists is the cornerstone of intelligent buying. In this chapter, you'll learn how to gather and analyze data about any artist's career accomplishments.

Every piece of art can be evaluated in terms of its basic physical characteristics. This chapter defines those characteristics and explains how they impact a work of art's value and desirability.

Two of the most important, least-understood, and most abused documents in the art business are the certificate of authenticity (or COA) and the appraisal. Here you will learn what constitutes a valid COA and a valid appraisal, and how to recognize meaningless or inappropriate ones.

The ownership history of a work of art often affects its value and collectibility. Learn how to piece together such a history, evaluate it, record it, and maintain proper files on every work of art you own.

Experienced art buyers prefer works of art in perfect condition and not susceptible to problems in the future. This chapter talks about how to spot damage and potential condition problems, how condition affects value, and how to care for works of art so that they don't deteriorate over time.

Forgeries, scams, and misrepresentations are a small but significant part of the art business. Learn about different types of forgeries, how forgers operate, how to spot questionable works of art, how art can be misrepresented, how to recognize questionable sales practices, and how to avoid being taken advantage of.

This chapter explains the relationship between art and money and addresses topics like liquidity of art, art as investment, the different ways to value art, and why art prices fluctuate.

The markets for various types of art differ due to factors like stability, longevity, supply, demand, how accomplished artists are, how broad collector bases are, fashion, and what influential art experts do and say. This chapter compares various segments of the art market to certain types of equities in order to help clarify how value, collectibility, salability, and significance of those art market segments fluctuate over time.

Every work of art for sale has an asking price. This chapter teaches you how to evaluate the fairness of that price. Learn what to ask sellers about art prices, and how to use art price references to locate relevant sales records, track an artist's sales history, analyze price data, and assess an artist's or type of art's potential future in the marketplace.

Acknowledgements

A substantial number of people aided me in the writing of this book including art experts, art collectors, art dealers, other fine arts professionals, and everyday people who are interested in learning more about art. Much of their help was in the form of discussions, debates, questions, and the sharing of beliefs, feelings, and opinions about how art should be bought, sold, and collected. Their feedback on so many different topics was instrumental in the completion of my task. I would like to thank the following people for contributing to this book.

First of all, thanks to my wife, Louise. Without her support, this book would have been far more difficult to complete. Second, thanks to my two sons, Elliot and Nicholas, without whom I would have taken far fewer spontaneous breaks from my research and writing.

Special thanks to all the people from across the country who respond to my Art Talk column and to those from around the world who contact me through my website, *www.artbusiness.com*, with their letters, phone calls, faxes, and emails. You are the individuals who encouraged me to go beyond *Buy Art Smart* and who continue to guide me in my writing with your questions and requests for information about art, artists, and art collecting. Thanks also (in no particular order) to the art librarians at the main branches of the San Francisco and Oakland public libraries, the art librarians at the San Francisco Museum of Modern Art, Mark Simpson and Sally Mills of the Fine Arts Museums of San Francisco, Charles Campbell, Stacey Roman, Susan Friedewald, Kevin Mac Donnell, Paul Hertzmann and Susan Hertzig, Scot Levitt, Scott Haskins, Bob Conway, Thomas McKenna, Steve Rubenfaer, Bill Currier, Edan Hughes, Tom Hoepf and Connie Swaim of Antique Week, John Garzoli of Garzoli Gallery, Lisa Peters of Montgomery Gallery, Ruth Braunstein, Dr. Joseph Baird, Steve Newman, Ray Lewis, Mark and Colleen Hoffman of Maxwell Galleries, Tom Rarick, George Stern, and Harris Stewart.

Preface

Once upon a time, owning original art was not much more complicated than seeing something you liked, paying for it, taking it home, and hanging it – no questions asked. But that carefree era is gone. These days, buying art is serious business, and today's buyers are more concerned than ever about getting good art and good value for their money. Simply put, people want to spend wisely, no matter what they buy, and that's exactly what *The Art of Buying Art* teaches you when it comes to buying art.

Over the years, the basic principles involved in deciding whether or not to buy a work of art have stayed pretty much the same. Evaluation techniques and procedures remain constant. What has changed dramatically is access to information. On the whole, today's art buyers are (or can be) more informed than ever about what they buy. The internet is in large part responsible for these changes, especially with the proliferation of online art, artist, art gallery, art price, and art research databases. In that regard, you'll find the entirely revised, enlarged, and updated Appendices more than helpful.

While knowledge is far more accessible, so is misinformation – sometimes unintentional, other times deliberate. This means wending your way around the art world to find art that's right for you can get tricky every now and again. In response to this, you'll find plenty of updated tips, instructions, precautions, and recommendations to make sure your art-buying experience is a rewarding one. So prepare to become an educated, informed consumer and to learn *The Art of Buying Art*.

Part I: Define

The Art of Buying Art is a book for everyone who appreciates original art and would like to own some. You or anyone else can learn to locate quality works of art that you love and pay fair prices for them; no previous knowledge about art is necessary. In order to accomplish this goal, however, realize at the outset that the art business has become increasingly complex in recent years, and figuring out what you like in art and how to find it are not quite as straightforward as they used to be. These introductory chapters contain basic information that will help orient you as you begin your search for those special works of art that will provide you with a lifetime of enjoyment.

CHAPTER 1

Anyone Can Master The Art of Buying Art

There is no right or wrong art; there is no right or wrong reason for wanting to own art; and there is no right or wrong way to go about buying art. With these thoughts in mind, you are about to begin a book that deals not in rights and wrongs, but rather in suggestions and recommendations which stem from two basic assumptions about people who buy art:

- People prefer to buy good-quality art.

- People prefer to pay fair prices for the art that they buy.

All techniques and methods described in this text follow directly from these assumptions as a starting point. If you are like the great majority of art buyers, you too want good quality at fair prices – you want to master the art of buying art.

Unfortunately, most beginners feel anywhere from inadequate to totally helpless about the prospect of buying art "intelligently." Worse yet, they have little faith in their abilities to ever accomplish this goal. To them, art is a mysterious and incomprehensible commodity, the secrets of which are understood only by art dealers, scholars, critics, and other highly educated experts.

As a result, beginners all buy art in pretty much the same way – impulsively. They buy what they like, or what they think they like, wherever they happen to see it for sale, the first time they lay eyes on it. Any questions they might have are put to the sellers; whatever answers they get are instantly accepted. No further efforts are involved. They buy this way because they aren't aware that alternative methods exist and that they can actually control their art-buying destinies.

Here's the truth: *You – or anyone else – can research and evaluate any work of art you see for sale entirely on your own and determine whether you are spending your money wisely if you decide to buy it.* No previous knowledge about art or the art business is necessary. Everything you need to know is laid out right here in an easy-to-understand, easy-to-follow, and logical progression.

Facts About This Book

This book is a beginning. However involved you decide to get with art, what you are about to learn will serve as an introduction. You can spend a lifetime mastering the skills necessary to build a substantive art collection, but first you need a good solid foundation – and this book happens to be a great place to get it.

This book is a consumer guide to buying art. It approaches art from a product standpoint and it approaches the buying and selling of art from a business standpoint. As in any other consumer situation, when you buy art, you deserve to be treated fairly, you deserve to know what you're buying, and you deserve a quality product for your money.

This is a generic art book. It is specially designed to guide you through the intricacies of the art world regardless of your tastes. No matter what you want in art, the procedures for familiarizing yourself with its peculiarities, learning about the artists who create it, and learning how to buy it effectively are remarkably similar in many ways.

The term "art" as used in this book is whatever you want it to be. Whether your interest centers on Old Master paintings, sporting scene lithographs, abstract sculptures, wildlife prints, art that moves, etchings of Paris street scenes, or _____ (you fill in the blank with what you want to buy), this book will serve you equally well. The only requirement for our purposes here is that the art be original and artist-created, not mass-produced by mechanical means in factory-type settings (See Chapter 2 for more information on how to distinguish original works of art from reproductions and copies).

This book favors no artists, and it favors no art. In order to keep you from becoming biased or unduly influenced in the direction of your art buying, artist names you see in the text are fabricated, and facts about artist careers are fabricated. Only occasionally, in examples at the ends of chapters, are actual artists' names mentioned and only then to make points about how the art business works, not about those artists. Words describing different types of art (paintings, lithographs, sculptures, etchings, watercolors, etc.) are also used interchangeably throughout the book. All are treated equally, the point being that the entire text is applicable to all art and that no one medium is better to buy than any other.

This book applies to art in all price ranges. Whether you are chasing after multimillion dollar masterworks or have a per-piece budget of $200, the ways you learn about and ultimately buy your art are essentially the same.

This book introduces you to how the art world works. It teaches you general truths about art, the art community, and the business of buying, selling, and collecting. Wherever you go to buy art, whoever you meet in the process, and whatever you hear, the great majority of what you read here will apply to your experiences.

This book is about safe, sensible, low-risk ways to begin buying art. A conservative approach is necessary, because when you don't have much experience, you can be taken advantage of in too many ways. You can overpay, get stuck with forgeries, buy inferior pieces, be fooled by get-rich-quick schemes, buy art with severe condition problems, buy copies or reproductions when you think you're buying originals, and so on. Once you build yourself a good solid base of knowledge from which to operate – once you master the fundamentals – you can branch out, take risks, and experiment with more advanced methods of buying art.

This book is primarily about buying art at established art galleries. These are the best places for novices to begin because galleries provide personal attention, offer ample learning opportunities, and protect buyers with guarantees that are difficult to get elsewhere. You will find occasional references (and several chapters) throughout the book to alternative sources for buying such as directly from artists, over the internet, at flea markets, garage and estate sales, resale outlets, auctions, and so on. The message about those resources, here and elsewhere, is that you're welcome to explore them, but you really should wait until you gain some experience and become more comfortable buying art before you patronize them on a regular basis. You can use what you learn here to buy art anywhere, but when you're just starting out, established galleries are the safest way to go.

This book is about *buying* art for your own personal enjoyment, not "investing" in it. It is not about making money. If anything, it's about keeping you from losing money. Those of you who don't have a fundamental love, appreciation, fascination, and passion for art to begin with – feelings that are totally unrelated to dollars and cents – should get out now, because in the long run you'll lose. Although financial aspects of art are important and will be discussed at length, they should never be the primary consideration in deciding whether nor not to buy a work of art.

The Four Steps to The Art of Buying Art

A lot can happen in the time interval between the moment you get the inclination to buy art and the moment you exit an art gallery with your first purchase in tow. Two approaches you may take are 1) you can buy at random and hope for the best, or 2) you can order your activities, logically proceed from one step to the next, and assure yourself the best possible outcome. This second approach is also known as the art of buying art. If you happen to be of the art-of-buying-art persuasion, the way to accomplish this goal involves your following four important steps exemplified by four key words, as described below.

Define: The first step to follow once you get the urge to buy art is to *define* those types of art that attract you the most. You need concrete ideas of what your tastes are and of what in art really affects you in a deep and meaningful way. Part I of this book teaches you how to define the characteristics of the art that's right for you.

Select: Your next step is to locate and *select* specific works of art for possible purchase, art that appeals to you according to the guidelines laid out in Part I. In order to accomplish this, you need a working knowledge of how the art business operates. Familiarizing yourself with the art community, art personalities, art dealers, art galleries, artists, and learning your responsibilities as an art buyer are all parts of the selection process. Part II of this book teaches you how to understand and navigate the art world in a way that maximizes your chances for selecting those works of art that are best for you.

Research: Once you make your selections, you have to learn about them by *researching* them. In order to make informed decisions about whether or not you really want to own these works of art, you need to acquire specific information about the art itself, the artists who created it, and a variety of other general background information relevant to that art. Part III of this book teaches you basic art research techniques.

Buy: All works of art that remain appealing to you at this final stage in your decision-making process become subject to one last consideration: price. Before you make that ultimate determination, *to buy or not to buy*, you need to understand general dollars and cents aspects of the art business and, in particular, the financial consequences of your potential purchases. You also need instruction in how to complete those purchases that you do end up making – that is, how to complete them to your best advantage. Part IV, the final part of this book, teaches you how to evaluate art prices and how to buy art advantageously.

Define, select, research, and buy – that's what the art of buying art is all about. This book will not transform you into an instant art expert – that takes time, effort, and plenty of practice. It will, however, transform you into an informed consumer, protect you from making bad buys, and help you locate the best art for your money. So take some time to read this book, follow the instructions, and learn art-business basics. Don't rush out to spend your money until you have a handle on how to spend it wisely.

Seasoned collectors will tell you that the "work" involved in defining, selecting, researching, and buying the right art for their collections is not really work at all, but more like pleasure, adventure, mystery, and discovery all rolled up into one. In fact, most everyone will go on to say that the final act of buying is anticlimactic to the events that lead up to those moments. Collectors across the board further agree that the learning process is self-perpetuating – the more they learn, the better they get at collecting, the greater their rewards, and the more they want to continue learning in the future.

A Look Ahead

The Art Of Buying Art is about how to buy original art, but if you have little or no experience looking at art, how do you know whether what you're looking at is an original work of art or a reproduction or copy of that art? Unfortunately, the fine art marketplace is full of "fine art reproductions" that may look and sound like original art, but are no more original than newspaper or magazine illustrations. The next chapter teaches you how to tell the difference between original works of art and reproductions or copies of original works of art.

CHAPTER 2

Original Works of Art Versus Reproductions

Once upon a time in the not-too-distant past, Adam Adams, the owner of the Three Star Printing Company went to a fancy art opening at a downtown art gallery. The gallery was showing paintings by a well-known artist. Adam looked at one of the paintings, saw the selling price, and was amazed at how expensive it was. He walked around the entire gallery, looked at all the other paintings, and saw that they were equally expensive. He got to wondering whether other art galleries sold expensive paintings like this gallery did, too.

The next day, Adam went back downtown to see more art galleries and find out how much the paintings cost that they had for sale. He saw all kinds of paintings and they all cost a lot of money. On the way home from his day of gallery-hopping, Adam had a fantastic idea!

"Instead of printing travel brochures with beautiful little color illustrations of far away places and selling them for a few pennies each like I do now, I'll make beautiful big color prints of paintings like the ones that I've been looking at in the art galleries. Each print will cost about the same amount of money to produce as a travel brochure, but I'll sell the prints for hundreds of dollars each. That sounds expensive, but compared to the prices of the paintings that I've been looking at, the prints will seem like bargains. I'll sell them to people who like the paintings but can't afford them. These people will think they're getting great deals and I'll make tons of money!"

There was one slight problem with the Adam's idea, however. His prints were not original works of art like paintings or watercolors are. They were copies or reproductions of paintings that were mechanically printed the same way that the illustrations in his travel brochures were printed. His prints were no different than calendar prints, posters, newspaper and magazine illustrations, or any other mechanically reproduced images like the kinds that were selling at frame shops and poster stores for only a few dollars each. Paying hundreds of dollars a piece for his prints made no sense.

"I can get around this price issue," Adam thought. "I'll change the name of my business to the Three Star Fine Art Publishing Company instead of the Three Star Printing Company. I'll print my prints in finite quantities that I'll call *limited editions*, print them on heavy papers like the kinds of papers that artists use, and have the artists who paint the originals sign and number the prints. Instead of marketing them as copies or reproductions, I'll call them *artist-signed and numbered, limited edition fine art lithographs*. That's technically what the prints are, anyway, so I'm not misrepresenting anything. They'll sound important and people will think that they're getting original works of art just like paintings. My costs will be a few dollars more per print than if I print them on regular paper and don't have the artist's sign them, but that's nothing compared to the amount of money I'll make when I sell them."

So the commercial printer became a "fine art publisher" and began producing his prints and advertising them in full-page color advertisements in art magazines. He designed his advertisements to look and read just like the ones that the art galleries used to sell their expensive original paintings. People saw his advertisements and, sure enough, they believed that his prints were original works of art, too. They also believed that they were saving huge amounts of money compared to what the original paintings cost, so they bought without having the slightest idea that what they were really buying were only reproductions or copies of original works of art. Meanwhile, the Three Star Fine Art Publishing Company made tons of money, Adam Adams never had to print another travel brochure again, and he lived happily ever after in a great big house on a hill.

This may or may not be how the "limited edition fine art print industry," or, as I prefer to call it, the copy-print business, got started, but it's probably not far from the truth. Today, copy-print sales represent a substantial percentage of all art business transactions with the larger publishing companies having annual operating budgets ranging well into the millions of dollars.

Here are the facts: *These limited edition prints are not original works of art. They are not made by the artists who conceive of and create the originals. They are copies of original works of art that are printed by printing companies. You do not get original works of art when you buy them; you get signatures of artists on mechanically produced copies of original works of art.*

Certain reproductive processes involve a degree of handwork, but the handwork is almost always that of publishing company employees, not the artists themselves. Advertisements sometimes claim that the artists "oversee" or "closely cooperate" in the copying of their originals, but the artists that actually do participate are in the small minority. Their participation is rarely hands-on and it usually involves little more than making sure that the colors and finished copy-prints are accurate copies of the originals. The overwhelming majority of artists play little or no part in the reproduction process – all they do is sign and number the finished copy-prints.

Publishing companies use a variety of techniques to obscure this minimal artist involvement and also to obscure the fact that the prints are copies and not originals. The most obvious two techniques have already been mentioned – they print the copies in limited quantities and then have the artists sign and number them. This gives the copy-prints the same basic look as original prints, like etchings or lithographs that are entirely conceived, created, and produced by hand by fine artists known as "printmakers."

To enhance the illusion that copy-prints are original works of art, marketers create names for the prints like offset lithographs, continuous-tone lithographs, repligraphs, canvas transfers, canvases, serigraphs, collotypes, multi-media prints, laser-scanned lithographs, lithoserigraphs, and giclees (digital prints). Those names are used in combination with a bewildering array of ambiguous words and phrases like "hand-signed," "consecutively numbered," "hand-pulled," "acid-free paper," "no-fade inks," "certificate of authenticity," "100% rag paper," "limited edition art," "subscription edition," "commission offering," "authentic," "original," "produced in close cooperation with the artist," "hand-accented," "blind embossed," "deluxe embellished edition," and so on. For example, an *authentic, original, limited edition, offset lithograph* sounds important and accurately describes a substantial percentage of limited edition prints, but it also accurately describes most newspaper and magazine illustrations!

To complete the illusion, copy-prints are marketed and sold just like original art is sold. The prints are advertised in art magazines, sold out of stores that look just like art galleries, professionally hung and lit, beautifully framed, and treated like original art by the people who sell them. The big publishing companies thoroughly accomplish their objective – laypersons have great difficulty telling the difference between original art and copy-prints.

More facts about copy-prints:

- *Original prints made by artists are usually printed in editions of less than one hundred and rarely more than two hundred.* Copy-prints are usually printed in editions of at least 300-500 and occasionally in excess of 60,000! (For purposes of comparison, a book with sales exceeding 50,000 copies is considered a bestseller.)

- *The dollar values of copy-prints have no relation to the values of the original works of art that they depict even though the people who sell them would like you to think that they do.* Suppose, for example, that a fine art publishing company makes a limited edition print of the Mona Lisa. Granted, they can't get Da Vinci to sign it, but let's say that the chief printer and a museum curator sign it. Do you believe for one moment that the print's value has any relation to the value of the priceless Mona Lisa? Of course it doesn't!

- *The great majority of copy-prints cost less than $20 each to produce and often as little as a few dollars each.* Serigraphs are the one notable exception, but even the most expensive serigraphs cost well under $100 each to produce. The great majority of copy-prints sell for hundreds and often thousands of dollars each. They're advertised as affordable when, in truth, they're overpriced for what they are!

- *Publishing companies, not artists, receive the bulk of the revenues generated by sales of copy-prints.* The artists receive modest royalties, assuming they don't sell the reproduction rights to the original works of art (and sometimes even the original works themselves) outright.

- *Copy-prints are not art; they're big business.* Every time a publishing company sells a copy-print, one less artist sells one less original work of art.

Now that that's out of my system, let me add that the great majority of copy-prints are beautifully produced, highly decorative, and perfectly acceptable to buy and collect. If you love a particular image and buying the copy-print is the only way that you can own it, go ahead and buy it. Have no illusions, though, about either the originality or the financial prospects of what you're buying. At best, copy-prints are not much more than collectibles relating to the artists who sign them, in much the same way as an art book or gallery exhibit catalogue would be if it was signed by an artist.

How to Recognize Limited Edition Copy-Prints

Until recently, recognizing limited edition copy-prints was not that difficult. Since they were printed in the ways that were very similar to how most commercial illustrations are printed, all you had to do was look closely at their surfaces, with magnification if necessary, for dot matrix patterns – the same types of patterns you see when you look closely at newspaper or magazine illustrations. This test still works for many, but certainly not all, copy-prints because today's printing techniques have become increasingly sophisticated.

Some of today's dot matrix patterns are so fine that you need a jeweler's lupe or hand-held microscope to see them (Radio Shack sells a good 60-100X pocket microscope for about $10). Special textured papers can obscure these patterns and make them difficult to detect. Printing techniques such as serigraphy, continuous-tone lithography, and some of the more advanced digital reproduction processes eliminate dot patterns altogether. In other words, simple identification tests no longer work across the board.

One identification technique, however, has always worked and will continue to work for as long as copy-prints are produced. If you ever have doubts about whether what you are looking at is an original work of art or a copy-print, ask the seller the following question: *Is this print a copy or reproduction of an original work of art?* If the seller is not sure or is unable to give a satisfactory answer, have her contact the publisher. Better yet, ask both the seller and the publisher and get their answers in writing along with a money-back guarantee that their representations are correct.

Other Types of "Art" That are Not Original

Variations on the limited edition copy-print method of moneymaking pervade nearly all segments of the art trade. Although the following items are often advertised and marketed as affordable "art," once again, they're overpriced for what they are, and they're not original works of art – they're copies of originals. If you want to buy original works of art, several such products to avoid are listed below.

Reproductions of famous works of art. Any type of art from any time period can be reproduced including bronzes, paintings, prints, antiquities, metalwork, ceramics, and porcelains. Contemporary recasts of Remington bronzes, reissues of Currier & Ives or Audubon prints, and other reproductions of famous works of art are occasionally marketed using words and phrases like "limited," "authorized," "collector editions," "precision-crafted using the finest materials and techniques," "unique," "special," and so on.

No matter how these are marketed, they are copies. They have no connection to the originals other than being similar in the way that they look. The original artists are not involved in their production – most died many decades ago.

Textured reproductions of paintings. These items also tend to be copies of famous works of art, but they deserve special mention because of the ways that they are marketed. Potential buyers are told that these copy-prints look just like the originals, that their surfaces are textured just like the paint on the originals, that they're framed just like the originals, that some art experts think they're originals, and that owning these copies is like owning the originals.

These claims are nonsense. First of all, anyone who knows art can instantly tell the difference between these copies and the original works of art. Second, these are produced by machines, not by artists. Third, they may sound cheap when compared to the originals, but they cost little to produce and for what they are, they're way overpriced.

Limited edition copy-prints with small amounts of highlighting. This is a relatively recent arrival on the copy-print scene. The printing processes are the same, but small amounts of paint are then added by hand to the surfaces of the finished prints. Marketers have a field day promoting these because, in a sense, each print is unique. Highlighted prints sell for at least several hundred dollars more than what their signed and numbered counterparts with no added paint sell for.

The truth is that the few added brush strokes take a few minutes at most to apply. Furthermore, the highlighting may not even be done by the artists who created the originals. Dollar for dollar, these prints are even more overpriced than ordinary copy-prints. If you have any doubts about what you are looking at, ask the seller the following question: *Is this a copy or reproduction of an original work of art that has been retouched by an artist?*

Remarqued limited edition copy-prints. These are also copy-prints with handwork. Instead of altering the images, though, the artists add small sketches to the copy-prints, usually in pencil and along the bottom margins where the prints are also signed and numbered. These sketches are rarely much larger than a square inch or two and usually take a few minutes to complete. Nevertheless, they increase per-print prices by at least $200, and often more, in the great majority of cases. For you math fans in the crowd, an artist who charges $200 for a sketch that takes five minutes to finish is making $40 per minute or $2,400 per hour or $4,992,000 per year (assuming a 40 hour work week).

Reprints of vintage photographs. Another recent entry into the copy-print market is reprints of vintage photographic images. These are often enlarged from the originals and are occasionally signed, titled, numbered or accompanied by certificates of authenticity. The original photographers are often famous and may or may not still be alive. The original photographs themselves are often valuable or collectible, and their subject matters are often historical or significant. Images of famous sports figures and early panoramas of cities, for example, are among the more popular subject matters currently being sold by copy-photograph dealers.

Copy-photographs can be made from any existing photographic image including negatives, positives, digital files, and moving picture film. As is the case with other forms of copy-art, marketers use ambiguous sounding terms and phrases to sell copy-photographs such as "original glass negatives," "never before published," "certificate of authenticity," "archivally printed," "hand titled," "numbered," "exclusive limited edition," "original prints," and so on. Selling prices can range well into the hundreds of dollars per image and, as with other limited edition copy-prints, copy-photographs are billed as affordable when compared to what the originals would cost.

The truth is that copy-photographs rarely cost more than a few dollars each to produce. Other than the way they look, they have no connection to the original photographers or to the dollar values or the collectibility of the originals. They're worth about as much as they cost to print and nothing more. If you have doubts about what you're looking at, ask the seller: *Is this a copy or a reproduction of an original vintage photograph?*

As an aside, copies of well-known photographic images can make great decorative additions to collections, especially when the originals are either in museums or are prohibitively expensive. Many museums and institutions with photography collections or archives, including the Library of Congress, offer what are called "photo-duplication services." Anyone can contact these institutions directly and buy copies of famous photographs in their collections for prices starting as low as $10 to $12 each. The Library of Congress, for example, has over *ten million images* in its archives.

A Word About Giclees

A "giclee" is a print-out of a digital file located on a computer's hard drive, a floppy disc, or a CD-ROM and printed by a digital printer that's connected to that computer. The word "giclee," is derived from the French verb "gicler" which means "to squirt, spirt, or splash." Giclee prints are not only popular with collectors, but also with fine art printing companies.

Collectors like giclee prints because of the way that they look. Digitally produced prints have a unique appearance about them that is difficult to achieve by using conventional printing processes. Colors can be strikingly vibrant, details can be crystal clear, and the overall visual impact of a digital image can be highly dramatic.

Printing companies like giclee prints because they're more economical to produce than prints printed by conventional means. Giclees can be printed individually rather than in runs of hundreds or thousands (as is necessary with conventional printing processes) which means that printing companies don't have to tie up thousands of dollars in printing costs and storage space, and then hope that the prints they produce sell. If a digital image sells poorly as a giclee print, all the printing company loses is a few megabytes of space on a computer hard drive, and they can move on to marketing the next digital image in hopes that it will sell better.

From an art standpoint, there are two types of giclee prints. The first type exists only as a computer file, that is, it is created by a digital artist on a computer. These giclees are original works of art and are usually sold by the artists themselves or by galleries specializing in original digital art. The second type is a digital reproduction or copy-print if a work of art is in another medium. That is, it is made by taking a piece of art like a painting or a watercolor; either photographing or scanning it, converting it into a digital file on a computer, and then printing that file out on a digital printer. These giclees are basically equivalent to photocopies and are usually marketed by commercial printing companies.

If you love the look of giclees and want to buy them, make sure that you understand the difference between original giclees and copy-print giclees. When you're not sure about what you're looking at, ask the seller: *Is this an original image created by a digital artist on a computer or is it a reproduction or copy of a work of art like a painting or a watercolor?* Reviewing the artist's career accomplishments is another good way to check for originality. Resumes of digital artists usually discuss their experience creating computer graphics; resumes of conventional artists usually talk about their paintings or watercolors.

A Look Ahead

Now that you have some instruction in how to tell the difference between originals and copies, you're ready to go out, start looking at art, figure out what you like, and define the types of art that you would most enjoy buying. The next chapter talks about how to set aside any preconceived notions that you have about art and approach the art world with an open mind.

CHAPTER 3

Discover the Art World

The great majority of people who decide to buy art are relatively unaware of the incredible variety that's available for purchase. Their tastes are the products of happenstance, past experiences, and limited arbitrary encounters with art. They operate according to preconceived notions about art collecting, art buying, and what the art they want to own looks like – notions that they've held for years or even decades. This is best illustrated with an example.

Suppose that you're back in kindergarten and that your art class assignment on this day is to draw an apple. You eagerly take out your purple, green, and black crayons and draw a green form shaped like a figure eight with black and purple lines coming out of it. Then you make purple, black and green dots all over the back side of the paper, crush the whole thing up, and confidently place it on the desk in front of you. For whatever reasons you have at that moment, this is an apple. More importantly, it's your apple, you're proud of it, and you believe you did a great job making it.

When the art teacher comes by to critique your work, you find out differently. You are gently but firmly informed that you don't crush up your paper and that an apple is round and red with a place on top for the stem and maybe a leaf or two. You sadly accept this fact, throw away your apple, take out a new sheet of paper, and draw the art teacher's apple in place of yours.

The combined effect of this and similar experiences is that your definition of art becomes narrower and narrower and narrower. You are told that art should look a certain way, be made a certain way, mean certain things, be this size, that shape, these colors, have this texture, and so forth. If it fails to satisfy any of these criteria, it's bad, incompetent, a bunch of scribbles, trash, junk, stupid, and, of course, it's not art.

Take a few moments here and jot down *your* preconceived notions. Include what you think the art you're interested in buying looks like, who the artists are, where you might go to buy it, how much it costs, and any other relevant specifics. Be as thoughtful and detailed as possible and *save these notes*. They define your official starting point and will serve as a reminder of where you were when you began this book.

Done writing? Good. Now take your piece of paper, fold it up, put it in a drawer, and forget about it. While you're at it, imagine putting everything else you know about art into that same drawer and forgetting about it, too. Your current knowledge may well come in handy later, but for the time being, let's start with a blank slate. Approach your quest to define what you like as though you've never read or heard a thing about art before in your life, as though you have no opinions about it whatsoever.

Whatever you think, forget it for now. Don't let your brain get in the way. With brain in full gear, you look at a painting, print, or sculpture and hear little voices in your head saying things like "My friends will stop speaking to me if I buy this," or "This thing will never increase in value," or "I have no idea who this artist is – his art can't be any good." Screening out all this interference allows you to begin at the very beginning and survey your most basic gut reactions to art.

An empty mind permits you to see, feel, and experience pure emotion. The art controls you. You do not filter your response to the art through a belief system that may or may not have a basis in fact. By letting your raw feelings guide you, you take the first major step in defining what you really like. After all is said and done, of course, you may find that you are attracted to the exact same art you were before you started, but then again, you may discover that your true tastes are for art that you never imagined you could appreciate.

Look, Look, Look

Now that your mind is out of the picture, let's get art into the picture. You've got to familiarize yourself with the product you intend to purchase. *Your first assignment is to begin the definition process by getting out there and seeing as much art and as many different kinds of art as you possibly can.*

Either you can take a systematic approach to your looking and see one particular type of art at a time or you can see many different types in no particular order. Whatever you feel comfortable doing is fine, but remember, don't be selective in your viewing – look at everything everywhere.

Visit places specifically to see art such as museums, historical societies, art galleries, arts organizations, artist associations, and corporate collections. But don't stop there. Wherever your day-to-day activities take you – shopping malls, banks, doctors' offices, on the internet, hotel lobbies, restaurants – keep a constant eye to the walls, the pedestals, and the display areas. At this early stage, the art you see in a shopping mall is just as important to study as what you see at a museum.

See old art, new art, abstract art, big art, little art, bright art, and dark art. Look at paintings, sculptures, etchings, prints, and watercolors. Look at "works of art" that you're not even sure are art. Once again – *look at everything.* Don't try to understand it, analyze it, read about it, find out who the artists are, figure out what it is or how it's made, or ask other people what they think about it. Just plop yourself down in front of it and look. Monitor you reactions to it – that's all.

Do you like it or not? Does it make you feel happy, sad, calm, angry, exhilarated? Do you love it or hate it or have no reaction to it at all? Does it make you think about certain issues? Does it transport you to other realities or to far away places? These are the internal reactions that you are looking to define.

THE ART OF BUYING ART

Two additional pointers:

- *Study art you hate as well as art you like.* Recognizing what you want to avoid is just as important as recognizing what you love.

- *Don't ignore certain types of art you are already familiar with because you think you know what your reactions will be and believe that nothing about them will ever change.* That's your brain getting in the way again. View it as though you are seeing it for the very first time.

How to Look

Looking at art means more than giving casual glances as you pass it by. You've got to spend time studying individual pieces.

Stand up close and focus on small areas of the art. Stand back and look at the whole thing. Stick your nose right up to the canvas or wood or paper or bronze and study the minutest details. Back away slowly and watch how the art changes. Move so far away that the art fades into its surroundings.

Look at the colors, subject matters, sizes, styles, frames, pedestals. Look at single brush strokes on a painting, single lines on an etching, single details on a sculpture. Look at the materials making up the art; see how it's put together.

If you happen to see something you really like, note what it is, where you saw it, how it looks, and why it attracts you – nothing more. You'll have plenty of opportunity to return and learn more about it later.

Resist the temptation to speak with people about whatever you're looking at. Start asking questions and you'll be right back in that rut of letting your mind or the minds of others control your responses. Avoid exposing yourself to opinions on what's good, what's bad, what to buy, or what to avoid. At this formative stage, no one has the inside track on what's best for you better than you do.

Don't read literature or brochures about the art you are looking at. Don't look at name plates, titles, or price tags. Pay no attention to the names of artists or how famous they are. All this information interferes with your gut feelings. Suppose, for example, you see a painting and hate the way it looks. Then you come closer, read the label, and find out that Picasso painted it, and it's selling for $14 million. Do you change your mind all of a sudden and decide that you really like it? Of course not!

Remember, all you're doing here is looking and feeling. You are not committing yourself in any way; you can change your mind about what you like at any time. You are simply getting in touch with how you feel when you look at various types of art. *The goal of "looking without thinking" is this: By experiencing a little bit of everything that's out there and taking some time to*

31

study it in detail, you begin to acquire strength of conviction and begin to define
what really thrills you.

Out of all the millions of art pieces that have ever been and have yet to be created, you will choose to own maybe one, maybe five, maybe one hundred. And you'll choose them because they mean something special to you and you alone. Now is the time to acquire a feel for where that special meaning lies, and to identify what qualities in art attract you the most.

Example 1:

The most sophisticated collectors I know are the ones who spend the most time looking at art. Some focus only on the art they collect, while others are more adventurous and are constantly on the lookout for new and exciting pieces to add to their collections. One man in particular makes a point of looking at and studying a far greater amount and wider range of art than he collects. He stays in shape, so to speak, and, as a result, is able to evaluate many different types of art on a variety of levels, whether he collects them or not.

This man began by collecting impressionist paintings by American artists, moved on to regionalist art of the 1930's and 1940's, from there focused on abstract and abstract expressionist art, and is now collecting contemporary art. By keeping informed about current events in the art world and considering whatever art is brought to his attention – whether he knows anything about it or not – he has developed an uncanny ability to spot and act on trends in the marketplace before most other collectors. Two big benefits of his buying ahead of the market are that he has a larger selection of pieces from which to choose and the prices he pays are often reasonable due to the fact that not that many other collectors are buying in his chosen areas.

Example 2:

An incredible amount of art is bought by people who have never bothered to formally identify their true preferences. They buy because someone tells them to, because they think they're going to make a bundle of money when they resell, because they think the artists are "famous" and that they'll impress their friends, and so on. Buying art this way hurts just about everyone:

- The buyers themselves suffer because they are being controlled by outside forces. They have no idea whether or not they are buying what they like.

- Artists suffer. Rather than select from the great variety of art that artists produce, inexperienced buyers put their money into those few names that they already recognize, that happen to be trendy, are hyped the most, get the best news coverage, and so on. Many outstanding artists who are not that publicity-oriented have difficulty selling art because so many people are blinded by glitz and glamour and buy like sheep.

- Dealers who deal in quality art suffer. The market gets flooded with art that is not necessarily good, but that satisfies mass tastes – whatever buyers think is the thing to buy at the moment. At worst, money goes to slick business people who know more about marketing what's hot than they do about art.

What's important here is that you come to understand the incredible variety of art that's available in the marketplace, pinpoint your tastes, cultivate an independence of intention, and avoid jumping into the market before you have a good solid footing. Develop confidence in yourself. Then begin buying.

A Look Ahead

As you begin to get an idea of what those qualities of art are that attract you the most, the time is right to start getting practical – to let your brain back into the picture. Putting thoughts to your feelings once again becomes necessary because that is the only way you'll be able to communicate your needs, acquire information, and in the end, buy art. Your next step in defining what you like, therefore, is to identify and describe what it is that you really want to buy.

CHAPTER 4

Define What You Like

So far, you have experienced art on a purely emotional level, evaluating how it looks and feels to you with no interference from the brain, that is, the intellect. You have seen and noted particular works of art that possess a certain magic for you, that impress you in ways you find appealing. Defining what you like means putting the characteristics and qualities of this special art into words.

Not only do you have to define it, but you have to be specific. The better you are able to pinpoint your preferences, the better the art community is able to understand and serve you.

Begin this procedure by reviewing any notes that you took during your Chapter 3 adventures. Return to locations where you saw art you liked. Look at that art again and find out basic information about it. If you have questions about specific works of art, have experts such as curators, art dealers, or experienced collectors explain and clarify whatever details you're unsure of. Record all relevant data for future reference. Avoid getting involved in any serious discussions about art (it's a little premature for that), and confine your fact-gathering mission to the following:

- Find out where the art originates. Is it American, European, South American, Japanese? Is it from Texas, from Detroit, from New York City?

- Find out the names of the artists.

- Note when the art dates from. Is it from the nineteenth century, early twentieth century, contemporary, or some other period?

- Note the style or styles of the individual works of art. Are they abstract? Realistic? Impressionistic? Pop Art? Surreal?

- Identify the mediums that the art is created in. Are they watercolors, bronzes, oil paintings on canvas, etchings, color woodcuts, wood carvings, and so on?

- Identify the subject matters. Are they landscapes? Seascapes? Still lifes? City scenes? Busts of famous politicians? Geometric abstracts?

- Find out the dollar values of any works of art that are for sale or that private owners can price for you (as opposed to art on permanent display in museums or other institutions).

- Note any other relevant physical characteristics that are consistent from one piece to the next such as what sizes, shapes, and colors they are.

Once you have assembled this information, combine it into a concise opening statement that you can make to anyone who is interested in knowing what you prefer in your art. As conversations progress, you can fill in the additional details as required. Here are some examples of good opening statements:

"I'm interested in contemporary oil paintings of spring scenes in the French countryside."

"I love New Orleans scenes that were painted before 1920 by Louisiana artists."

"I'm looking for abstract sculptures executed by New York City artists between 1940 and 1960."

"I want to buy etchings and lithographs of sporting scenes that have waterfowl in them, preferably ducks."

Make sure your statement provides adequate introductory information about your needs. Suppose you are in an art gallery and the owner asks what you are interested in buying. You answer: "Seascapes." You feel perfectly comfortable with that answer because the central feature of every work of art you like is a large body of water. But if you think for a moment, "seascapes" happens to cover a huge amount of territory. Your statement is too general – the dealer has virtually no information to work with. He could show you hundreds of seascapes, none of which you would find acceptable.

The dealer has no idea whether you want coastal scenes, clipper ships tossing about on stormy seas, or peaceful sunsets over tropical beaches; large pictures or small ones; bright pictures or dark ones; contemporary examples or ones that were painted decades ago. You can only carry on a constructive conversation about your tastes in art when you have a good opener and plenty of specifics to follow it up with.

Don't worry that defining your preferences too narrowly at this early stage will eliminate huge amounts of art from consideration before you even get going. This is not the case and, in fact, the opposite often occurs. Once you begin focusing on specifics, you realize that a lot more is available within that particular realm of collecting than you ever imagined existed. And remember, just because you define your interests now doesn't mean that you must stick to them for the rest of your life. You can modify your opening statement or change your preferences at any time.

The general rules for buying art are pretty much the same no matter what you decide to collect. By setting an initial direction now and following through to the point of purchase, you acquire the basic skills necessary to form a quality collection of whatever type of art you eventually choose to focus on.

Be Realistic

An important part of defining your likes is making them workable in the real world of buying art. By setting realistic, reachable goals for yourself, you maximize the chances of your being able to find exactly the art you are looking for. If your preferences in art are great in theory, but impractical in terms of buying, you've got to adjust them appropriately. Below are some factors you should take into consideration.

Make sure that you can afford what you want to buy. As soon as possible, figure out your budget; decide approximately how much money you are willing to spend per work of art. If the art that thrills you the most is too expensive, look for something more affordable that has similar characteristics to those favorites.

Suppose, for example, that you love French Impressionist paintings, but that your per-piece budget is only $5,000. Average French Impressionist works start in the upper hundreds of thousands of dollars each and quickly proceed upward from there. For your $5,000, you can't even buy a scribble on a scrap of paper. You could solve this problem by looking instead for impressionist-style pictures by contemporary artists that approximate the look of those you like and that sell in the $5,000 range. Your opening statement would be "I want to collect oil paintings by contemporary artists done in the manner of the French Impressionists that cost between $3,000 and $5,000 each."

Make sure that you can buy a reasonably good piece of art on your per-piece budget. If you can't afford good-quality examples of what you like the most, lower your sights accordingly. Collectors across the board will tell you that regardless of your budget, buy as close to the top of your chosen area of focus as you can.

For instance, if good-quality examples of the art you like the most cost $8,000 to $10,000 each and you only have $2,000 to spend, you won't be able to get very much for your money. You'll be forced to buy closer to the bottom of the market for this art than the top. Find art you like just as much where $2,000 buys the best or at least a better example of what's available, not a mediocre one.

Make sure that what you like is readily available and that you have a good selection to choose from. You won't find anything to buy if the type of art you're looking for is so rare that it hardly ever comes onto the market.

Make sure you choose your art for art reasons, not money reasons. Buy because you love the way the art looks, you are fascinated by the history behind it, and so on. If you like specific works of art because you think they'll go up in value, think again. For one thing, only a small percentage of art increases in value over time (as you will see in Chapters 19 and 20). Additionally, getting all caught up in money matters can destroy the fun of buying art.

Keep your preferences conservative at first. Focus on art that dealers and collectors generally accept as being collectible. The more you learn and the more experienced you become, the more experimental you can afford to be in your buying.

Be Thorough

Be complete and thorough when defining your likes; don't overlook any important details. You must be fully aware of the qualities that you want in your art and of the basic principles that will be guiding your buying. The truth is that some art buyers are not aware of these things and, consequently, the art they end up owning is quite different from the art that they originally set out to buy.

Suppose that you meet a collector who tells you, "I love to collect paintings of Florida coastal scenes done between 1890 and 1980." You visit him at his home, he gives you a tour of his collection and at first glance, all his pictures seem to be exactly what he told you they were. But as he presents each piece and describes it, he finishes with statements like, "Paintings by this artist sell for $1,250 and up – I paid only $150 for mine at the flea market," or "I got this one at an estate sale for a tenth of what it's worth."

Whether or not this collector originally intended it, a guiding principle behind his collecting – one that belongs in his opening statement – is that he purchases only those coastal scenes done between 1890 and 1980 that he can buy cheaply enough to brag to his friends and acquaintances about what great bargains he got. A more appropriate statement about his collecting would be, "I love to buy Florida coastal scenes done between 1890 and 1980 that I can get for much less than they're really worth," or "I collect bargain paintings that happen to be Florida coastal scenes done between 1890 and 1980." He cannot legitimately title his collection "Florida Coastal Scenes Painted Between 1890 and 1980."

This fellow may need to re-evaluate his buying strategies if he's not fully aware of how much the bargain requirement is controlling his selection process. By limiting his purchases to "bargain" paintings, he automatically eliminates all non-bargains from consideration. This could possibly result in his compromising quality for price or in depriving himself of important coastal scenes or art by particular artists that simply can't be found at bargain prices. His obsession with bargains may adversely affect his collecting.

Here are examples of two other constraints that can and do significantly alter the intended courses of many a collection:

1. Only purchasing works of art that a particular person – wife, mother-in-law, best friend, employer, etc. – approves of. The

resulting selection is more indicative of the tastes of the approving person than of the buyer.

2. Buying all art from a single gallery. A buyer who patronizes only one gallery does not really buy what he or she likes; that collector buys what the gallery likes.

A Look Ahead

Defining what you like, tempering it with the realities of your buying situation, and explaining it in a manner that the art community understands completes the first step in the process of buying art. The next step – which is the goal of Part II – involves your selecting specific works of art for possible purchase according to your requirements. In order to make the best choices, however, you need basic training; that is, you need an introduction to how the art world operates.

Part II: Select

Selecting a work of art for possible purchase is easy. Since you are now able to identify what you like, all you have to do is walk into a gallery, take a look around, see something interesting, and say to yourself, "I wouldn't mind owning that." Selection process completed.

The hard part is locating that gallery in the first place; knowing what to do once you get there; being able to tell whether you have encountered a good dealer or a bad one; effectively interacting with anyone you meet before, during, and after your visit; and knowing how to behave in order to maximize the quality of each visit. Consequently, the goal of Part II is not to teach you how to select art – you can do that already – but rather to provide you with the information you need in order to assure that your selection process has a positive outcome. Part II is a basic course in understanding and navigating through the art community. The truth is that you can't come face to face with and select the art that's right for you until you know how to get around.

CHAPTER 5

Who Says it, What They Say, How to Take it

So far, you've kept pretty quiet about your art interests and intent to buy. Everything you've done, you've done pretty much on your own. Keeping your contacts brief has allowed you to wander from place to place, make initial observations about what you like, and acquire basic information about it with little or no interference from outsiders. Sooner or later, though, you must deepen your contacts, make your intentions known in greater detail, and progress towards buying art.

Once you begin to do this, the way the art world relates to you changes. You are no longer a looker – you are now a participant. People start taking vested interests in how you should think, feel, and react to art. They declare, expound, criticize, hold court, pass judgments, share beliefs, emote, foretell the future, and say whatever else comes to mind regarding your particular situation. They want a say in your selection process.

Speaking with others about art can be quite difficult at first. You hear many different things from many different people, and you're never quite sure how to respond. You don't really know who's right and who's wrong, who knows what they're talking about and who doesn't. You have little choice but to take whatever you hear at face value because you don't yet have the knowledge to analyze and digest.

So what do you do? You jump right in and start talking. You tell people exactly what you know and exactly what you're looking for. That's the best practice you can get and the only sensible way to begin. By participating in conversation after conversation, you eventually figure out how to evaluate what you are hearing, extract the information you need, formulate your own opinions, and determine whether the art that you've selected is really right for you.

When you don't know much about art, however, and the people you are talking with do, you are at a continual disadvantage. They find out more about you faster than you do about them. They control the conversations and have a variety of options in responding to whatever you say, while you have very few.

Imagine putting on a pair of boxing gloves and stepping into the ring with a professional fighter. He can give you a painless and highly educational lesson in how to box, he can exit the ring without saying a word and leave you standing there, he can pound you to a pulp, and so on. You can listen, run, plead for mercy, or put up your gloves and see how long you last – and that's about it. Depending on his response to your situation, you can leave the ring knowing more than when you stepped into it, you can leave learning nothing, or you can end up staring at the ceiling.

This is similar to what you encounter as you begin to speak with people about art. You step into the art ring with professional after professional, tell them about your situation, and listen to their responses. Some help you, others tell you nothing, a few take the opportunity to hinder you or manipulate you to their own ends.

Your task is to separate the helpers from the hinderers as quickly as possible and to use what you hear to locate the art you want to buy. Sooner or later, you acquire the necessary skills to accurately assess all that people tell you. This chapter is about how to make it sooner.

Who Says it

Figuring out whose views to accept and how much to accept them is difficult at first. Everyone can sound like they know what they're talking about as long as they present themselves in reasonably competent and trustworthy manners. You can't really apply any quick and easy rules to diagnosing a situation, but you don't have to operate blind, either. Knowing a little about the structure of art interactions comes in handy here.

To begin with, be aware of conflicts of interest. In any conversation, know when another person stands to benefit from having you see things their way and having you focus on the art they want you to select. The greater the profit potential is for a person – monetarily, psychologically, or otherwise – the more inclined that person is to give you a biased view of art.

Art scholars, museum curators, and others who are not involved with the art business, but rather with the academic, scholarly, and historical aspects of art, can usually be relied upon for accurate, unbiased information. They do not profit from having you believe their views about art, do not ordinarily take sides, and purposely steer clear of the business side of art. When you ask their advice, they attempt to present the issue fairly and allow you to make the necessary decisions for yourself.

Individuals involved with the art business are different. People who sell art for a living such as art dealers, gallery employees, and auction house staff people profit directly by having you believe what they believe. With such people, you have to be a little more careful about who and what you listen to and believe. Most sellers represent their art fairly and tell you exactly what you need to know. But remember that the possibility of their making sales always looms on the horizon. If they see that they can influence your selection process, they probably will.

Much of what sellers tell you relates specifically to the art they sell. Even when you speak with them casually, outside of direct selling situations, be aware that they believe very strongly in what they sell and present consistently positive cases for owning their type of art and less positive cases for owning other types of art. They want you to like what they like, whether you buy it or not.

Keep in mind also that sellers don't always know that much about types of art outside their fields. They know plenty about what they sell, but are not necessarily well informed about what other people sell. When you ask sellers about art they don't deal in, you won't always get accurate answers. But you will get answers, answers that you should always corroborate with more knowledgeable experts before accepting.

Sellers are most helpful in educating you about the art and artists they represent. When you speak with them, keep conversations focused on their specialties. Whether or not their types of art turn out to be the right art for you, they can tell you just about everything you need to know about it.

Art collectors are much like sellers in that they also prefer having you see art the way they do. Suppose, for instance, that a private collector is giving you a tour of his collection. He believes certain things about the art he has purchased, and it's in his best interest that you believe him, too.

Let's say you agree with his views on collecting (that is, you approve of what's in his collection) and decide to select and buy similar art for yourself. In doing so, you indirectly increase the value of his art by increasing the demand for that art in the marketplace. The more people agree with this collector's views on collecting and buy what he buys, the greater the demand for that type of art becomes.

This collector also benefits from your support in a psychological sense – you make him feel good about himself and his collection when you agree with him. If you don't see eye to eye on a particular point, he'll most likely attempt to convince you he's right. Knowing that you disagree with him about the art he has chosen to buy may make him feel uncomfortable because he may feel that perhaps he has not spent his money wisely.

Collectors feel strongly about what they collect and that's fine; but once again, you've got to decide whether believing them works as well for you as it does for them. They may have quality collections and know what they're talking about – in which case, you're safe following their leads. On the other hand, they may think they have bought wisely when, in fact, they haven't. They may think their art is worth a lot more than it actually is, or they may think it's a lot better than it actually is. You certainly don't want to follow any leads in either of those circumstances.

Be careful when speaking with collectors for the simple reason that they frequently do not know as much about art as full-time art experts. They buy in their spare time and do not spend their lives amassing knowledge about art the way that people in the business or museum curators and art scholars do. Furthermore, their focus is much narrower than that of most experts. Although some may speak with strong conviction and sound like they know everything there is to know, be cautious and check out what they tell you before accepting it as fact.

Artists are somewhat like dealers and collectors rolled up into one in that every artist is both a major collector and dealer of his or her own work. As with collectors, artists tend to focus on their own art to the exclusion of all else. As with dealers, they have an obvious conflict of interest when advising you on what to buy. They want you to understand, appreciate, and buy *their* art. When you collect a particular artist's work, it is important to know that artist for purposes of better understanding her art. If, however, you are speaking casually or in generalities with an artist whose art you do not collect, keep in mind that she is heavily invested in converting you into a fan of her art.

Speak with as many dealers, collectors, artists, auction house and art gallery personnel, museum curators, and other experts as possible. By listening to everyone, you acquire a well-balanced picture of what you want to select and eventually buy. Accumulating information from a great variety of sources protects you from coming under the influence of any one or two in particular. Weigh all points of view on a continuing basis so you can progressively strengthen your convictions.

What They Say

You hear plenty about art as you move through the art world from one person to the next. What you hear can be broken down into three basic categories:

- Facts about artists or works of art.

- Emotional reactions to artists or works of art.

- Market information about artists or works of art.

Facts are easy to evaluate. They are either true or false and can almost always be verified simply and directly. Sometimes the people who state the facts offer that verification themselves. Other times, you have to corroborate what you hear by independently contacting art experts or researching at museums, libraries, online, and other resources.

The operative word here is *verify*. Any time you are presented with new or unfamiliar information, check it out – do not automatically accept it as gospel. Make sure that whatever you are told is true and generally accepted by the art community. Unfortunately, you can't believe everything you hear.

For example, an art dealer tells you that an artist she represents is famous. You speak with four collectors, two independent art experts, several art dealers, and contact several art museums to see whether you can corroborate this information. You come up with the following results: No expert or collector has ever heard of the artist, one art dealer thinks he recognizes the name but isn't sure, no museum can provide any information about the artist. You have to conclude that, at best, the artist is not quite as famous as the initial dealer would have you believe.

Emotional reactions to art are a little more difficult to evaluate than facts. You will hear everything from raw, spontaneous reactions to the most highly informed and educated reactions (commonly referred to as art criticism). Just as you verify facts, you have to learn to verify – or more accurately, qualify – emotional reactions in order to determine how they might influence your selection-making process. This qualifying may seem difficult, but it's really not. It just involves a little reading between the lines.

Basically, you have to figure out how qualified the people doing the reacting are. Are they knowledgeable experts who are having legitimate educated responses, or are they casual observers who just happen to be passing by and have no idea what they are looking at? How much do the reactors know about the art they are reacting to? That's the key.

Suppose, for instance, that you are attending an art opening at Triple-A Fine Arts Gallery and overhear a man remark that the abstract paintings on display are terrible and don't even deserve to be hung in a monkey cage. You politely tap him on the shoulder, introduce yourself, and ask him to explain why he feels this way. He tells you that he hates bright colors and that his six-year-old daughter brings home better pictures from first-grade art class.

This is probably not an explanation you should take too seriously. It shouldn't affect your decision about whether or not to consider one of these abstracts for purchase. If, however, this fellow goes on to say that in all his years of curating shows at the Municipal Art Museum he has never seen such amateurish work, you could have an entirely different situation on your hands. Suddenly you realize that you're dealing with someone who could well know what he's talking about. Not necessarily, though.

As a curator, he certainly qualifies as having experience in the art world, but before you can take him too seriously, you have to find out exactly where his expertise lies. If he turns out to be a curator of Greek and Roman antiquities, for instance, he may not be qualified to criticize the abstracts on display at this opening. An expert in one field of art is not automatically qualified to judge art unrelated to that field.

If, however, he's an expert on contemporary abstracts and curates contemporary art exhibits, you listen. But don't blindly accept what he has to say. Politely request that he support his initial reactions with facts. This is how you learn. Perhaps he'll mention a book you should read or name several other artists who accomplish the same results much more skillfully, or he may tell you where you can go to see really good abstracts.

When evaluating emotional reactions, always find out the answers to these three questions:

- How qualified is the person doing the talking?

- Can the reactions be supported with concrete proof that they are valid?

- What is that proof?

Market information is the toughest of all to evaluate. A primary reason for this is that many people who give you price data have vested interests in what they tell you. Another problem is that you can easily be misled by people who think they know about prices, but actually don't. And if that's not enough, many people are reluctant to give you price information in the first place. They want to keep what they know to themselves and use it to their advantage. Part IV of this book treats money matters in depth, but a brief summary is appropriate here.

As in evaluating emotional or critical reactions to art, you must qualify the sources of any market-related information you get. Ask people who talk prices to back up everything they say with facts. Figure out whether they have any vested interests in telling you what art is good to buy, what art isn't, and what art is worth how much. Find out the extent of the experience they've had dealing with the monetary aspects of art. For example, a private collector who buys but never sells may not give you as reliable information about the art market as will someone who sells or appraises art for a living. You will also see in Part IV that standard art price references which place specific dollar values on works of art are available to the public and that you can use them to substantiate what people tell you.

How to Take it

At present, digesting what you hear about art is not easy. You probably don't know that much, you haven't met that many people, you're not sure whom to trust, and you haven't established any long-term relationships. You're still operating pretty much in the dark, and you never quite know how to take what people tell you.

And you hear what you hear in so many different formats. Some people seem completely trustworthy, congenial, and sincere (making you inclined to accept anything they tell you, true or not). Others have strong feelings and no qualms about imposing them on you, whether you're interested in hearing them or not. The more adamant among them can literally attempt to steamroll you into submission (making you inclined *not* to accept anything they tell you, true or not). Most people happen to be helpful and supportive, but not everyone is going to treat you with respect. Be prepared for anything.

Never take what people tell you personally. No one is out to get you. Getting all caught up in why someone treats you disrespectfully is a monumental waste of time. Sure, you'll meet a few people who have to make your life difficult in order to feel good about themselves or prove how much they know. Consider that their problem, not yours.

Listen to and reflect on *everything* people tell you. Get a well-rounded art education. Most people happily soak up any information that already supports their beliefs but pay little, if any, attention to divergent points of view. This is fine if you ascribe to the "ignorance is bliss" philosophy, but ignorance does not come in handy if you expect to master the art of buying art. Resisting or discounting opposing viewpoints before checking them out is not a healthy practice.

You don't have to believe everything you hear, follow every bit of advice that anyone gives you, or change direction at the slightest provocation. You do, however, have to catalogue the data. No matter whether it seems right or wrong, makes sense or not, sounds sincere or condescending, assume at the outset that it has value and deserves your attention.

Let's say you are interested in the artist John Doeman and are in the process of learning as much as you can about him. In your art travels, you speak with people who have heard of Doeman, people who claim to be experts on Doeman, people who have never heard of Doeman, and people who think they have heard of Doeman and will gladly comment on the artist if you would just refresh their memories as to who he is. Everyone has something to say.

So what do you do when the subject of Doeman comes up? You listen. That's the best way to go. Even if you know more about the artist than the person you are speaking with, listen. Even if someone insults you, listen. The more you listen, the more complete your picture of Doeman and his art becomes. You get an idea of where he stands as an artist, where his strengths and weaknesses lie, and what the prognosis on his future is. You learn why people like him, why they hate him, and why they don't care one way or the other.

Whenever someone gives you information about any art or artist, you also learn just as much about the person giving you the information (or opinion) as you do about the art. You learn whom to trust and whom to avoid, who knows what they're talking about and who doesn't. Mastering the art of buying art means knowing how to evaluate art people as well as knowing how to evaluate art.

Example 1:

Some sellers say anything to sell art, and sometimes what they say is not necessarily true. One way they occasionally distort the facts is by comparing the art they have for sale to art by more famous artists. Imagine hearing any of the following reasonings from an art dealer:

"The painting you are thinking about buying is just as good as a Jonathan Johnson painting. Johnson's paintings sell for between $25,000 and $30,000 each. At only $3,000, that makes this painting an absolute bargain."

"If Jonathan Johnson had painted this, it would be worth $30,000. I'm only asking $3,000 for it."

"You can't touch a Jonathan Johnson at this price."

None of these statements are valid. Jonathan Johnson did not paint the painting you like, and his price structure has nothing to do with the value of that painting. Though the two may look alike, they are totally unrelated and the dealer is attempting to establish a connection in order to increase the painting's attractiveness and make the asking price seem more like a bargain.

Even if the painting happens to be as good as a Jonathan Johnson, the dealer's arguments still hold no water. Much more goes into determining value than how one piece of art compares in quality to another from a visual standpoint alone. The dealer is making a frivolous and irrelevant value comparison for the sole purpose of selling you this piece of art.

Carry this logic to extremes and imagine a seller telling you the following: "If Vincent Van Gogh had painted this, it would be worth $25 million. I'm only asking $3,000 for it." Does Van Gogh have anything to do with this seller's painting? Are you getting an incredible bargain if you buy it? Of course not!

Example 2:

Over time, you learn who you can and cannot trust in the art business. One dealer I know does not always tell the truth. She sometimes tells me several conflicting stories about the same work of art; other times she gives me information that cannot be confirmed by other sources. I can never be sure about what I'm hearing, and experience has taught me to accept nothing she says until I verify it independently.

She sounds like someone I should terminate relations with, but I don't. I continue to work with her from time to time because she happens to be a competent dealer, and she happens to buy and sell interesting and worthwhile art.

Aside from the fact that I can accept nothing she tells me at face value, she's great. If I am interested in a work of art she has for sale, I find out the price and that's it. I listen to everything else she says – I don't want to be rude – but then I do the necessary research entirely on my own.

Unfortunately, if you were to meet this dealer for the first time, you would have no idea what to believe and what not to believe. She's entertaining and knowledgeable, and she speaks with great conviction and always sounds sincere. Other art dealers won't warn you about her unless they know and trust you – you have to learn by yourself (dealers rarely gossip casually in public about fellow dealers). If you buy art based on her advice alone, you might end up with a great piece of art at a fair price. But you might also significantly overpay for a mediocre example. She makes everything she sells sound equally appetizing.

A Look Ahead

Now that you've had an introduction to art people, you're ready to go out and meet some of them – particularly those who are involved with types of art that relate to your buying interests. The majority of these people happen to be art dealers, and you will meet them as you shop from gallery to gallery comparing the selections they have to offer.

As you have seen, the more people you meet, the more you learn about art and the better balanced your art education becomes. In the same vein, the more galleries you visit, the better able you are to select just the right art to purchase and the better balanced your art buying becomes. Naturally, you need instruction in how to locate as many of the right galleries and meet as many of the right dealers as possible, and these topics are covered in the next chapter.

CHAPTER 6

Comparison Shopping for Art

Knowing what types of art you want to buy and being able to select specific pieces that suit your lifestyle do not necessarily go hand in hand. So far, you have seen art you like at certain galleries, museums, online, and in other public places. But you have only seen that art as a result of random exposures, not organized, systematic visits. What you have seen to this point is only the beginning.

Shopping for art is like shopping for anything else. Now that you have defined your likes, you need to find out who sells that type of art, speak with them, see what they have to offer, and make gallery-to-gallery and dealer-to-dealer comparisons. You have to survey what's available in the marketplace. In order to select worthwhile works of art – ones that are priced fairly and that you won't get tired of looking at – you've got to stifle every impulse to buy immediately and instead make it a point to comparison shop.

Think about how gallery owners select their art. Out of all the millions of art pieces available for sale, they have to decide what to show and which artists to exhibit. Passion, feeling, and visual impact, of course, play significant roles in their selection processes, but there's more. When they see art they like, they research it, evaluate its quality, see what else is available in that category, compare prices, and ultimately determine whether they can remain competitive with other galleries by buying and then selling it. They comparison shop for art that has the most value from business, aesthetic, and quality standpoints. Shouldn't you?

Why Everyone Doesn't Comparison Shop

Many inexperienced buyers make the mistake of buying art without comparison shopping. They do so primarily because of a misconception they have that I call the "uniqueness myth." They believe that since every work of art is "unique" – one-of-a-kind – they might as well buy what they like when they see it because they'll never find anything else exactly like it.

This myth is only partially true. Any original work of art is unique in the sense that no other work of art looks *exactly* like it, but that's about as far as you can go with this line of reasoning. In spite of its "uniqueness," that work of art also happens to be similar to plenty of other works of art. Let's say, for example, that you see a painting of a Paris street scene. Even though no other Paris street scene painting is a precise duplicate of the one you saw, hundreds of artists have produced countless thousands of Paris street scenes over the years. And, if you take the time to look, you can find a number of street scenes that are similar to that one particular scene.

Whatever works of art specifically attract you, you can *always* find a number of other pieces out there that look approximately (and often remarkably) the same. The more art you see, the more you will realize how true this is.

Related to the uniqueness myth is another reason why beginners tend not to comparison shop; they mistake initial attraction for everlasting love. They believe in love at first sight; they believe that they can find "perfect" art, and no other art can ever provide them with as much satisfaction and enjoyment. This rarely happens with anything else people buy, so why should it happen with art? Veteran art buyers will tell you it doesn't.

Whenever you see art that attracts you, know that you are being attracted only in the moment, that you are experiencing the love-at-first-sight phenomenon. For this reason, you should avoid the impulse to buy and instead test that attraction by comparison shopping. Compare the art to similar pieces at other galleries; compare it to totally different pieces at other galleries. You may find art that attracts you just as much; you may find art that attracts you more. You'll discover this once you begin looking.

Lastly, some art buyers don't comparison shop because the galleries they patronize discourage comparison shopping. These establishments don't want their clients to know that worthwhile art can also be found elsewhere. They manipulate by saying things like, "Buy this now because you'll never find another one like it," or "This is the best one you'll ever see." They use the "uniqueness myth," the love-at-first-sight phenomenon, and whatever additional ploys that they have at their disposal to in order to keep you inside their galleries and sell you art. These sellers prefer buyers who ask few questions, blindly accept what they are told, and are convinced that the best art can only be found at certain galleries (theirs in particular). We're getting a little ahead of ourselves, though. You'll read more about these sorts of tactics in Chapter 7, "Dealer Dealings" and Chapter 12, "How Not to Buy Art."

Established Versus Offbeat Resources

The number-one rule to follow when learning how to comparison shop for your selections is this: *Stick with established galleries when you're just starting out.* You need all the protections you can get at this early stage, and you will see in the next chapter why established galleries are among the best and safest places to begin buying art.

Beating the bushes for art, as so many collectors love to do, can be hazardous to your wallet. Avoid art liquidations, estate sales, yard sales, flea markets, unqualified online resources, and auctions of all types. Stay away from second hand stores, places that sell art on the side but really specialize in other merchandise, and so on. Don't shop out of newspaper classifieds or at the homes of private collectors. These are all high-risk ventures, and you need plenty of experience buying art before you start to shop wherever you happen to see art for sale.

Locating Galleries That Sell What You Want

Comparison shopping for art does not mean that you have to spend months contacting galleries and meeting dealers around the world. Your search depends upon the type of art you have chosen to buy. For example, if you want to buy art by local artists who are active only in your area, you certainly don't have to make national or international efforts to find out who sells it.

As for how exhaustive or comprehensive you want to make your search, that's up to you. You can go out and locate every gallery that sells your type of art or you can approach the assignment more casually and locate only a few. Know, however, that the amount of effort you put in is directly proportional to the amount of knowledge you will accumulate about your art and about the marketplace for that art, and to the quality of the selections you will eventually make. In any event, do whatever feels most comfortable. A variety of gallery-locating techniques are listed here. Choose and follow whichever ones are applicable to your particular situation.

A good place to begin any art gallery search is by looking at advertisements in major national or international art magazines and newspapers. See Appendix I for a partial listing of major art-related periodicals and brief comments about each. Many city, state, or regional art-related periodicals are also available. Check with local art galleries or public libraries to see whether any are published in your area. These periodicals often contain extensive gallery advertisements and provide the best coverage of local and regional art scenes.

Most art-related newspapers and magazines are available at main branches of major public libraries. Libraries that don't shelve them can often borrow them for you from other libraries or tell you where to find them. If spending time in libraries doesn't suit you, you can find most of these periodicals at major book or magazine stores either in your local community or online.

Focus your attention primarily on art gallery advertisements. The articles won't help you all that much at this early stage, but if you happen to see one that catches your eye, either read it or note what magazine it appears in and save it for later. The articles are much more helpful after you know your way around the art business a little better.

Some periodicals will appeal to you more than others. Your best tact is to sample them all at first, and eventually subscribe to the ones you enjoy the most and find most helpful to your art buying. In the meantime, browse thoroughly.

If you are interested in art from foreign countries, locate and study a copy of the *International Directory of Arts*. This annual publication is a worldwide guide to museums, art-related institutions, dealers, galleries, and much more. You can find it at most major libraries. (*International Directory of Arts* is published by the German firm of K. G. Saur. The 31st edition, 2007/2008, contains approximately 2,500 pages in three volumes.)

Here are several additional resources for locating galleries:

- Your local Yellow Pages and those of nearby major cities under the heading "Art Galleries, Dealers & Consultants."

- Entertainment sections of local newspapers and city, state or regional general-interest magazines. These publications often contain gallery advertisements, notices of art openings and ongoing shows, art-related events, and so on. Look for special sections where art galleries list current offerings or exhibits.

- Membership lists of regional, national, and international art dealer organizations. The major national and international ones can be found in the *International Directory of Arts*, the *American Art Directory*, and also in the annual directories published by magazines like *Art in America* (also see Appendices 2 and 5). Check local galleries and regional art publications for names and addresses of city, state, and regional gallery associations.

- Online searches. General online searches can be pretty daunting, but typing in "Art Dealers Association" on Google (*www.google.com*) gives good results. Searching specific dealer art sites like *Art Dealers Association of America* (*artdealers.org*) or all-purpose art sites with large databases like *ArtInfo* (*artinfo.com*) can be far more productive. A number of art websites provide a variety of search options such as by artist, medium, dealer, and subject matter. See Appendix VII for a listing of internet art resources.

- Referrals from collectors, museum curators, and knowledgeable members of the art community. Referrals from museum curators and other nonbiased professionals are especially helpful. You may not know many experts or authorities yet, but the more involved you become with collecting, the more of these people you'll be introduced to. Much of your most valuable information will eventually come by word of mouth.

Making Contact

As you research, make a working list of all galleries that seem to offer art or artists similar to what you are interested in. Write down full names, addresses, phone numbers, emails, websites, and include any other relevant details such as where you read the ads, why the ads attracted you, who referred you, and so on. Include the following types of galleries on your list:

- Galleries that represent particular artists whose work you have already seen and like.

- Galleries that offer the look you like by whatever artists happen to be producing it, whether you recognize the names of the artists or not.

- Galleries that sell art you find appealing, even though you may never have heard of the artists.

- Galleries that sell art you like in your price range.

- Galleries selling what you like that have been in business for long periods of time.

Next, contact these galleries. The four ways you can reach them are by phone, letter, email, or personal visit. Tell everyone you meet where or how you heard about them, what attracted you, and ask for promotional information about the various galleries. Your primary objective here is to view the art for sale by the galleries – personally, in brochures, or online – and see how much you like it. If you happen to see a selection of art you really like, get basic facts about it and nothing more – the in-depth research and decisions about whether or not to buy come later.

With first contacts like these, keep interactions simple; find out what each gallery sells, and get an idea of whether it's right for you. Don't get involved in long discussions about art. Don't let anyone start selling to you. If you prefer making contacts by phone, mail, or email, don't let anyone pressure you to come in for personal visits – ask them to send you any promotional material available on the gallery's art, and that's that. Personal visits are best, however. As soon as possible, visit all galleries that appear to have what you want.

If you're curious about how much a particular work of art costs and the asking price is not readily apparent, ask. This is a good time to begin getting a basic feel for prices. Don't immediately eliminate a gallery if a price quote is way over your budget. They may also sell art with a comparable look and feel that is more in your price range. Keep price discussions simple, though. Advise gallery personnel that you are just beginning your art quest, are curious about what sells for how much, but that you're not yet ready to buy and don't want to get much more involved than that.

Comparison shopping for art is the process that exposes you to a variety of dealers, a variety of galleries, and a variety of ways of doing business. It gives you an overall understanding of how the marketplace operates and what it has to offer. Comparison shopping provides you with ample opportunities to make intelligent selections and informed buys.

You may never do business with many of the galleries you locate and visit. You may decide to buy your art from only two or three or four after all is said and done. No matter how many dealers you eventually patronize, at least you will have made the contacts and had the experiences of meeting them and seeing their places of business. All this gives you a significant advantage over other collectors who never bother to broaden their horizons beyond one or two dealers.

Example 1:

Art of superior quality is the hardest to find; plenty of people are looking for it. When a desirable work of art comes onto the market, many people may want to own it, but only one lucky person ends up with it. That person is usually a serious comparison shopper – one who keeps constant contact with a wide range of galleries. Good art sells fast, and you want to be first in line when it arrives at a gallery.

One very thorough collector I know maintains constant contact with many galleries. He stays on top of the market by sending out periodic want lists of the art and artists he is looking for to all dealers who he thinks could possibly come across pieces that might interest him. When new dealers open their galleries, his list is one of the first things to arrive in their mail. He follows every mailed list with a phone call or a personal visit when appropriate, introduces himself to the gallery owner, and clearly restates what he is looking for. He is able to point out a number of fine examples in his collection that he has acquired as a result of his diligence.

Example 2:

You can actually save money on art by comparison shopping, keeping a wide range of contacts, and knowing many dealers who sell what you like. A significant amount of art is bought, sold, and traded between dealers before it ends up in private collections. One reason for these gallery-to-gallery transactions is that dealers are constantly on the lookout for art they know their customers will buy. Dealers scour the market and buy this art wherever they happen to find it, and such an approach includes buying from other galleries.

Let's say that Dealer A knows what you like to buy. He sees a good example of that art at Dealer B's gallery, a gallery you have never visited. Depending on how sure Dealer A is that you will buy the art, he either buys it outright, trades for it, or asks to have it on consignment so that he can offer it to you.

When Dealer A gets the art from Dealer B he will, in the great majority of cases, raise the price and offer it to you for more than Dealer B is selling it for. If you buy the art from Dealer A, you pay that difference in price for never having met dealer B. If Dealer B had already known you and was aware of your interests, she would have offered you the art before passing it on to Dealer A. You could have paid Dealer B's cheaper asking price rather than Dealer A's more expensive one.

In this example, the art passed through only two dealers before being offered to you. Sometimes art passes through four, five, or even more dealers before it finally ends up in private collections. And the more dealers that handle an art piece before it reaches its final destination, the more expensive it gets. Each dealer adds on a profit margin in the form of a percentage markup, a commission, or a brokering fee. If you can keep that dealer-to-dealer chain short, you can save money.

A Look Ahead

The first stages of comparison shopping involve your locating places that offer selections you like and cataloguing the most likely of these resources for return visits. Initial contacts are brief, but as you move closer and closer to buying art, interactions become increasingly complex and involved. For your more serious encounters, you need basic information about art dealers and art galleries, the similarities or differences you will find between one gallery and the next, and how to interpret those findings. This information, which is discussed in the next chapter, will protect you from advantage-takers and help you make the most of your gallery contacts.

CHAPTER 7

Dealer Dealings

Art dealers and art galleries are a fact of the art business. The art business cannot exist without them. You have to shop their establishments, and you have to interact, communicate, and negotiate with them at various points in the process of buying art.

Unfortunately, some art buyers, especially those who are not that knowledgeable about the art business, believe that dealers are a necessary inconvenience that must be tolerated. They think that all dealers do is buy art cheaply, mark the price way up, stick it in their galleries, and sell it expensively. To them, dealers are nothing more than merchants who always want their piece of the action, mechanically acting as middlemen between one owner and another.

The truth: Art dealers are experts at what they do. Art dealers are professionals who provide a structure to the art business and are eminently qualified to handle art in the marketplace. They know how to properly transfer art from artists or private sellers to art buyers and then transfer it again if those buyers ever decide to resell it. Without them, purchasing art in any organized manner would be extremely difficult. The art-buying public would have no one to supply them, no one to give them advice, and no formalized settings in which art transactions could take place.

In many ways, art dealers are similar to stockbrokers, real estate agents, and other merchandise brokers. All keep current with their respective markets, know how to place dollar values on art they deal in, know how to locate quality art and make it available to interested buyers, and are qualified to advise buyers as to what best suits their needs. The best among them spot trends and even dictate tastes.

A word of caution: Art dealers are not oracles to be obeyed without question. As in any business, a few dealers make their livings by taking advantage of unsuspecting clients. Sooner or later you find out who these dealers are and learn to avoid them. The majority, however, are respected professionals who attend to your particular situation as it relates to the art market in general.

"But buying art from established art dealers and galleries is expensive," you say. "I know what I'm looking for, and I'm going to see whether I can find it elsewhere for less."

Be extremely careful if you're new to the art world and this is what you're thinking. Art is not necessarily cheaper outside of galleries. Yes, prices may seem lower at places like secondhand stores, frame shops, online, artists' studios, resale outlets, antique malls, and so on, but look a little closer. What you frequently see are inferior works that art dealers have already passed on or would never consider selling in the first place, not to mention the possibilities of condition problems or being outright forgeries.

This is not to say that all art outside of galleries is damaged, inferior, or fake. Quality art *is* out there, but it's not easy to find, and plenty of savvy dealers and collectors chase after it. What happens all too often, unfortunately, is that when amateur art buffs invite art dealers to comment on their backwater bargains, the standard dealer response is, "I hope you can get your money back."

Of course, if you buy from galleries, you won't be able to impress your friends with what a super bargain you found at the local secondhand store, nor will you realize instant appreciation on your purchases by paying full gallery retail. But just in case you're interested, the great majority of art gallery art fares *much better* financially over time than "wherever you happen to find it" art. So in the end, you usually get the most for your money anyway.

"But art is a matter of personal choice," you say. "What I like is my business and no one else's. I don't need any art dealers to tell me what I should be buying."

Not true. Recognizing quality in art and selecting and eventually buying worthwhile pieces is a learned, not an innate, ability. You must learn what makes art "likable" (good) or "not likable" (bad) in order to make intelligent "personal choices." Art dealers come in mighty handy here for a number of reasons:

- Art dealers see countless thousands of works of art. All they do is look at art, and when they take a break from looking, they talk about art. Their recommendations come from a broad-based knowledge of the art market.

- Art dealers are qualified to give you specialized financial advice about whatever art you are considering buying.

- Art dealers screen all art that is offered to them and sell or resell only the best.

- Art dealers educate you. They answer your questions, explain specific art and artists in depth, recommend books to read, and share other important knowledge. They want you to gain experience.

- The best dealers offer money-back guarantees of authenticity, full condition reports, trade-back arrangements, free updated appraisals, consultations on the scope and direction of your buying, and other amenities. Try getting *those* at the flea markets or estate sales.

Now supposing that some years after you start buying art, you decide to sell some of it. Your tastes have changed, you're moving into smaller quarters, you're upgrading your collection, or whatever. Dealers come in mighty handy in these instances, too. This book is about buying art, not selling it, but nevertheless, you should know at least a little about how dealers help you sell as well as buy.

"But I know how much my art is worth," you say. "I can sell it on my own without any outside help." Believing this is a big mistake — in fact, it's three big mistakes.

First mistake: Private sellers think that with no professional help, they can accurately determine how much their art is worth. The dollar values they come up with are generally inaccurate (usually too high) and almost always based on inadequate and arbitrary research. *The facts*: You have to know an artist and his or her market inside and out in order to accurately value the art.

Second mistake: Sellers believe they can locate the perfect private collectors for their art. They take out classified ads in newspapers and magazines, they hang out at antique shows or art auctions looking to see who the big buyers are, they read articles about collectors and then write them letters, and so on. *The facts*: Contacting private collectors personally is difficult; private collectors prefer to remain private.

Third mistake: Sellers believe they can sell their art to collectors at full retail or, what's even more absurd, to dealers at full retail. *The facts*: Selling to private collectors is harder than finding them. Collectors pay retail to long-established galleries they know and trust. They pay retail for the amenities that galleries provide, and they are not inclined to buy art with no guarantees from total strangers. Dealers, on the other hand, buy at wholesale and sell at retail — they obviously do not buy art at the same price they sell it for, or they wouldn't be in business.

Dealers help you sell your art in ways you can't help yourself. They know the market for your art, they know detailed information about the artists, and they know who collects those artists. And there's more:

- Dealers recognize how important your art is, how that art fits into the artists' careers, whether it is high or low end in terms of quality, and so on.

- Dealers recognize the strengths and weaknesses in your art and the strengths and weaknesses in the markets for that art.

- Dealers know which collectors would like to own your art. They understand the individual needs of those collectors and know how to properly present your art. Dealers stand a much better chance of selling your art to those collectors than you do.

- Dealers give you a realistic idea of how much money you can expect to sell your art for.

- Dealers often net you more for your art than you can by selling it to "private collectors" on your own. Believe it or not!

Art dealers are in business to help you whenever your situation involves a transaction in art. Whether you're buying, selling, trading, or collecting, take advantage of the services that dealers offer and the insight they provide.

All is not wonderful in art-dealer-land, however. In a perfect world where everything was fair, buying art would be easy. You could visit any art gallery, present your situation, state what you wanted to buy and how much you wished to spend on it, make your selection, write out the check, and take your new acquisition home with you. Unfortunately, we do not live in a perfect world, and buying art is not quite that straightforward. Not every dealer is fair.

The art business, like any other business, is populated with great dealers, good dealers, average dealers, worse-than-average dealers, and a few terrible dealers. The art they sell ranges, in like fashion, from excellent to awful (most of it being closer to excellent than it is to awful, of course). Prices range, too. Most are fair and reasonable, but a small percentage are ridiculously inflated. Major goals of your comparison shopping are to meet, understand, and communicate with dealers and, ultimately, to differentiate between who sells good-quality art at the right prices and who doesn't – and who has the best (and worst) selections for you.

Characteristics of Good Art Dealers

Good dealers listen to what you have to say. They allow you to lead the discussion about what you are interested in buying. They want to know what you are looking for. They show you any art they have in stock that could possibly interest you. When they don't have anything in your field, they refer you to galleries that do.

Good dealers want you to learn. They determine how much you know, offer advice where it is needed, and suggest where you need help. They either tell you who is qualified to teach you, or they teach you themselves.

Good dealers discuss options. They offer you a variety of alternatives as to which direction you can take with your art buying. They discuss the good and bad points of each option. They never make you feel pressured to move in any particular direction.

Good dealers give you plenty of facts. They discuss the visual, scholarly, aesthetic, and historical aspects of the art you are interested in. They compare and contrast artists, quality levels, works of art, and art prices. All your questions are answered in a direct and straightforward fashion.

Good dealers provide you with outside tools and resources for continuing your education on your own. They recommend books to read, museums to visit, experts and collectors to meet, and collections to see. They present you with information not only from their own galleries but also from other galleries. They do not try and convince you that their galleries are the only ones you should ever patronize.

Good dealers speak your language and work with you at your own pace. You never feel compelled to buy. You are always free to make your own decisions. You leave their galleries knowing more than when you arrive, and feel that they are genuinely concerned about your success as an art buyer.

Dealers to Avoid

Unfortunately, not all art dealers have your best interests in mind when they attempt to sell you art. These sorts of dealers can be avoided, though. Certain telltale signs almost always mean you should exit the gallery you're in and move on to another.

Avoid dealers whose sales presentations focus primarily on the emotional. These dealers speak only about the way the art looks – the beauty, the drama, the color, the intensity, the feeling. If you listen carefully, however, you notice that important details are conspicuously absent from the presentation, namely facts about the art, the artist, and the market for the art.

Watch out for dealers who avoid price talk. They're usually evasive for a reason, most likely because what they sell is overpriced and they prefer not talking about it. They would rather haul you into their private viewing rooms and tell you how their art transports you into unique and marvelous worlds (the financial world not being one of them). Interrupt the travelogue with price questions and you can get some rather strange and occasionally ugly responses. Any time you hear phrases like, "If you have to ask the price...," or "It's worth many times that in beauty alone....," or "How you feel is what's important, not how much it costs," you're in trouble.

Dealers, of course, have a right to say whatever they want about the price of the art they sell. No law forbids them from believing that price is irrelevant and what counts is the mystic, cosmic interplay between you and the essence of the artist as embodied in the art. But the facts are that any art piece has a corresponding fair and reasonable dollar value, one that anyone familiar with that artist's market will agree on, give or take a little.

Watch out for dealers who focus their sales presentations *only* on money. These are the exact opposite of those who avoid price talk. All these dealers do is talk money. The worst offenders go so far as to totally ignore the way the art looks and sell artwork as if it were stocks or bonds. In the extreme instance, galleries tell prospective clients that they will enjoy set percentages of appreciation over specific time periods – which is a ridiculous, misleading, and borderline fraudulent way of selling art.

In a way, the people who buy art based on financial reasons alone are as much to blame as the dealers for the proliferation of dollar-oriented selling. A good percentage of buyers, especially first-time buyers, are attracted to art by the possibilities of financial gain, and such buyers make easy marks for investment-style selling. Dealers simply play into their fantasies about buying art now and cashing it in for big profits later.

Typical statements you hear during the course of a make-big-bucks-fast sales presentation are:

> *"Who cares whether or not you like it. In eighteen months it'll be worth twice what you're paying for it."*

> *"As soon as this artist has a show at the Municipal Art Museum, you won't be able to touch one for this price."*

> *"Buy one now while you can still afford it."*

> *"This piece has a retail value of $10,000 on the open market, but I'm going to let you have it for only $3,500.*

> *"This artist isn't going to be around for much longer. As soon as he dies, his prices are going through the roof."*

> *"This edition is almost sold out. Cash in while we still have some left. Once it sells out, prices will double."*

> *"This is the only one of its kind. You can either buy it or forget about ever being able to buy one as good for as little money again."*

> *"This piece will make a great investment."*

> *"You could buy these for a song ten years ago. Think what they'll be worth ten years from now."*

These types of statements are not only basically untrue, they're also disgusting. To portray a piece of art as nothing more than a speculative commodity or an artist as a person who will hopefully die soon and boost the value of his own art is the basest way to operate an art business. Anytime you find yourself in these sorts of situations, no matter how much money you are being told you can make, leave immediately.

Watch out for dealers who attempt to qualify you as a buyer. They decide how much of their time is worth spending on you based on the amount of money they believe that you have to spend with them.

One gallery I know that specializes in selling overpriced art to unsuspecting out-of-town buyers uses a couple of well-placed questions to get to the bottom line. When you visit this gallery, shortly after your entrance, a sales person asks you the question, "Are you in town attending the medical convention?" A medical convention may or may not be taking place, but that's irrelevant. The question is a lead-in to finding out what you do for a living and, therefore, whether or not you can afford this gallery's art. If you answer no, the staff person responds with "I thought for sure you were a doctor. You certainly look like one. What do you do for a living?" or "What brings you to the city then?" or "I've been seeing doctors all week, and I'm ready for a change. What do you do for a living?" If your answers indicate that you've got money, get ready for an aggressive sales presentation.

Avoid dealers who are not sensitive to your needs and who don't listen to you. These dealers often force you to look at art you are not the least bit interested in. Rather than admitting they don't sell what you want and referring you to galleries that do, they try to change your mind and force you to buy what they sell.

Watch out for dealers who focus on one or two artists, ones they represent or for which they carry stock, and avoid all others. No matter what you say, the conversation always returns to these few artists. You get a very one-sided picture of the art market from these dealers. Avoid them unless, of course, they happen to be dealing in artists you collect.

Avoid dealers who pressure you, who need your sale to make their next commission, or who are constantly on top of you to buy. Being victimized by a hard sell is always painful. Galleries that are more concerned about their bottom lines than serving your needs are a sad fact of the art business. When you feel that the art wants you rather than you want the art, just say no.

Watch out for dealers who find out how little you know about certain art or artists and then go to work educating you whether you want to learn or not. Once these dealers see that you're not experienced, anything goes. You may be introduced to a "world famous" painter, one that the seller can't believe you've never heard of. You may get spoken to in "secret technical art lingo" that you don't understand, but can have the privilege of learning if you decide to patronize that gallery. Never let anyone bully you with their supposed expertise.

Finally, avoid art dealers who answer any of your questions about their art with the reply "I don't know." This answer is *never* acceptable no matter what the question. At the very least, it's an indication that the dealer is uninformed about some aspect of what he or she is selling. It's also a convenient way of dodging a touchy question such as whether the art is worth what you are being asked to pay for it. At worst, "I don't know" is a great way for a dealer to avoid telling you something he doesn't want you to know.

Example 1:

Antique dealers occasionally call me when they meet private individuals who have art for sale. One time, an out-of-town dealer called to tell me about a middle-aged couple who had a group of paintings for sale and asked me to come out and take a look. I wanted to make sure the trip would be worth my while so I asked him to find out some particulars about the art and call me back.

The next day he called to tell me that the paintings had originally come from an elderly lady who had apparently acquired them over a twenty- or thirty-year period. He then gave me basic information about some of the paintings like sizes, subject matters, artists' names, and how much the couple was asking for them. Several of the artists were collectible and all asking prices were reasonable. What I heard sounded good, so I decided to make the trip.

I arrived at the couple's home and introduced myself. The husband led me into a rear room and, with a sweep of his hand, directed my attention toward the paintings, all of which were leaning against a wall and stacked one in front of the other. I began looking through them and immediately realized that this trip was going to be a complete waste of time.

The paintings by name artists were either outright forgeries or terrible examples. The rest were by complete unknowns. I had even seen some of these paintings for sale at various shops over the past several years which meant that on top of everything else, the "elderly lady" story was a lie.

I looked through the collection, bought nothing, politely thanked the couple for their time and left. The sad part of this story is that several weeks later I was at the home of a relatively inexperienced collector who proudly told me he had beat the dealers and made a great art buy out of a private home. He showed me his three latest acquisitions and – you guessed it – they had all come from this out-of-town couple. One of the paintings was a forgery that he had paid almost $2,000 for. The other two were junk.

Example 2:

Some collectors prefer buying their art directly from the artists to buying it from dealers. They enjoy meeting the artists in person in their studios and negotiating purchases without dealer interference. This is fine, but once again, be aware that if you buy without dealer assistance, you'd better know what you're doing first. There are drawbacks to buying directly from artists.

First of all, artists are not art dealers (with a few exceptions), and artists' studios are not art galleries. Artists are experts at creating art and not necessarily at selling it. Most are far removed from the business of buying and selling art.

Artists may know plenty about the lives and the art of their fellow artists, but they do not stay on top of current events in the art business. They do not usually provide amenities that galleries do such as trade-back policies or free updated appraisals, and they cannot provide you with an overview of the market the way that dealers can.

Artists focus primarily on their own work. They often give you very biased ideas about what your buying options are. You would not, for instance, expect an artist to suggest that her work is not right for you and then refer you to another artist whose work she thinks would better suit your tastes. In the great majority of cases, her work is what suits you, and that's that.

As for you, arbitrarily picking artists whose work you happen to like is not the way to collect. Until you acquire a good overview of the market, you'll have difficulty recognizing which artists to collect, whether or not to pay their asking prices, whether you are getting the best-quality work for your money, and so on. Have dealers help you make those sorts of decisions while you're still in the learning stages. Once you've developed a feel for what you're doing, buying from artists can be a very rewarding experience. You'll learn how to buy directly from artists in Chapter 10.

A Look Ahead

Being able to distinguish between one art dealer and the next is a big step towards selecting the right art, but it's only part of what you need to know. Dealers operate and sell art from their galleries, places where you will be spending significant amounts of time viewing art, learning about art, and eventually buying art. Understanding what art galleries are and knowing how to use them to their full potential is just as important as understanding the dealers who operate them. Chapter 8 will help you to attain this goal.

CHAPTER 8

Insider Tips on What to Do Inside Art Galleries

When you step into an art gallery, you encounter much more than an art dealer standing in a room full of art. You leave the everyday world behind and enter a unique microcosm of reality. The term *art gallery* is almost too mild a description of what confronts you once you are inside. Most galleries could more accurately be described as shrines to art or art temples. They are places where art is hallowed above all else and where devotion to that art is embodied in the ceremony of dealers passing it on to collectors in exchange for money.

Galleries are designed to focus your total attention on the particular art or artists they represent. When they do their job well, you are aware only of what's going on right before your eyes. Your life, for those brief moments consists of art, art, and art.

Whenever you're inside a gallery that displays art you find appealing, you feel compelled to a certain extent to select a piece or two that you might consider buying. A portion of that compulsion may be attributed to your genuine desire to own the art and another portion to the gallery's efforts to convince or induce you to own it. Some of the more intimidating galleries can actually interfere with and alter your normal decision-making process in favor of their art.

Controlling your own destiny inside galleries is not always easy. Meeting art dealers on their home turf can be difficult, especially for beginning buyers. The dealers and their staffs know plenty; you hardly know anything. They have dealt with thousands of customers; you've barely had a chance to get your feet wet. They have all their sales tools right there at their fingertips; you have nothing. They see certain qualities in you the moment you walk through their doors; you don't have the vaguest idea of what these galleries are about and what to expect from them. They have all the advantages.

This is not to say that art dealers lie in wait in their galleries, ready to play on your inexperience and manipulate the way you think. The overwhelming majority don't. But they are in the business of selling art, and if they can figure out how to talk you into buying some, that's exactly what they'll do. In order to understand the art of buying art, you have to know how to navigate your way through art galleries; understand what happens within them; and know what to look for, what to watch out for, and how to interpret it all.

Gallery Interiors Versus the Rest of the World

Art gallery interiors present art at its absolute highest level of appeal. The track lighting is perfectly focused, the walls behind the art are plain, and the carpet or flooring is simple. You see little, if any, competition from the surrounding environment. These are important points to keep in mind because under such circumstances, just about anything looks great. When properly displayed and lit, a sack full of trash can look like a masterpiece worthy of a place in any of the world's great art museums.

Another fixture of gallery interiors is the gallery owners and staff. The information they present you with is designed to heighten the beauty of their art even further. They believe in the art they sell, and they know exactly what to say in order to sell it.

Finally, you have the art gallery viewing room, the place where art looks even better than it does in any other location on the gallery floor. Galleries without viewing rooms also have special spots where their art looks best. When you and an owner or staff person head over to the viewing room or viewing spot, art in tow, for a closer look under these perfectly ideal viewing conditions, you see and hear about that art at its absolute unobstructed finest. At this point, you have to be completely sure whether you want to own it or not, because the deck is definitely stacked in the gallery's favor.

Keep in mind that if you buy the art, you have to remove it from the protective environment of the gallery and take it out into the cold, cruel world where it is no longer the center of the universe and no longer has a supporting cast telling you how great it is. It gets no special treatment in your environment; it becomes just another thing in a room full of things. Suddenly, it has to stand on its own and prove that it is really as great as the gallery made it look and made you think it is. The truth is that sometimes it is and other times it isn't.

Many inexperienced collectors, unfortunately, do not account for the affects that ideal viewing conditions of art gallery interiors combined with overwhelmingly positive employee input can have on art. They buy art on the spot without ever seeing it outside gallery settings and away from the hype, display it in totally different settings, and expect it to thrill them just as much as it did at the galleries. Several weeks or months later, they begin to wonder why it doesn't look as great as they originally thought it did when they bought it. At worst, they actually regret buying it.

What you have to do in order to prevent this from happening to you is to take any selections you are considering buying out of the viewing rooms, out of the galleries, away from the sales people, and into your own environment – and keep them there for a few days – *before you buy them.* You see and hear how great they are from the sellers. Now you must let gallery influences fade into the background, let your personal feelings come to the foreground, and decide whether or not the art really means as much to you as the gallery presentation led you to believe it does.

How do you take a selection out of a gallery without having to buy it? Easy. Art galleries offer a courtesy, known as *"taking art home on approval,"* that allows you to keep art, at no financial risk, for anywhere from several days to a week or two for the sole purpose of deciding whether or not you are sure you want to own it. Some galleries ask you to leave deposits or even pay for the art in full when you do this, but all will completely refund your money if for any reason you decide not to buy. Taking art home on approval, for example, is absolutely essential when buying over the internet, as you'll see in Chapter 11.

When you're just starting out in your collecting, always take art you have selected for possible purchase home with you on approval first. You will see for yourself how drastically gallery interiors and sales presentations can sometimes influence the way art looks, and you will discover that some art you initially thought you wanted to buy is really not for you at all. One word of caution: never take art home on approval unless you are serious about buying it.

Art Gallery Back Rooms, Storage Areas, and Offices

Almost all art galleries have more art for sale than what you see on display in their public viewing areas. Galleries often have additional works of art stored in stock rooms, back rooms, office areas, separate warehouse storage facilities, and so on. Some galleries keep photo albums of art that they have in storage, pieces they have access to out of private collections, and art they can purchase for you through other dealers. A gallery may have ten additional pieces available or it may have ten thousand.

Whenever you are in a gallery and don't see art that interests you, don't turn around and walk out. Introduce yourself to the owner or a staff person, state exactly what you're looking for, and find out whether they have access to any art you desire even though none is currently on display. You do yourself a major disservice every time you browse in silence and then leave because you miss seeing everything for sale that is out of public view.

See back-room selections and actually go into storage areas with dealers whenever possible. These experiences add to your knowledge of how galleries operate and to your understanding of the range and variety of art that galleries have to offer. Other advantages to seeing art that is not on display in public viewing areas are as follows:

- A gallery may have large holdings in an artist or type of art that you like, but may not currently be showing it.

- A gallery may have large holdings in an artist that you are not that familiar with, but whose art you might find appealing once you have a chance to see multiple examples.

- You may notice art you like that gallery owners forgot they even had for sale.

- You may find art you like that is out of place in a particular gallery and that the owner is willing to let you have at an attractive price.

- You are afforded opportunities to learn about art and artists whose work gallery owners keep in stock but rarely display in public areas.

- Dealers understand from how you respond to the full scope of their art how best they will be able to help you in the future.

As with storage areas, offices can also be interesting and informative. So whenever you have the opportunity to see and speak with gallery owners or staff people in their offices, do so. Visiting office areas and seeing the centers of operations increases your understanding of what art galleries are all about. It also makes you less intimidated and thus better able to make decisions regarding the substance and direction of your collecting.

Another advantage to office access and access to places other than the main floor is that you sometimes get the chance to see new arrivals and hear about the latest developments before the general public does. When things happen, they happen in offices and back rooms first. Acquiring this sort of inside access takes time and is part of the process of developing long-term working relationships with dealers, but as you get to know certain dealers better, you'll find yourself receiving special attention that ordinary clients do not normally receive.

Art Gallery Libraries

In any gallery, pay attention to all books, exhibition catalogues, and other art reference materials out on display for public use. More importantly, look for the gallery art library. A gallery library may consist of five books or it may consist of five thousand. It may be in an office, in a work or storage room, or out on the main floor. Libraries are usually in plain sight, but when you can't find one, ask whether one exists and, if it does, whether you can see what it looks like.

An art gallery library contains art books, exhibition catalogues, art periodicals, and other materials that relate to what the gallery sells. Art dealers use these references when they have to research particular artists or works of art. A comprehensive library is indispensable to a good art dealer and an excellent indication of how serious that gallery is about knowing the history and details behind the art it sells and having the means on hand of conveying that information to their customers. In fact, there's a saying in the art business that goes, "You're only as good as your library."

Good reference libraries should contain standard references like those you will learn about in Part III. The more of those you see, the better. Also, the more a gallery refers to them and shares that information with you, the better. The best galleries support any claims they make about their art with substantial documentation from standard reference materials that are recognized and accepted by those in the art community.

Better gallery libraries also contain substantial price reference materials which you will learn about in Part IV. Briefly, the more standard and widely accepted price references you see, the more galleries refer to them, the more they use them to determine sensible selling prices for their art, and the more they tend to share that information with you, the better.

Get into the habit of asking gallery owners or staff people whether they can provide you with printed information about particular art or artists they have on display that you are interested in. Make them use their libraries. This gives you the chance to see how they do research and also allows you to learn what books and catalogues provide the best answers to your specific questions. Most dealers are experts at art research; learn from them whenever you get the chance.

One caution, though. Ask for library references only when you're seriously considering buying art. Avoid making frivolous requests or forcing dealers to haul out book after book when you're only using them for personal research or are not really interested in learning about or buying the art you're asking questions about.

Beware of galleries that have no libraries to speak of. Galleries with minimal reference materials on hand are often more interested in merchandising art than in educating and cultivating informed collectors. A poor or nonexistent gallery reference library is never a good sign.

Tips on Recognizing the Best (and Worst) Galleries for You

The goal of all gallery visits is to identify those establishments best able to supply you with the art you want to buy. As you progress from brief initial contacts to in-depth interactions, you will be choosing those places where you will most likely do business in the future. Here are the two most important characteristics you want those galleries to have:

- Wide selections in particular artists or types of art that you find appealing.

- Personnel who have a wide range of knowledge about that type of art, have substantial experience selling it, and who show sensitivity to your collecting needs.

Galleries that do not meet these two conditions are not good places for beginners to shop.

Avoid establishments that offer only isolated examples of art you like; avoid gallery personnel who are not informed about it. While you're in the learning stages, you need to surround yourself with experts. You take serious risks if you don't.

Suppose, for example, you walk into a gallery because you see an attractive bronze statue by a sculptor whose work you like on display in the front window. You take a look around and see no other work by this artist. You ask the owner about the sculpture, and during the course of conversation you find out that it's the only work by this sculptor that he has ever had for sale, that he has learned most of what he's telling you only since he acquired it, and that he has only seen several other pieces by the artist during his entire career. Conclusion: This dealer does not qualify as an authority on the sculptor and, unless you are, you would be ill advised to buy the sculpture without doing further research.

Avoid galleries that have no direction or focus in what they sell. These places are easy to spot because they display many unrelated pieces of art by many different artists, spanning many time periods, styles, and so on. When the selection gets too general, the amount of knowledge the dealer has about that selection is usually too general as well.

Example 1:

A collector once came to me with a "bargain" painting he had discovered while rummaging through the back room of a local art gallery. He said the dealer appeared to know a little about the artist but was not that familiar with his market and how desirable his art was. That was why the price was so low.

I took one look at it and saw that it was a fake – a good fake, but a fake nonetheless. I recommended that he return it as soon as possible, but just to be on the safe side, I had him contact another dealer first in order to confirm my suspicions. The dealer agreed with my assessment, the collector returned the picture to the gallery, and fortunately, was able to get his money back without any problem.

What happened here was that this collector was not yet experienced enough to be buying odd works of art out of dealer back rooms. He knew that this particular artist was highly collectible and had seen a few examples of his work, but that was about all. He automatically took the word of the dealer (who didn't know enough about the artist either) and ended up getting fooled by a good-quality forgery.

A big problem with dealers who are not experts in what they sell is that they can inadvertently buy and sell forgeries. These dealers think they are buying and selling authentic art, but in some cases, do not know enough to tell the difference between the real thing and skillfully executed fakes.

Example 2:

A collector once asked me about a sculptor whose work he was interested in purchasing. He had visited a gallery, seen the artist's work for the first time and liked it very much. The gallery owner had fueled this collector's enthusiasm by showing him a book that contained an entire chapter on the sculptor. The collector believed from this presentation that the artist was extremely well known and almost famous.

I was familiar with this artist and told the collector that he had been given the wrong impression. Although the artist was known and respected, being categorized as "extremely well known" or "almost famous" was definitely out of the question. Seeing that much of his excitement seemed to be based on the one chapter that had been written about the artist, I asked what book the dealer had showed him.

He gave me the name of the book and I immediately recognized it as one that was not taken very seriously by members of the art community. True, the sculptor did have a chapter in the book, but the artists included were not necessarily there because they were famous. They were included primarily because they had been friends of the author. The book contained little scholarly information, but was rather a collection of anecdotes about how various artists lived their lives.

Dealers occasionally misuse their libraries when documenting the art they sell. By showing only selected references, they attempt to inflate the notoriety of their artists in order to justify unreasonable asking prices. Read everything dealers show you, but unless you know and trust them, do not assume that they're giving you either a balanced presentation or all the information you need to know.

A Look Ahead

Understanding art dealers and art galleries well enough to choose the best ones for your needs is essential to intelligent buying. You do not, however, simply decide who you're going to buy from, sit back, and wait for the art to roll in. In order to assure yourself of getting the best treatment possible in the marketplace and of being shown the greatest number of selections relating to your requirements, you have to know how to be a good customer. Some tips on being a good customer are next.

CHAPTER 9

How to Be a Good Customer

A dealer-customer relationship is a cooperative venture. You each have obligations to fulfill in order to make it work. Dealers supply you with art, educate you about that art, and, through their galleries, provide amenities, guarantees, and protections on the art you buy. Throughout this process of locating and selling you art, dealers prefer that you cooperate with them and follow certain guidelines. By doing so, you make their job of serving you so much easier.

In general, dealers like doing business with people who are serious about art and willing to learn. They offer these clients many fringe benefits that average buyers never receive such as showing them newly arrived art first. These sorts of arrangements do not develop overnight – some relationships take months or even years to mature – but once they do, buying art becomes less of an effort and even more of a pleasure.

Things Dealers Like

About the most important favor you can do for dealers is to learn what they ask you to learn. The better you understand the language and the history behind what you buy, the better you are able to communicate your needs. Informed, educated buyers are easy to work with – it's that simple. Observe the additional directives listed in this section and hasten your attainment of "most favored buyer" status among dealers.

Always be as specific as possible about what type of art you are looking for. Specify, for example, that you're looking for nineteenth century paintings of horses by English artists, contemporary watercolor scenes of the Mississippi River Valley, sculptures done by Brazilian artists since the 1940's, European etchings of African big game animals, or whatever. As you gain experience, become progressively more detailed in defining your needs. Tell dealers about your favorite artists, subject matters, colors, sizes, shapes, and any other characteristics you prefer in your art. Also keep them informed as to any changes or new developments in the direction of your buying.

Respond as quickly and directly as possible to all art that dealers show you. Tell them whether or not you like it and why. Be as precise as you can and say everything that comes to mind (as long as you don't become overly negative). Don't feel shy or embarrassed – you learn by speaking with experts. For instance, spending half an hour with a dealer evaluating the plusses and minuses of a particular painting can be a highly enlightening and educational exercise.

Know your budget and never mislead anyone about your ability to buy. Be fair with dealers on this issue, and they'll return the favor. For example, if you are in a gallery that has little for sale under $10,000 and you have a limit of $1,500 per acquisition, say so. Nobody's going to throw you out. Most likely, people at the gallery will still be happy to speak with you about their art and artists, and maybe on some future visit you'll be able to afford a piece of their art.

Encourage dealers to call you, to extend special invitations to you, and inform you about new arrivals. You are never under any obligation to buy. Of course, if you don't buy something at least every once in a while, they'll stop calling you, but by that time, you may have settled on other dealers who you prefer doing business with anyway.

Act immediately when dealers call you about art they think you might be interested in, whether you want it or not. Dealers appreciate quick responses because then they can either sell you the art or if you don't want it, proceed to call whoever's next in line. If you make dealers wait for days before you respond, you can bet they won't be calling you back in the future.

Buy art! Buy art from galleries that offer what you want, in terms of art, art education, and other amenities. Galleries that take the time to teach you expect something in return. If all you do is take without giving, you'll find that gallery owners will eventually reduce communications with you.

Be loyal to the dealers that help you the most. This does not mean that you blindly buy from one or two dealers and ignore the rest of the art world. Get to know your favorite dealers, visit their galleries regularly, solidify relationships, work together whenever possible, make sure they know how much you appreciate everything they do for you, and generally keep in touch. Continue to meet new dealers at all times, and buy from whoever happens to come up with what you want; but maintain and deepen good relations with those who have been helping you the longest.

Pay for what you buy when you say you are going to pay for it. Whether you are supposed to pay over several months or within three days, pay on time. Dealers need to know when and how much money is coming into their galleries so that they can gauge their own purchases and pay their bills on time.

Listen to the advice dealers give you, even when it may not be what you want to hear. This doesn't mean that you instantly accept whatever they say, but rather that you show a willingness to consider new input and ideas that may diverge from those you already have. Much of what dealers tell you is for your benefit, and by keeping an open mind, you allow yourself to grow as a collector.

Things Dealers Don't Like

You want dealers to like you. When they don't, you and your art buying suffer. Dealers who don't like you behave in ways that are counterproductive to your buying, for example:

- They spend as little time with you as possible.

- They don't educate you.

- They don't care whether they sell you quality art or not.

- They don't inform you about the latest developments in the art market.

- They don't speak favorably of you when your name comes up in conversations with other dealers or collectors.

- They may purposely mislead you.

Observing a few specific cautions, as outlined below, will keep you off of dealers' "least-favored clients" lists.

Don't be a silent customer, a mystery person. When you visit galleries, introduce yourself, ask questions, and state what you're looking for. No one appreciates people who are cagey or secretive about their intentions.

Don't take information without offering something in return (in other words, buying art). Dealers know when they are being hit up for free advice and they don't like it. You can ask dealers you already do business with for informational favors, but make sure that in the long run, you compensate them for their time.

Don't talk a big game about how much money you have to spend or are willing to spend and then not spend any. Dealers are not interested in listening to how much money you have either before or after you spend it. Even when you do spend it, they are quite capable of figuring out your financial situation all by themselves – they don't need you to tell them. By the way, as far as dealers are concerned, you have no money to spend until you spend it.

Avoid playing dealers one against the other. Ask dealers to comment on each other's art or tell dealers what other dealers are saying about each other's art, and you'll find yourself in trouble fast.

Don't be cheap. If you know that $1,000 is a fair price to pay for the art you want, don't offer $500 for it. First of all, you'll never own any art. Second, you'll waste everyone's time including your own. Third, you'll get a reputation as a cheap buyer, and those dealers who continue doing business with you will only offer you cheap art – cheap in quality as well as in price.

Don't attempt to hide your enthusiasm about art you really like. Some collectors think that if they remain totally unemotional, show no feelings, and express take-it-or-leave-it attitudes, dealers will drop asking prices and sell for less. First of all, dealers show the greatest consideration to customers who are excited and completely satisfied with what they buy. Second, dealers love to know when they pinpoint tastes exactly. Third, the deadpan routine rarely fools anyone. Start playing sneaky games with dealers, and they'll respond with a few of their own.

Avoid showing off good buys you make from other dealers. If you find a bargain somewhere, great. Suppress the urge to brag about how clever you are. Act like you know so much that you can buy art without dealer assistance and guess what, dealers will stop assisting you. Smart collectors savor their bargain buys quietly.

Don't tell dealers that you can find art just as good as theirs at other galleries for less money. Buy art where you get the best quality for the best price, and that's that. Going public with gallery-to-gallery price comparisons irritates dealers. Besides that, you probably aren't telling them anything they don't know already.

Don't respond rudely to art that dealers offer you. If you don't like the way a piece of art looks, say something like, "It's not quite my style," or "It doesn't have the right feel to it." Go into graphic detail about how your eyes ache when you look at it or complain that it makes you nauseous, and you'll lose a dealer's support quickly. Insult the art, and you insult the dealer who is selling it.

Don't treat dealers like servants or hired help and feel that they should pay homage because you have graciously singled out their galleries with which to do business. Dealers respond to this treatment by either avoiding you altogether or taking your money and returning as little as possible above and beyond what they sell you. You don't do dealers any favors by buying their art.

Example 1:

Gossip is a fact of the art business. The art world is small, and many dealers know each other and often speak among themselves about their clients. If you buy art on a regular basis, sooner or later the dealers who specialize in the art you like find out who you are. Some of them hear about you before they even meet you.

When I meet potential buyers for the first time, I often ask other dealers about them. I basically want to protect myself from people who could possibly cause me trouble, waste my time, or try to take advantage of me. Dealers warn me when I'm in for a rough time, and on occasion I decide not to do business with certain people. In the worst instances, I'm warned about problem buyers ahead of time and, based on the strength of those warnings, decide not to do business without ever meeting them!

Dealers also have good things to say about their customers. They talk about those who are eager to learn, who pay their bills on time, who know how to recognize quality art, and so on. I look forward to doing business with these people and am inclined to show them special considerations, even when I hardly know them.

Make sure that you treat dealers fairly and with respect, because in the art business your reputation often precedes you. Having dealers hear negative things about you before they know you can do a great deal of harm. On the other hand, when they hear good things about you, you have an automatic head start in building a gratifying working relationship.

Example 2:

I know a collector who would rather buy a lot of inexpensive paintings than a few expensive ones. Consequently, he ends up sacrificing quality for quantity. Most of his pictures are so mediocre that even for how little he spends, they're still wastes of money. Unfortunately, he refuses to listen to constructive advice from dealers who suggest that he buy fewer good-quality pieces instead of many mediocre quality ones.

Dealers have long since stopped trying to educate this fellow and instead, supply him with exactly what he wants – cheap, mediocre paintings. They don't waste their time showing him anything that's any good because they know it will always be "over his budget." Remember, most dealers want to see you advance as an art buyer, so seriously consider any advice they give you about improving your buying habits.

A Look Ahead

Some people prefer buying their art directly from artists to shopping at galleries. They like to search for art at art shows, visit artist studios, meet artists, see artists create art, discover new types of art, socialize with artists, and become directly involved in the artist community. However, buying directly from artists is very different than buying art at galleries. Chapter 10 talks about what those differences are and instructs you on how to proceed when the artist is also the dealer.

CHAPTER 10

Buying Art Directly From Artists

Buying art directly from artists is a great way to collect art. Many artists never show at galleries, due mainly to the fact that there are far more artists than there are galleries to show their work. Any art dealer will tell you that he or she is only able to give shows to a fraction of the artists who bring in their portfolios for evaluation, and that many of the artists who they have to turn away have talent.

Two admonitions regarding buying from artists are in order before we get going. First, don't view this option as an opportunity to eliminate dealers (and their commissions) from your art-buying adventures. As you've read in previous chapters, dealers play an essential role in the art world's structure and hierarchy. Continue to visit galleries, interact with dealers, and learn about art.

To briefly recap, dealers sift through countless works of art in order to bring the most deserving examples to the public's attention. They present art in ways so that the public can more easily understand it – ways that few artists are capable of doing on their own. Dealers educate, inform, and provide valuable overviews of art, artists, and the art market for the art-buying public. The best among them set trends, build great collections for their clients, advance the careers of the artists they represent, and increase the public's overall awareness, appreciation, understanding, and demand for quality works of art.

Second, do not attempt to go around dealers and buy directly from the artists they represent. Seeing an artist's work on display at a gallery, for example, and deliberately trying to exclude the dealer from a sales transaction by contacting the artist directly on your own is totally inappropriate. It's extremely poor art business etiquette, and you'll end up alienating the dealer, the artist, and ruining your reputation as a trustworthy buyer.

Meeting Artists in Group Settings

Meeting artists in group settings, as opposed to one at a time, is the best way to begin an artist art search. Check local arts organizations, art periodicals, community arts websites, public service announcements, and weekly calendar or entertainment sections of local papers for dates and times of art fairs, art exhibitions, street fairs, and juried shows offering prizes for the best art. These events can be anything from a few artists selling art at a small local street fair to highly competitive shows with strict admissions requirements. Hundreds of major shows and thousands of minor ones take place annually across the country at local, regional, and national levels. They are held at locations like museums, community galleries, community centers, exhibition halls, public parks, malls, state and county fairs, and so on.

For beginning collectors, convenience and anonymity are two plus points of group settings. The work of dozens and sometimes hundreds of artists is on display at one location, thereby allowing you to see plenty of art with very little effort. You can compare and contrast specific pieces you like without having to travel from gallery to gallery or place to place. And you don't have to speak with anyone until you're ready – you'll be just another face in the crowd.

The ability to compare prices is another big advantage of group settings. You see what amount of money buys you what amount of art from a variety of different artists. Learning about art and money is far easier when you acquire data from numerous sources all at once than it is when you confine your activities to single galleries showing only one or two artists at a time.

On average, selling prices tend to be lower at group art shows than they are at retail galleries. This is true not only because so many artists are competing for sales at the same locations, but also because organizers are often groups like non-profit or community-service organizations who have more interest in showing art than they do in making money. As a result, they tend to charge artists modest entrance or exhibition fees and take smaller percentages of final selling prices than galleries do, assuming they take any percentages at all.

Juried shows and awards competitions have an additional advantage. The best pieces in the show are already selected and labeled by panels of art experts which makes your job of evaluating what's "good," "better," and "best" a lot easier. If you really want to enhance your art education, talk to show organizers, participants, or judges about how prize-winning pieces are selected and what selection criteria are used.

When you see a piece of art you like at a group show, don't buy immediately. Find out what else the artist has to offer. The artist may only be showing a piece or two at a show, but have dozens or even hundreds of pieces at other locations. Find out, for example, whether you can visit the artist at her studio and see her full range of work. At the studio, you might find pieces you like even more, or ones you like just as much at more affordable prices. Studio visits also bring you closer to artists and give you a better understanding of their art.

Meeting Artists at Open Studios

You can make appointments to visit individual artists at their studios or, better yet, you can meet groups of artists at their studios all at once by attending events like "open studios," "art walks," and "art trails." These events are held in places with significant concentrations of artists like major cities, communities known for their "artist colonies," locales where multiple artists maintain summer studios, and so on.

Once or twice a year, many such groups of local artists get together and open their studios to the public at the same time. These are special opportunities for you to meet dozens and sometimes hundreds of artists in person, speak with them about their art, tour their studios, see how they live, and see the best selections of their art available anywhere. There's no easier way for artists to sell art than right out of their own studios. Therefore, an additional benefit of these events is participating artists can afford to be flexible with their selling prices.

Open studios allow you to get as close to artists as you can possibly get in brief encounters, and, of course, the festive atmosphere makes the events great fun. For those of you who want personal involvement with the artists you patronize, nothing beats the access provided by open studios.

Dealing directly with artists is perhaps the greatest advantage of open studios, but it can also be a drawback when you don't know that much about art. This is because you're pretty much on your own and have no professionals like dealers or other art experts available to provide critical overviews of what you're looking at. If you're not careful, you can end up patronizing artists who know how to sell a lot better than they know how to make art. Avoid this problem by attending your first few open studios with people who know the territory.

Another occasional problem with open studios is that artists can respond inappropriately to the increased public exposure. For example, some mark their prices up over what they normally charge for their art. Others put more reasonably priced pieces out of sight and only show their most expensive work. If you find yourself in a situation where you like the art, but can't afford it, state your budget and your preferences. See whether the artist is flexible on prices or can show you additional, more moderately priced selections.

Whenever you visit an artist's studio, whether at open studios or one-on-one, let the artist show you art the way that she likes to show it. Pay special attention when she explains particular pieces. Never be too quick to dismiss art without hearing the story behind it because a piece that you don't find attractive at first, may take on new meaning, beauty, or significance once you understand what it's all about. Ask for selling prices of pieces of art that appeal to you, and assuming you really like what you're looking at, have the artist set aside those pieces that you like the most, even if one or two may be a little over your budget. When you're done, sit down with the artist, review your selections, and ask any remaining questions you might have. Making final selections will be addressed below in the "Getting Down to Business" section.

Maybe the art that you're looking at comes close to what you want, but doesn't quite satisfy you and you'd really love to have a particular type of piece that you believe the artist is capable of making for you. Describe it, and ask whether that's possible. If the artist says yes, allow her to create the piece on her own terms and without any further coaching on your part once she understands your preferences. Be prepared to accept the final product, even if it's not totally to your liking. Remember, you asked for it, and the artist took her time and tried her very best to make it for you. (Commissioning artists to produce particular pieces is not generally a good idea for beginning collectors.)

Open studios are usually highly publicized within local arts communities. Find out if and when they take place in your area by contacting artists, art schools, college art departments, art galleries that specialize in exhibiting local artists, and by reading the art listings in the date book or entertainment section of your local paper.

Additional Ways to Meet Artists

Assuming that you enjoy meeting artists and feel comfortable buying from them, you can explore more adventurous ways to meet them such as by placing classified ads in art periodicals like those mentioned in Appendix I and on community art websites like those mentioned in Appendix VII. Shopping for art directly online will be discussed in greater detail in the next chapter. A well-worded classified should include your preferences in art (size, subject, medium, etc.), your budget, and appropriate contact information. You may wish to mention that you're a private party (as opposed to a dealer), although that's not really necessary.

Advertising your wants on community bulletin boards is another, more advanced way to meet artists, especially when you're interested in buying within particular geographic regions. Contact area arts councils, art schools, art galleries, art supply stores, and museum sales and rental galleries to find out the best places to advertise. For example, many major cities have converted warehouses or warehouse districts where artists live and work. Find out where these are, and get names of local businesses where artists get together or do their shopping. You'll find community bulletin boards at many such studio, warehouse, and business locations.

Profile of an Artist with which You Can Work

Wherever your art adventures take you, sooner or later you'll meet artists who create art that you're interested in buying. At that point, begin making more in-depth contact. Introduce yourself, talk with the artists about their art and, when appropriate, make appointments to see more work at their studios. Your goal is not only to locate art that you like at prices you want to pay, but also to identify those artists who respect your requirements and who you'll be able to get along with.

THE ART OF BUYING ART

Every artist you meet has his or her own ideas about what you deserve and how much they are prepared to give you in terms of art, time, attention, and respect once you tell them what you're looking for and your budget. At one end of the continuum is the artist who sits down with you, answers all of your questions, wants you to have a good piece of art, stays in touch with you after your purchase, keeps you updated on his or her career developments, and so on. At the other end of the continuum is the artist who offers you as little as possible, based on your budget, and can only be bothered with you for as long as it takes to sell you art.

If you're like most people, you'd rather do business with the first artist than the second. Not only do you end up with more art for your money when you buy from these types of artists, but a higher percentage of them succeed in their careers than do more self-centered artists. Artists who tend to be positive, selfless, generous, flexible, interested in enriching people's lives with their art, and not obsessed with making money or getting ahead attract the attention of the art community. Artists who are difficult to deal with, on the other hand, impede their own progress.

Below are the types of responses that you should look for when speaking with artists:

"For me, an important part of making art is sharing it with others."

"The more collectors who own my art, the better."

"I enjoy meeting everyone who likes my work, whether they buy it or not."

"I have art in all price ranges."

"Show me the pieces you like the most, and I'll find others for you that you might also like."

"I love to talk about art and show people what I do and how I do it."

"If you can't afford that piece, then let me show you some less expensive ones."

"If you have any questions about what I do or what particular pieces of art mean, I'll be happy to answer them."

Artists You Should Avoid

Some mention has already been made of qualities in artists that make for poor relationships and ill-advised buys. Most are centered around money and ego issues, but to be more specific, avoiding artists who exhibit the characteristics listed below will help keep you out of trouble.

- The artist refuses to be flexible in selling prices.
- The artist talks down to you or makes you feel inferior.

89

- The artist is only willing to meet with you if he's relatively certain that you are going to buy art.

- Money is a central aspect of everything the artist says and does.

- The artist wants to charge you gallery-type prices for her art even though she's just starting out in her career and has no gallery representation.

- You feel pressured to buy something.

- The artist thinks he should be better known than he is.

- The artist compares her work to that of expensive, well-established artists, claims that it's just as good, and bases her asking prices on what those artists charge.

- The artist has bitter or hostile feelings about the way the art world works or the way his career has progressed.

- The artist has nothing good to say about fellow artists.

- The artist flat-out refuses to consider making a smaller, less detailed or less expensive version of a piece that you really like but can't afford.

- The artist has a take-it-or-leave-it attitude about your interest in any particular piece of his art.

- The artist is willing to sell you something for what you want to pay, but complains or is unhappy about it.

- The artist only offers you the most insignificant pieces in his studio and stresses how little he has to give for what you want to pay.

Getting Down to Business

Suppose you get along well with an artist, you've chosen a piece of art to buy, and you're ready to write out the check. Before you proceed, you should make sure that you're paying a fair price for a good-quality piece of art. You'll learn how to research and evaluate art, artists, and art prices in Part III, but, for our purposes here, you want to make sure that you have the necessary information on-hand in order to perform that research and evaluate the art effectively.

An important part of purchase-oriented interactions is to review the artist's resume, or, better yet, get a copy to have for your files. An appropriate resume should include information about the artist's education, participation in group and one-person shows, appearances in print, awards won, grants received, organizational memberships, names of individual collectors and institutions that own the artist's art, and other art-related accomplishments. Make sure the resume lists names, dates, and locations. Also ask to see any articles or news stories that include the artist. An artist's statements regarding her personal philosophies about how and why she creates art and about what she expects to accomplish through her art are nice to know, but, at this point, you want facts.

Using appropriate tact, politely ask the artist to talk about her price structure, how she sets her prices, why particular pieces of art are priced at the levels they are, what types of art are the most popular with collectors, and so on. You're looking for indications that the artist regularly sells art comparable to the piece or pieces you're interested in buying for dollar amounts comparable to what you're being asked to pay. You should also look for signs that the artist regularly produces and sells a variety of works of art, or, in other words, that she's serious about being an artist.

If you really want to own a specific piece, but would like to pay a little less than the asking price, observe the following guidelines to assure an optimal outcome (read more about negotiating for art in Chapter 22):

- *When you the like the art, say so.* Artists take extremely well to compliments. You may think that artists will hold firm in their prices if you show your enthusiasm, but the opposite is much more often the case. They'll be more flexible.

- *Be truthful about your financial situation.* Artists will work with you. There is nothing they want more than to sell their art to people who really enjoy it.

- *If you can't afford to pay all at once, ask whether you can pay over time.* Most artists are amenable to these sorts of arrangements.

- *Never disparage a work of art to get the price down.*

- *Never criticize an artist's pricing policy or compare it in negative terms to how other artists price their art.*

- *Don't insult with an offer that's far below the asking price.*

Barter

Barter is one of the better-kept secrets about buying from artists. Art insiders are aware of it, but relatively few novice buyers or people who buy exclusively at galleries are aware of the barter option. Simply put, galleries rarely accept barter for art; artists, on the other hand, do.

Artists love to barter. They barter art among each other and with their friends all the time. Virtually all artists will accept goods or services from anyone in exchange for their art. Barter is a great way to own art that you don't have the money to pay for.

While speaking with artists whose art you like, politely bring up the subject of barter. When they say that they'll consider barter, find out what sorts of things they need and tell them what types of goods or services you have special access to. The wider the range of options that you can offer, the more likely the chances that barter will play a part in your transactions.

When barter appears to be a possibility, don't insist on all-barter, no-cash arrangements unless the artist is really enthusiastic about making a complete trade with no cash. The likelihood of an artist accepting barter increases exponentially when you pay a portion of the purchase price in cash. This way, the artist gets the best of both worlds.

Regardless of how you complete your final transaction, always get a written statement from the artist describing the piece that you've bought. Also make sure that you get a receipt that describes the art, a copy of the artist's resume, and copies of any additional relevant information such as magazine or newspaper articles that talk about the artist and his work. You'll learn more about how to document your purchases in Chapter 23.

Example 1:

I once attended an art show where the great majority of the artists were established in their careers. Average painting prices ranged from $5,000 to $20,000 – more than I was willing to spend. I really liked the art, though, and looked closely at every piece. After a while, I came across a very competent and appealing watercolor. I looked at the price and had to do a double-take – instead of $6,000 to $8,000 like I thought it would cost, it was priced at only $800!

When I inquired about the piece, I was told that it was not painted by one of the artists in the show, but rather by the son of one of the artists. He was only about 18 years old, but yet his work was comparable in quality to much of the art on display. Apparently, the asking price was based more on the artist's age than it was on the quality of the art – a reasoning that made good sense, but, in my opinion, was taken to the extreme in the case of this watercolor. I bought the picture without hesitation and learned, in the process, that you never know what you'll find at a group art show, no matter how good the artists are or how expensive the majority of the art is.

A Look Ahead

The internet is the new frontier of art collecting. Right now, it's pretty much a disorganized, unregulated, free-for-all, with many thousands of websites selling art. To the uninitiated art collector who buys exclusively at traditional art galleries or directly from artists, searching for and buying art online is confusing at best and nearly impossible at worst. In this next chapter, you'll be given basic facts about how online art buying works.

CHAPTER 11

Buying Art Over the Internet

Buying art over the internet is unquestionably the wave of the future. When you think about how much art you can see online in one day on your computer and compare that amount to what you can see by physically transporting yourself from gallery to gallery in your area, you begin to see how pervasive online commerce in fine art will eventually become. A day of gallery-hopping in most American cities won't show you much more than several hundred works of art by a handful of artists. On the internet, you can see thousands of pieces in all price ranges and in all mediums by hundreds of artists from all corners of the globe with the click of a mouse.

The most basic level of internet art shopping is visiting galleries in your own home town at their online locations first (most established galleries and plenty of minor ones have websites). You can look at representative works of art, get a feel for what individual galleries are like, and find out which ones sell the type of art that you buy – all from your computer screen. When you find a gallery's selection appealing, you can then go and visit them in person.

The online art market is promising for artists as well as art buyers. For the first time ever, artists can show their art to people from around the world with minimal effort, at modest out-of-pocket expense, regardless of the level of success that they've attained in their personal careers. With this huge increase in exposure, more artists than ever before have better chances of selling their art. For example, artists with talent who can't get gallery representation where they live can get exposure on the internet and, by doing so, let the public decide whether their art has merit and is worth collecting. In much the same way, unproven garage bands use the internet to bypass record company executives, get their music out into the public domain, and let the listeners decide whether or not they like it.

Not all is peaches and cream in online art land, however. Perhaps the most confusing aspect of shopping for art over the internet is figuring out what a piece of art on your computer screen actually looks like in person (especially if you haven't been buying art for very long). Another problem is figuring out how to navigate the huge number of commercial websites offering art for sale. To complicate matters further, no easy system exists for evaluating either the art websites themselves or the art that they're selling. Once you get a feel for how to shop for art on the internet, though, and you locate those art sites that interest you the most, progressing to the point where you're ready to make your first online purchase is not that difficult.

Alan Bamberger

First Steps in Locating Art Online

A good way to begin your online art buying adventures is to make a list of larger, better-known commercial art websites such as those listed in Appendix VII. You can get additional names from art periodicals such as those listed in Appendix I. All major arts publications not only have ads for websites that sell art, but they also review them regularly. Commercial art websites may also sponsor art events in your community like open studios or outdoor art fairs, so always check program listings or handouts when attending these events to see who the sponsors are. Word-of-mouth in your local art community is another great way to find out the names of better art websites.

Searching for general types of art on major search engines like Yahoo or Google is not a great idea unless you know the name of the artist (assuming it's not a famous artist like Picasso or Warhol), the type of art, and other specifics. Just about any art search, using general art key words like landscape painting or limited edition print or bronze sculpture, but without artist names, will net you at least thousands (and sometimes hundreds of thousands) of matching web pages that, unfortunately, are displayed in no particular order. Tech people may understand how art websites get ranked, but the average art person has no idea why one site ends up being ranked at number 6 in your search while another site that's just as good or even better gets ranked at number 12,775. Trying to find general types of art online through major search engines is frustrating at best, even for experienced dealers and collectors who know their way around the traditional art world.

The Different Types of Art Websites

The five basic types of commercial websites that sell art at fixed prices are juried sites, non-juried sites, non-profit or community sites, all-purpose art websites, and individual artist sites (buying art at online auction websites is discussed separately in Chapter 25). Juried, non-juried, and non-profit or community art sites show art work, often provide resources for artists and collectors, and give contact information for anywhere from a few to several thousand artists. All-purpose art websites are just that – places offering a wide variety of goods and services including art, articles, advertisements, databases, consulting, and more. An individual art site, of course, is a website dedicated entirely to the work of one artist.

Juried commercial websites sell art only by artists and from art dealers who have applied for representation on those sites and have had their art and their career credentials reviewed and approved of by art experts, or jurors, employed by those websites. Jurors are usually composed of respected members of the art community. Most juried sites provide the names and qualifications of all of their jurors. When shopping for art on a juried website, make sure you know who the jurors are and why they've been selected to evaluate and accept the art that you're reviewing.

Art that you see for sale on juried sites is usually by artists who are either emerging (beginning to get recognized) or established (already recognized) and have documented track records of showing and selling art. Some such sites also include promising young artists who are just starting out and have no exhibition records or gallery representations to speak of. Juried sites, therefore, are good places to shop for art by artists who either have potential for recognition, are in the process of becoming recognized, or who have already been recognized by experienced dealers, collectors, curators, and other influential members of the established art community.

Non-juried commercial websites sell art by any artist who requests representation, pays the required fees, signs the necessary agreements, and abides by the rules of the site. Non-juried art websites are an integral part of the online art community because they allow any artist, regardless of experience or reputation, to establish a presence and exhibit their art at a known location on the internet. Since all art and all artists are allowed on a non-juried site, the overall quality of the art can, at times, be uneven and the credentials of the artists can, at times, be minimal. Non-juried commercial art websites are good places to shop for art by artists at all stages of their careers, but especially those who are just starting out, less well-known, undiscovered, experimental, unusual, out-of-the-mainstream, or who may otherwise operate outside the constraints of the established art community.

Nonprofit or community art websites often serve both as resources for local or regional artist communities and also as places where artists can show their art or add their names to local or regional artist directories or databases. For artists, nonprofit art websites provide information like tips on how they can market their art, articles about different types of art or art techniques, calendars of local or regional art shows, information about upcoming competitions where artists can enter their work, discussion forums about art issues, and classified advertisements about art classes, art supplies, studio space for sale or rent, and so on. For art buyers, nonprofit art websites are similar to non-juried commercial art websites in that artists, without qualification, can either show their art on the site or describe the types of art that they produce, and provide necessary contact information for interested collectors. As with non-juried commercial art sites, the art on exhibit at nonprofit sites can, at times, be uneven in quality and the credentials of the artists who show or list there can, at times, be minimal.

All-purpose commercial art websites are large databases of art-related information. These sites are similar to traditional art magazines in that they provide news and articles about the art world along with paid advertisements placed by artists, art dealers, and traditional art galleries. The ads are usually for gallery or individual artist websites where individuals can shop for art and then contact the artists or galleries directly when they find art that they're interested in buying. All-purpose art websites are not usually juried and they

95

tend not to get involved in the actual buying and selling of art; the advertisers independently handle art sales directly with buyers.

The most extensive all-purpose art websites offer services like daily fresh editorial content, researchable artist and art history databases, directories of art institutions, art price databases, auction tracking services, on-site art auctions, worldwide calendars of art exhibitions and art auctions, art consulting, and more. Some of these services are free and others are fee-based. All-purpose art websites fall somewhere in between juried and non-juried sites in that those sites that are the most expensive to advertise with tend to attract higher-quality art dealers and artists, whereas those charging more reasonable rates tend to attract a mixed bag of advertisers.

Individual artist websites are the true chaos of the online art world. Countless thousands of artists from every corner of the globe and of every level of artistic accomplishment, from the most famous to the most wacky, to the most totally unknown, display their art and offer it for sale in an astonishing variety of formats. Shopping online at individual artist websites is not for the faint of heart and is recommended only for experienced online art buyers or collectors who are already familiar with the artists, know exactly how to reach their websites, and know what they'll find and how to proceed once they get there.

Online Art Shopping Basics

Commercial art websites are open 24 hours a day, 7 days a week. You can spend as much time on them as you like, browse at your own pace, look at all the art you want to, and never feel obligated to make a single purchase. You won't ever get on anyone's nerves or take up too much of anyone's time no matter how long you hang out at an internet art gallery.

When you first visit a website, get a feel for what types of art they have to offer and focus on facts rather than fluff. Whether you're reading the site's customer service policies or stories about artists' careers, pay particular attention to factual, verifiable, concrete statements. Also pay attention to client references or testimonials from satisfied collectors. A website's philosophies and beautifully written descriptions of their art may be fun to read, but what you really want is proof that you've come to a place where you can buy good-quality examples by artists with documented track records – or at least as documented as you would like them to be.

As mentioned above, the best places to begin online art adventures are at larger commercial websites. Not only do they show thousands of works of art by hundreds of artists, but, compared to smaller commercial sites, they offer a wider range of services, are better organized and easier to navigate, have standard operating policies, offer secure payment options, provide limited, money-back guarantees, and are the closest thing to established traditional art galleries that the online art world has to offer. Other amenities of larger sites include art articles, news, discussion groups, links to museums, and more. These sites also give their artists pointers on how to price their work, which results in overall price structures being more reasonable and easier to understand than at smaller group or individual websites.

When you visit a large site, the first page you come to, known as the homepage, is usually a pretty busy place. Homepages are similar to tables of contents in books or magazines in that they tell you about featured locations on the websites where you can go to look around. For example, you'll find "links," or connections, to current featured artists, special on-site art exhibits, art education sections, site services and policies, museum shows, real-life art events, on-site gallery areas showing particular styles of art or art in specific price ranges, and more.

Once you've studied the homepage, a good place to go next is to the site's educational section. Most large art sites devote space to such topics as art appreciation, art history, biographies of well-known artists, strategies for art collecting, learning about artists and about how artists make art, learning how to recognize and define different types of art, and so on. The overall goal of educational sections is to make visitors feel less intimidated about the art world and more comfortable not only about buying art online, but about buying art anywhere.

When you feel that you've been sufficiently educated, you're ready to take a look at the art that the site has to offer, so head back to the homepage. Most sites get you started by inviting you to look at particular types of art, spotlighting certain artists, and pointing you towards selections in certain price ranges. Many also provide search engines of varying capabilities that allow you locate art according to your own specifications using parameters like medium, price, size, color, subject matter, style, artist's name, and other characteristics. A few sites offer highly sophisticated features such as those where you can click directly from specific pieces of art that you like to selections of similar pieces by other artists. These types of features can greatly increase your searching capabilities and speed since you would have had great difficulty trying to locate such items on your own.

Take your time and look at plenty of art. Don't try to see too much too fast, and don't be in a huge rush to buy. You'll find so much art online that you can easily overdose or get confused, so when you start getting tired, turn off the computer and come back later when you're refreshed and ready to go. Remember to bookmark, your page so you can pick up where you left off.

Buying Art Online

When you see a piece of art you like, you can usually enlarge it on your computer screen so that you can study it in more detail. When you see a piece of art that you really like, note who the artist is and where you saw it, so that you can return to it later. When you see a piece of art that you really, really like, most larger sites allow you to click directly from the art to pages where you can learn about the artist who created it. When you see a piece of art that you really, really, really like – so much that you think you might want to buy it – evaluate it according to the research and pricing chapters in Parts III and IV of this book.

Assuming that the art satisfies all necessary requirements and you continue to be enthralled, you now confront the great disadvantage of buying art online – so far, you've only been able to see it on your computer screen and you have no idea what it looks like in person. The people who run the websites are, of course, well-aware of this situation and are prepared to work with you in a variety of ways so that you can see the art you like with the greatest possible ease. The time has come to review the website's shipping, money-back guarantee, membership, and return policies. The greater the number of options, such as those listed below, that a website provides, the better you can feel about doing business with them.

- *Easily verifiable seller credentials.* Make sure that you can verify a website's credentials. You want to know that you're buying from a reputable source with ample contact information, a documented art business track record, and references to prove it. (If you're buying from a traditional gallery or an artist advertising on a website, follow procedures laid out in Chapter 10 and in Part IV.)

- *Good customer support.* The site should provide phone numbers, preferably toll-free, that you can call in order to speak personally with art consultants and ask whatever questions you have about the art, both *before and after* you buy it.

- *Time to live with the art before you decide whether or not to keep it.* Better sites offer approval periods lasting from one to three weeks. The minimum acceptable approval period should be one week.

- *Payment options.* The art website should accept major credit cards and have mechanisms in place for secure online ordering. Better sites also allow buyers to call in with credit card numbers.

- *A full money-back guarantee if, for whatever reason, you return the art in the condition in which you received it, before the approval period expires.*

- *Ease of shipping.* The better art websites make shipping and returning art as easy as possible. For example, some sites pack their art in special easy-open, easy-close crates and make returning art no more complicated than filling out brief return forms and calling shipping services to pick up the art at your home or place of business.

- *Cost of shipping.* Shipping art, especially larger pieces, can be expensive, so make sure that you really like a piece of art and that you're pretty sure you're going to keep it *before* you have it shipped. Find out what your shipping costs will be and whether, should you decide to return the art, the website pays the return shipping costs (some sites do; others don't).

The following are some additional points to keep in mind when shopping for or buying art online:

- *Study a website's membership policies.* The larger commercial art sites allow you to register and become a member. Depending on the site, membership benefits include personal art consultation, art newsletters, special art previews, early buying opportunities, 0% financing, ways to group and view your selections online, and so on.

- *When you see art that you like and it's described in a certain way using art terms that you're not that familiar with, remember those terms and use them in subsequent searches.* Sometimes finding art online that's right for you is merely a matter of knowing which terms to type into on-site search engines.

- *Some art sites allow you to make offers on the art that you're interested in.* Whether or not a site states that their asking prices are flexible, making an offer never hurts as long as you follow the guidelines laid out in Chapter 22.

- *Some sites let collectors make requests for specific works of art.* Those requests are then emailed to the site's artists and dealers either to see whether they have matching pieces at their studios or galleries, or to find out whether certain artists are willing to meet the requirements of those requests and create the art as commissions. When you know what you're looking for, consider emailing websites and allowing them to search for you. As previously mentioned, if you commission an artist to make art for your collection, you're pretty much obligated not only to keep the finished piece, but also to allow the artist to complete it with minimal interference from you. You should have some experience collecting before you decide to commission artists.

- *Shop only with online galleries, dealers, or artists who list the selling prices of all of the art that they have for sale.* Responding to sellers who mark their art with directives like "please inquire" or "price on request" instead of set dollar amounts is a no-win situation for you as a collector. When you inquire about art that is not labeled with a price, you tip off the sellers to the fact that you like that art, and the sellers, in turn, often take those opportunities to price it as high as possible in order to see how much they can make you pay. They have all of the advantages in any subsequent negotiations; you have none.

- *Be cautious when you're looking at a particular artist's art and you see that most of it is already sold.* In such cases, the artist is usually trying to create the impression that his or her art is really in demand. Collectors are rarely fooled by this tact. In fact, artists who show large percentages of sold works actually reduce their chances of making sales because when people see that most of the art is already sold, they get the feeling that the good art is gone and all that's left are the crumbs.

- *When you're on a website that offers both auctions and fixed-price art, confine your shopping to art that is priced and avoid the auctions until you become more experienced as a collector.* Read more about buying art at traditional auctions in Chapter 24 and at online auctions in Chapter 25.

The Future of Buying Art Online

Buying art over the internet is still in its infancy. More and more people are becoming comfortable with the idea of viewing and buying art online. More and more artists are realizing that they can reach far more people over the internet than they can by exhibiting at traditional shows and galleries. Expect to see substantial increases in online art sales in the years to come.

Even now, the largest commercial art sites have attracted so many artists, galleries, and works of art that they've become somewhat difficult to navigate. In response, programmers, software engineers, and website designers are hard at work to make buying art online increasingly more efficient and satisfying. At the top of the to-do list for these specialists is to create more sophisticated software and search engines in order to help online art buyers pinpoint the art that they like faster, with greater ease, and with minimal wandering. Insiders predict significant advances and improved accuracy in customized online art buying within the next several years.

Art sites are also experimenting with better ways to display colors, details, and even textures of art, and are striving for a level of accuracy that approximates studying art in person at close range. Ultimately, art websites are looking to present their art in ways that simulate actual art gallery experiences. Expect to see innovations in presenting art in greater detail and at higher resolutions as high-speed internet connections become more commonplace and websites are able to transfer larger amounts of data over greater bandwidths.

Regarding dollars and cents issues, today's online art buyers tend to be pretty conservative. The great majority of the art sold online is priced under $2,000. Although, if you want to spend $100,000 and up, you can find any number of pieces for sale at those levels, too. In the coming years, websites will unveil technologies and marketing programs designed to make people feel more comfortable buying pricier art online.

Example 1:

The evolution of the internet has changed art buying patterns for quite a few people. Experienced collectors, for example, use the internet to comparison shop for art. Before the internet, they comparison shopped mainly at local and regional galleries, and relied on a handful of dealers to supply them with quality art for their collections. Today, they can comparison shop among a far wider range of dealers and, as a result, buy better pieces for their collections at more reasonable prices. A significant amount of traditional dealer-to-dealer middle-manning and subsequent mark-ups is being eliminated because collectors are locating primary suppliers directly online.

Decorators and interior designers shop online to acquire art for particular interiors. In the old days, when a designer needed to create an international feel or find art with a specialized look, he or she would have to travel to far away places or take clients along on personal visits to gallery after gallery. Today, much of that "traveling" can be done online. Decorators can either locate and select the art themselves or have larger art websites select it for them.

People who have moved away from their birthplaces, but still feel connected to their roots use the internet to "return home" and shop for art that reminds them of where they grew up. Once again, buying online saves travel time and money.

One collector I know collects European prints from the 1940's through the 1960's, particularly by French and Italian artists. Unfortunately, these types of prints are not very common on the West Coast where this collector lives, so he does not have many opportunities to buy from local dealers. He now buys directly from European dealers who he discovered while searching online.

A Look Ahead

You have a basic knowledge, at this point, of how the art business works. You know about art dealers, art galleries, artists, online art resources, and what your responsibilities are in dealer-collector and artist-collector relationships. In order to further guarantee positive results in the marketplace, though, you need some additional instruction in how *not* to select and buy art – that is, how to avoid common pitfalls that all too many beginning buyers fall victim to. Chapter 12 summarizes basic art-buying mistakes and explains how to avoid making them.

CHAPTER 12

How Not to Buy Art

This chapter is about "don'ts." Just as you follow certain rules and procedures when buying art, you don't follow certain other rules and procedures unless you want to end up regretting the day you ever decided to get involved with art. Some of the don'ts you are about to read might sound almost too obvious to mention and others are being repeated just to make sure you remember them. Unfortunately, beginning buyers ignore them all the time and end up buying art they never should have considered in the first place.

The don't list teaches you how not to buy art. These don'ts are in no particular order. One is just as important as the next. They concern situations in which you could easily find yourself as you wind your way through the art world. Obey them, and you'll significantly increase your chances of acquiring good-quality art for reasonable prices; ignore them, and there's no telling what you'll end up with.

Don't buy art without thinking. Ask questions and get the facts about any selections you make before you buy. True, buying art should be fun, spontaneous, passionate, and so on, but that doesn't mean that you take leave of all reasoning capacities and abandon yourself to whimsy, ignorance, or impulse.

Don't confuse art with the environment you see it in. The circumstances, surroundings, and happenings taking place at a gallery are entirely separate from the art the gallery is selling. When you buy art, all you get is art; none of that glitz, glamour, baked brie, champagne, jumbo shrimp, sexy sales personnel, and other fun stuff leaves the gallery with you as you exit the establishment with your purchase.

Don't buy art under the influence of drugs or alcohol. Alter your consciousness and you impair your ability to judge the art that's right for you, both in terms of its appearance and the information that you are given about it. Ask dealers and collectors about buys they have made under the influence and those who are willing to talk will tell you some real horror stories. Few have more than one incident to relate, however, because once they buy in a condition other than sober and realize what they've done the next day, they never buy that way again. Say no to drugs and alcohol and yes to buying art intelligently.

Don't buy art at night. At night, you tend to be less focused on rational, practical issues and more interested in entertaining yourself and having a good time. The chances of your buying art impulsively are greater at night than they are during the day. If you see an art piece you like while browsing through a gallery after normal business hours, put a hold on it and return the next day to look at it again and research it properly.

Don't buy art while you're on vacation unless you investigate it as thoroughly as you do the art you buy while you're at home. People on vacation are more carefree and unconcerned about how they spend their money than when they're at home. They tend to relax the rules a bit. This is one reason why you see so many art galleries at popular tourist destinations. And guess what? Many of them stay open at night!

Another mistake art buyers make on trips away from home is that they buy art not necessarily because it's good, but rather to remind themselves of what wonderful times they had while they were away. Once again, remember that when you buy art, all you get is the art. You have to live with it long after the memories of that fantastic vacation fade.

Don't buy art simply because you're charmed, delighted, and entertained by the seller. When you buy art, you do not buy the personality of the gallery owner, the artist, or anyone else. Long after the seller is gone or that great time the two of you had together is forgotten, the art must continue to stand on its own as a quality example that's worth what you paid for it. If you're having trouble figuring out whether it's the art or the seller that is fascinating you more, take the art home on approval for a few days and study it in peace.

Don't buy art from sellers passing through town, at special closeout sales, at one-shot auctions, or through any other unestablished or transient outlets. No matter how attractive or reasonably priced the art for sale at these places or events may sound, confine your buying to respected dealers who have been in business for years and are known throughout the art community. Established dealers may not sell year-end, closeout, get-it-while-you-can, bargain art, but they do offer stability and amenities that transient sellers lack. Quality art does not change hands like leftover blouses on a sale rack.

Don't buy art on cruise ships unless you are an experienced buyer and have the means onboard to corroborate all information sellers provide. Otherwise, wait until you're back on land and at home to research art that interests you. In order to convince you to buy onboard, sellers may tell you that art is cheaper at sea than it is on land – but that may only mean cheaper than they can sell it on land, not cheaper than ANYBODY can sell it on land. You may save taxes or duties in which case, have the seller tell you exactly how much those are above the base price of the art. However, art prices themselves **do not** fluctuate depending on whether the art is on land or sea. They do not drop in value the moment the art leaves port and then increase in value the moment it arrives back on land.

If you're new to art buying, regardless of how much of a bargain, how important the artist, how rare the art, or how great the investment you think you're getting, wait until you're back home to confirm all such claims (and get those claims in writing before you disembark). Most importantly, do not allow yourself to be pressured (which includes not pressuring yourself). Verify claims; THEN buy the art – not before. When you're just starting out, the best procedure is to shop for art on land where you can compare prices and research the market, not at sea where you're presented with only one option.

Don't buy art at one-time estate auctions unless you have complete information and documentation about whose property is being auctioned, the circumstances that led up to the auction, and complete verifiable contact information for the auctioneers including street addresses (not post office boxes), phone numbers, auction licenses, and permits to sell (all of which must be verified before you bid). Unfortunately, some companies that conduct these sales simply rent houses or halls, pack them with new merchandise, present them as antiques or collectibles or as bargains, and sell them to unsuspecting buyers. Often these sales are easy to spot because they contain significantly more furniture and decorations than you would expect to find at a typical estate sale (ten dressers, for example).

Don't buy art because it sounds like a great bargain that's almost too good to be true. First of all, this type of art usually is too good to be true. Second, the fact that a work of art is presented to you as a "super deal" is not adequate justification for purchasing it. Look closer and chances are it's not such a great deal after all. Sellers who offer incredible bargains usually provide somewhat suspect explanations about why their prices are so cheap. Watch out whenever you hear excuses like, "I need money fast to finance a new art buy," or "I have major expenses coming up and have to raise money," or "I could sell this for a lot more if only I had the time."

Don't buy art based on claims from sellers without first verifying those claims. Sellers are obliged to substantiate whatever they tell you about the art they sell. In addition, any representations or claims must be verifiable outside the confines of the circumstance where the art is being sold. If an artist is supposed to be world famous, for example, get specific information (names, dates, places) from the seller to support that claim.

Don't buy art based solely on appraisals or certificates of authenticity unless you know how to read and interpret the information they contain. Chapter 15, "Certificates of Authenticity and Appraisals," explains the basics in this regard.

Don't buy art over the phone. This sounds unbelievable, but it actually happens. In spite of the fact that art is a visual and not an auditory commodity, dealers telemarket it and people buy it. The whole idea of buying an art piece based on the way a seller makes it sound during a telephone conversation is absurd to begin with. What's more, you have no idea who these sellers are, how reputable they are, what their galleries look like (assuming they even exist), how you would get your money back if you were not completely satisfied (even when they promise full immediate refunds), and so on.

Don't buy art by name only. You buy art because you like it, not because you hear that the artist is hot, that she's popular among investment bankers, that she's about to be featured in a national magazine, and so on.

The first thing you look at is the art. The last thing you look at is the name of the artist.

Don't buy art based solely on the fact that it's in a beautiful frame, on an expensive pedestal, or otherwise lavishly displayed. Putting bad art in great frames, on expensive pedestals, or presenting it in other sumptuous surroundings is a trick some sellers use to fool unsuspecting buyers. Evaluate the art separately from the drama of the presentation.

Don't buy art because you are impressed by the beauty of the gallery selling it. The furnishings, decorations, and interior design of a gallery have no relation to the quality of the art that is being sold there. Some of the best art dealers operate out of the most modest surroundings and some of the most unscrupulous dealers have beautifully appointed galleries.

Don't buy art when sellers change the price drastically with little or no provocation. Some galleries sell art by radically dropping prices right before your eyes. They appeal to the greed instinct. This procedure is designed to make you think you are getting a great bargain when in actuality, you are usually getting schlock at heavily inflated prices.

For example, suppose a painting starts out at $10,000 and within thirty minutes, the price has dropped to $6,500 because, according to the seller, you qualify for various special privileges. You mention that you're a collector, so the seller gives you a collector's discount; you mention that your aunt once worked in a frame shop, so he gives you a dealer discount; you tell him you work with computers, so he gives you the special high-tech Silicon Valley discount; and so on. The focus is off the art and on the plummeting price. Dealers who sell quality art rarely slash prices in this manner.

A corollary to this is **don't buy art at an auction where the prices start high and go down.** THIS IS NOT AN AUCTION, but rather a sales technique designed to make you think you're getting a bargain. Essentially, the "auctioneer" is setting the selling prices rather than the bidders (exactly the opposite of what an auction should be). Established auction houses that conduct regular sales start the bidding low and allow bidders to set the final prices by bidding against each other until only the high bidder is left. None start prices high and go down.

Don't buy art by famous, well-known, or collectible artists at online auctions from sellers you don't know unless you're an experienced buyer and know exactly what you're looking at. Unfortunately, online auctions remain a risky place for novices to buy these types of art. The exceptions here are if the sellers are reputable, established, brick-and-mortar auction houses, or if you're buying brand new art directly from the artists (self-representing artists are safe to buy from in the overwhelming majority of cases).

Don't buy art for monetary reasons alone. Serious collectors buy art because they love art, not because they think they will be able to cash it in for profit at some later date. True, some art increases in value over time, but this is never adequate justification for deciding to buy or collect fine art. Remember that art increases in value a lot less often than most people think.

Don't buy art under pressure. You should not select art for your collection based on the presence of a salesperson standing over your shoulder bombarding you with reasons why you should own it. When you begin to feel pressure to buy art, leave the gallery.

Don't buy any particular art or artist because all your friends happen to own one. Everyone has their own individual tastes and preferences in art. You buy what you like, and your friends buy what they like. When you buy what other people collect or tell you to buy, you deny yourself the thrill and pleasure of exploring, discovering, and expressing your own personal tastes.

Don't buy art that you see for sale in restaurants, hotels, department stores, or at other non-gallery environments. Confine your buying to full-time art dealers whose only business is buying and selling art. Just as you do not rely on art dealers for overnight accommodations, meals, or clothing and appliances, do not rely on hotels, restaurants, and department stores for art. Consider buying art at non-art venues only after you've had plenty of experience collecting and know exactly what you're looking for.

Don't buy art based on predictions. Beware when sellers begin talking about what's supposed to happen with art or artists at some point in the future. Base your purchase on past performance, not on conjecture about what may or may not happen in the future. Predictions about how famous an artist will become or how much the art will appreciate in value are almost always designed as appeals to the greed instinct and nothing more.

Don't buy art based only on emotional response. The initial emotional response that you have to any art piece is no more than a very rough indication of how much or how little you like it. Temper the emotion with reason and spend some serious time evaluating your reactions to any work of art before you buy.

Don't buy art unless you're absolutely sure you want to own it. As long as you have even the slightest doubts, do not buy. You want the love affair you have with your art to last. You don't want that art to end up in your attic several months after you buy it.

Example 1:

I know of a case in which an art dealer and an artist, both fascinating personalities, combined forces and sold plenty of art. They received a great deal of media attention and appeared at all the right functions. They were extremely popular on the local social circuit and much in demand. People loved to be around them and showed their appreciation by buying the artist's art. Together, this dealer and artist sold hundreds of paintings at prices reaching well into the tens of thousands of dollars each.

With the passage of time, the artist retired, the art dealer closed up his gallery, and both faded out of public view. The market for the paintings, which were never that good in the first place, faded right along with the dealer and the artist. Collectors who paid huge prices for their art thirty and forty years ago are now lucky if they can get even several hundred dollars each for them.

Make sure the art is at least as good as the personalities representing it. When it's not, as soon as the personalities are no longer available to stand by it while it is being sold, the market collapses. **Remember, when you buy art, all you get is art.**

Example 2:

I know an art dealer who tells the story of how he once bought art under the influence of a few drinks – once and only once. This happened while he was attending an opening-night benefit at a large antique show. While there, he saw a painting in one dealer's booth that he thought looked great. It was a reasonably priced mountain scene painted in the 1920's. At that moment, he believed he could tell from looking at it that it was good enough to sell at his gallery. He was sure he'd heard of the artist before and felt no need to check any reference books before buying.

Here is what this dealer discovered the next day:

The artist had no track record. He was not listed in any reference books. The dealer had apparently confused the name with that of a different, more collectible artist. Furthermore, when he saw this painting in a sober state of mind, he realized it was terrible. He was astonished that he thought it had looked as wonderful as it had in the antique dealer's booth just a few short hours before.

Example 3:

The phenomenon of "the art opening" deserves special mention because you can be misled by what goes on at these events in so many ways. If you become at all involved with art, sooner or later you will be invited to art openings.

In order to prepare yourself for the real thing, let's attend an imaginary one now. You find yourself at an art opening at a beautifully appointed gallery. You sip fine wine, nibble on long-stemmed strawberries dipped in chocolate, rub shoulders with beautiful people, meet the artist, and look at art. You are in the eye of the storm, the center of the universe for this artist and his art. Everything about the environment is designed with three purposes in mind: sell you art, sell you art, and sell you art. Nowhere on the face of the earth does this artist's art look more appealing than it does in this gallery at this moment. And you are there.

You notice a stack of beautifully printed full-color exhibit catalogues on the counter. You pick one up and begin reading:

Milton Mindholm's art transforms fact into fiction into fantasy and back into reality. He captures the highest essences of craftsmanship with techniques that unerringly undulate between brilliance and genius. He is unsurpassed in his ability to communicate direct mental images from his mind through his fingertips and outward onto blank canvas at which point they evolve into unmistakable being.

You are impressed. Mindholm's paintings are priced between $5,000 and $25,000. You are impressed again. Several pieces have little red dots next to them. You ask a staff person what the dots mean and she tells you that they indicate the art has been sold. "People are buying," you think to yourself.

This looks to you like an exhibition of serious art by a serious artist and some pieces are apparently being purchased for substantial amounts of money by serious collectors. From what you can see, money spent on Mindholm's art could well be money intelligently spent.

Now the facts:

- The long-stemmed strawberries and fine wine served at the opening have no relation to the quality of art that is being exhibited.

- The beauty, glamour, wealth, and fame of the people attending the opening have no relation to the quality of art that is being exhibited.

- The language used in the exhibition catalogue is only an indication of how good the writer is, not how good the artist is.

- The asking prices may or may not have any relation to the quality of the art.

- Little red dots are supposed to mean that art has been sold; however, that's not always the case. Some dealers place red dots on unsold art in order to make people believe that it is selling.

A Look Ahead

You now have all the basic tools necessary to successfully navigate your way around the art business, protect yourself from those who would take advantage, comparison shop, and in the end, select those works of art you find the most appealing. As far as actually buying that art, however, you're only half way there. You don't really know anything about the art you are considering other than what the sellers have told you about it – and that you like it. Acquiring additional information – learning the methods of art research – is the next major step in the art of buying art and is the subject of the next five chapters.

Part III: Research

Research is the cornerstone of intelligent art buying. So far, you have made some specific fine-art selections based primarily on how much you like the way they look. If you buy without researching them, however, you have no idea what you're buying, and you have no idea what you're getting for your money. Sure, sellers tell you plenty about your selections, but research corroborates these facts and can reveal additional information that perhaps the sellers have overlooked or, in worst-case scenarios, deliberately not mentioned. Art research supplies you with facts you need to know before you buy.

Why is research necessary? It's essential because facts affect value. Not only do you do yourself a huge favor by researching potential purchases and getting the facts first, but you also do the entire art world a favor. The more people research their art and buy intelligently, the more difficult it becomes for galleries that sell inferior art and thrive on uninformed customers who buy impulsively to stay in business. Informed shoppers breed fair dealers who sell quality art at reasonable prices.

"But research sounds like such a complicated process," you say. You feel intimidated at the prospect of having to research art. You have no idea how to start, where to go, or what to do once you get there. "Research is only for art scholars, and you need a Ph.D. to do it, right?"

Wrong.

Anyone can learn to research any work of art. Not only that, it's easy. You don't have to spend years training under museum curators and art historians. All the basic techniques you need to know are explained right here in Part III.

And not only is research easy to learn, but it doesn't take much time either. Once you get the hang of it, you can usually locate most of the information you need to know about a particular artist or work of art in less than thirty minutes. Sure, more detailed research is necessary on occasion, but more often than not, a few minutes are all it takes.

Research is also rewarding. The more you know about art, the more you're able to appreciate it and the more enjoyable collecting becomes. The simple truth is that you experience art more fully and completely when you understand the facts and the history behind what you are looking at.

One more thing: By mastering the techniques of art research, you establish your independence as an informed buyer. You eventually acquire the ability to analyze and evaluate every work of art you buy entirely on your own, with minimal help from dealers or other authorities. You make your own decisions and do what's right for you. You use effective research to master the art of buying art.

CHAPTER 13

Research the Artist

Behind any work of art is an artist, a human being. The product of that artist's career is art. Because of facts specific to her and her alone, the art that she creates is unique in ways that distinguish it from all other art. By understanding the progression of events in that artist's life and career, you understand her art. Add these facts to your visual appreciation of the art itself and you achieve a much deeper sense of what her art is all about.

On the practical side, facts about any artist, her career, and what she has accomplished relate directly to the dollar value of her art, its collectibility, and its salability in the marketplace. This type of information helps you decide whether or not to buy art that you like and find visually appealing.

The great majority of information you need to locate and evaluate is as basic as where an artist was born, where she studied art, how old she is, how long she has been an artist, what exhibitions she has participated in, and so on. You can learn plenty about an artist and her art from simple biographical data like that.

This procedure is similar to verifying the qualifications of any professionals you are interested in hiring before they perform services or supply products for you. You want to make sure you are getting quality services or products from people who know what they're doing. Just as you hire an attorney to handle your legal affairs or hire an accountant to keep your books, when you buy an art piece, you do, in a sense, hire the artist who created that piece. You pay that artist for services rendered – the product of those services being art. And if you're like most people, you want your art to be created by qualified artists who charge fees commensurate with their abilities and the quality of the products – or art – that they produce.

Buying art based on an artist's credentials is not necessarily a foolproof method of determining whether or not you are spending your money wisely; but in the great majority of cases, the more distinguished the artist's career, the more comfortable you can feel about buying that artist's art. Furthermore, accomplishments in art stand for all time and continue to affect marketability long after the artist has passed on. Below is an example of how even a small amount of biographical data can aid you in a decision-making process.

Suppose you have selected two very similar paintings for possible purchase, both the same size, subject matter, quality, and style. You like them both equally well and have decided to choose one to buy. Each is priced at $2,000. One is by an artist named John Doeman, the other by Henrietta Hooper. You find out that Hooper was born in 1930, began painting seriously in 1948, and that she has been an artist full time since 1958. Doeman was also born in 1930, recently took up painting, and is having the first public show of his work at the gallery where you saw the painting you like. What can you assume or conclude from these facts? Plenty!

Conclusions about Henrietta Hooper: She makes her living as an artist. She has been painting for decades and is established in her career. She has proven herself as an artist and survived financially for over forty years by selling her art. Chances are extremely good that she is going to continue painting and not give up art for another career. If she has sold successfully for so many years, she has certainly produced a substantial body of work, most of which is probably pretty good.

Conclusions about John Doeman: He is an unproven commodity. He started painting only recently, and even though the quality of the painting you like is comparable to that of Hooper's, you have no way to tell, due to Doeman's relative inexperience, whether he will be able to maintain that quality level in all his work and eventually be considered equal in stature and accomplishment to Hooper. In addition, you have no idea whether his art is consistently good and salable or whether he just happened to get lucky on the painting you like and other paintings in his opening show. You have no idea how many paintings Doeman has sold during his short career – certainly fewer than Hooper. You have no way of knowing whether he will produce a sufficient enough body of work to become recognized as an artist or whether he will stop painting next month and fade into permanent obscurity.

You rarely have so little information to go on as you do in this example, but you see how far you can get on a minimum of facts. Assuming you are concerned about how you spend your $2,000 and don't want to take any unnecessary risks (which is pretty much the way beginners should approach art collecting), buy the Hooper, not the Doeman. You get a work of art by a long-established and accepted artist if you go with Hooper. With Doeman, you're not quite sure what you get.

How would you decide between these two paintings knowing nothing about either Hooper or Doeman? You could flip a coin. You could put them side by side and stare at them hoping one might start looking slightly better than the other. No matter what you do, though, you'd be buying blind.

"But," you argue, "if I decide I like the Doeman, shouldn't I buy it regardless of what the facts are?" Absolutely. You're perfectly entitled to buy it, no matter how many facts you have and no matter what those facts are. What's important is that you have those facts, know what you are buying before you buy it, and that you have no misconceptions about Hooper or Doeman and their careers. Informed buyers make intelligent collectors.

How to Locate Artist Biographical Data

The primary source of artist data is printed information found in books, encyclopedias, directories, exhibition catalogues, online databases, CD-ROMS, price references, archives, newspaper or magazine articles, and so on.

All major public or university library art departments, art museums, and better art galleries have substantial amounts of these reference materials on hand. The references we are talking about here, the ones you will learn how to use, are standard and accepted by all in the art community.

For those of you who prefer to buy your own art reference books and would rather not use libraries, Appendix VI contains a list of dealers who specialize in art reference books and CD-ROMS like the kinds you will be reading about. For the computer-savvy, Appendix VII lists some of the better online art reference resources. Art museum bookstores are also a good source of reference books, but their art books tend to be a little more general in nature than those sold by Appendix VI dealers. Dealers in specialized art reference materials are good to know because if you decide to get at all involved in collecting, having certain basic references within easy reach is essential.

The types of references you will be using are briefly summarized by category here. Many of the more important basic references in each category are listed in Appendix II with brief comments about each following the listings. This appendix by no means covers all art reference books, but it is reasonably comprehensive and includes more than enough basic resources to get you started no matter what artist you are researching.

By the way, don't be intimidated by the total number of reference books listed in Appendix II. Once you know how to research, you develop a feel for which references in particular will be the most helpful to you on a case-by-case basis. You will rarely have to check dozens of titles, but rather just the few that relate to your specific situation.

Artist Indexes (See Appendix II). Artist indexes are a good place to begin any research. These references contain names of hundreds of thousands of artists of all time periods and nationalities. They are alphabetized lists of names, usually accompanied by brief basic biographical information such as birth or death dates, nationalities, and specialties (painter, sculptor, etcher, etc.).

Indexes are important because, along with basic data, some also list titles of additional art reference books that include more detailed information about whatever artist you are researching. You then locate these references and use them to assemble more complete biographical profiles. Be aware that art indexes do not always list every additional reference that contains information, so continue researching even after checking the books that indexes refer you to.

Each index lists artists slightly differently, but an average entry looks something like this:

Quinara, *Samaris; 1890-1969, Brazilian painter, EncArtAmer.*

From this entry you can see that Samaris Quinara lived from 1890 to 1969, that he was a Brazilian painter, and that further information about him can be located in a reference that is abbreviated as "EncArtAmer." Full bibliographical information (title, author, publisher, copyright date, etc.) about abbreviated resources can be located at the beginnings or endings of all indexes. In this case, EncArtAmer refers to an artist reference called *Enciclopedia del Arte en America*, which focuses on North, Central, and South American artists. Some indexes like *Davenport's Art Reference and Price Guide* also contain basic price data in addition to biographical data, but more about that later.

Artist Encyclopedias (See Appendix II). These multivolume sets supply information about artists of all time periods and all nationalities. The three most frequently used encyclopedias, *Benezit, Theime-Becker,* and *Theime-Becker's* supplement (called *Vollmer*) are written in English, French, and German, respectively, so you may need to have entries translated when you locate them. All three contain information about artists from around the world, although they are best for researching European artists. Other more specialized encyclopedias, some of which are listed in the appendix, include only artists from specific parts of the world. This is not a complete list, so check with art dealers, art librarians, or other experts for the names of additional specialized encyclopedias as you need them.

Artist Dictionaries (See Appendix II). These references, which are usually in one to three volumes, are more specific than general encyclopedias. They might include artists from only one country, one discipline, one time period, one state, one sex, and so on. For example, you can find dictionaries specific to categories such as the following: California artists, Ohio artists, Utah artists, Texas artists, Indiana artists, American Indian artists, Nineteenth Century English artists, women artists, New Orleans artists, marine artists, naive artists, and so on. Some of the major artist dictionaries are listed in Appendix II, but once again, this is by no means a conclusive list. As with encyclopedias, learn which dictionaries are most applicable to your specific needs.

Artist Annuals and Directories (See Appendix II). These references are published regularly and are constantly being revised, updated, and enlarged. Some are published annually while others are published every few years or so. Like dictionaries, artist annuals and directories list artists alphabetically and usually according to specific criteria such as the type of art they produce, the state or country they live in, and so on. *Who's Who in American Art*, for instance, is published every other year and includes only living American and Canadian artists and related visual arts professionals like curators, critics, collectors, and educators. Once again, the titles listed in Appendix II do not constitute a complete list of these types of references.

Art Archives and Files. Art archives and files are collections of documents, news clippings, correspondences, catalogues, writings, oral histories, and other miscellaneous information about art and artists. Archives and files often include data that is unpublished and is not available anywhere else. The major American art archives, called the Archives of American Art, is headquartered at the Smithsonian Institute in Washington D.C. (contact them at Phone: 202-633-7950; Website: *www.aaa.si.edu*). Many major national (and smaller regional and local) libraries, museums, historical societies, art associations, and art institutes maintain their own files and archives, as do some art dealers. Consult experts and check specific institutions according to whom you are researching to see whether relevant archives exist and, if so, where they are located.

Auction Records and Price Guides (See Appendix II). These references will be discussed at length in Part IV. Briefly, price references tell you whether works by particular artists have sold or been offered at public sales (primarily auctions, but sometimes through dealers) and either specifically or approximately what prices they sold for or were offered at.

When you first start researching artists, have art librarians, art dealers, and other professionals walk you through the basics, step by step. This is the best way to learn what you're doing, to identify the specific references best suited to your needs, and, eventually, to learn how to streamline the process. Experts can teach you how to use any reference book, CD-ROM, or computer database within a matter of minutes. Artist research is really that easy!

Even on your own, learning how to use books, CD-ROMS, and computer databases to research artists is not difficult. All you do is check those references listed in Appendix II and VII that appear relevant to your situation, one by one, preferably in the order they have been summarized here (indexes first, encyclopedias next, and so on). This way, you maximize your chances of locating the information you need on whatever artist you are researching. The next few paragraphs provide several additional research pointers.

Whenever you research, check as many relevant references as possible. This is especially true when you're starting out. Since you do not know which books to go to immediately and what their respective strengths and weaknesses are, you have to look up artists' names in every one that could possibly help you. This exercise also gives you practice researching and helps familiarize you with what specific references are all about.

If you find an artist listed in one book, don't stop looking and assume you have all the information you need. Different books often contain different information about the same artist, and combining what you find yields the best results. If you don't find an artist listed in the first two or three books you check, do not give up and decide that the artist is a total unknown. Continue checking; then decide.

Approach the task of gathering information as though you are writing an essay entitled "The Life of an Artist." Write down, print out, or photocopy every listing or entry you find. Do this whether or not you think that what you read has any significance or relation to the artist's art. The truth is that *everything* you find is relevant in one way or another.

Here's an extreme example of information that may seem irrelevant at first, but actually isn't. Suppose you have selected a work of art for possible purchase and discover that the artist murdered one of his models in 1942. This fact has nothing to do with art, but it may have something to do with whether or not you still want to own the piece that you've selected. Maybe you do, but chances are you want to own it less than you did before finding out that information. Regardless of your decision, a good percentage of collectors do not want to own art by an artist who committed murder, and that effect, in turn, decreases the artist's value and collectibility in the marketplace. The 1942 murder has no direct bearing on the quality of the artist's art, but it certainly affects its overall marketability.

You won't have to go much further than Appendix II references with the great majority of artists you research. The reason is that most artists are not that widely written about and are listed in few places other than in basic standard references, archives, and files. The more well-known artists are, however, the more they have been written about, the more information exists, and the more you need it in order to make informed decisions.

Information about better-known artists can be located in numerous books, exhibition catalogues, and other publications in addition to those references listed in Appendix II. The most famous artists are included in dozens of references; some even have entire books written about them (a book about a single artist is known as a *monograph* and a book that lists every work of art an artist produced during his or her career is known as a *catalogue raisonné*). If you intend to collect art by important artists, have experts teach you how to research and assemble data from multiple sources. Such advanced research techniques are beyond the scope of this book.

Interpreting the Results of Artist Research

Finding an artist listed in standard references is a good sign, but that fact alone does not bestow instant collectibility or justify the price that is being asked for a work of art. You must know how to interpret those listings in order to get an accurate idea of how accomplished the artist really is. Some of the general ways that information you find in books affects an artist's market and price structure are discussed here. Know that none of these is an absolute and that no single one being true is enough to base your final conclusions on.

The more books that include an artist, the more collectible his or her art is. An artist you find listed in twenty books is better known than one listed in only two books.

The more significant the references that include an artist, the more significant the artist is. For example, an artist listed only in a dictionary of Ohio artists and nowhere else is less important than one listed in all major international art encyclopedias.

The more mentions an artist has in any given reference and the longer those mentions are, the more collectible his or her art is. A detailed two-page listing is more significant than a brief two-line entry.

The longer an artist has been included in books, the more collectible his or her art is. For example, a contemporary artist who has been included in basic references ever since she started painting in the 1960's is more well-known and well-recognized than one who is the same age and has been included only since 1995.

The more detailed the listings are in terms of art-related accomplishments, the more collectible the artist. An artist who has participated in numerous national and international shows and exhibits, won awards in prestigious competitions, has work in museums, and has been represented by widely respected galleries is more important than one who has been involved in only small local or regional events, been represented only by one local gallery, and so on.

The more respected the authors and the more widely accepted the references, the more seriously you may consider the artists they write about. For example, museum curators, art scholars, and art historians who write legitimate scholarly texts are involved in the most non-biased sorts of writing. On the other hand, dealers who write and publish their own books or catalogues about artists they represent or promote in order to increase sales have personal interest and financial gain in mind. As a result, such publications are almost always prejudiced in favor of the artists and don't necessarily present the facts accurately. Check with experts whenever you have questions about whether a reference is legitimate and accepted as standard by the art community or is a vanity publication designed to make money for an art dealer.

The more respected the institution publishing the book, the more seriously you may consider the information you locate. For example, a listing in an important museum exhibition catalogue, book published by a major university press, or standard artist encyclopedia is more significant than a listing in a catalogue published by a small regional or local art association.

With respect to price records, artists who sell for more money are generally more important and collectible than those who sell for less. That's not much to go on concerning price, but it's enough for now. You'll read plenty more about art prices and how to evaluate them in Part IV.

Assessing the Facts

Once you have a general idea of what books list an artist, who wrote them, and how frequently and extensively that artist is listed, you have to focus on the individual facts you find. These facts fall into specific categories and mean certain things. Here are the categories of facts you normally encounter, a brief summary of what they mean, how to interpret them, and how they tend to affect an artist's market.

Birth and death dates. An artist's age is a good thing to know. From it you can determine how long he has been an artist, how old he was when he started, how old he is now, and so on. For example, if you like to buy conservatively, as you should in the early stages of your collecting, buying established artists who have been active for significant periods of time is less risky than buying art by young artists who are just starting out.

Where and with whom an artist studied. These facts are interesting to know, but they have little bearing on an artist's collectibility or reputation. Studying under famous artists or graduating from the finest art academies is a step in the right direction, but what really counts is what the artist accomplishes after completing that education. Self-taught artists with little or no formal schooling can be just as accomplished and collectible as those with years of training. Watch out for dealers who try to sell you on artists just because those artists had great teachers or graduated from the best schools.

Organizational memberships. The organizations an artist belongs to are not necessarily an indication of how collectible that artist is. Many groups or associations allow anyone to join. Certain memberships, however, do indicate a level of accomplishment on the artist's part, especially organizations that only admit new members by vote. For example, being elected to the National Academy of Design in New York City is a high honor and major accomplishment for any American artist. Whatever art you collect, find out the names of the most important and prestigious organizations that the artists who produce that type of art can belong to.

Where an artist has exhibited. The more recognized the institutions where an artist has exhibited, the better. For example, showing a painting at the Metropolitan Museum of Art is a more prestigious accomplishment than showing one at the Tinytown Zucchini Bazaar.

Group exhibitions versus one-person exhibitions. As an accomplishment, having a one-person show is superior to participating in a group show. For example, having a one-person show at the Metropolitan Museum of Art is a far greater accomplishment than showing one work of art at that same museum in a group show with three hundred other artists.

Awards received. Awards always speak well for an artist, but you have to differentiate between important awards and not-so-important ones. Winning a gold medal at a major international art exhibition is obviously more significant than winning the Minnie Ginchflower Award for Sunday Painting at the Acorn Valley Bake Sale.

Public or corporate collections that own works by an artist. The fact that museums or corporations own works by an artist is an indication that the art has been recognized as significant by certain experts and authorities within the art community. You have to be a little careful here because although most collection listings are legitimate, some artists claim to be in certain collections when, in fact, they are not. If you have any questions about collection listings, contact the specific institutions and ask whether work by the artist is actually in their *permanent* collections. One additional point: Make sure that listed corporations and other non-art-related institutions are known and recognized for the quality of their art collections.

Private collections that own works by an artist. This is a sticky area. Basically, major private collections known for having quality art are good for an artist to be in and good for you to know about. Other collections, even though they sound impressive, may mean nothing. For example, suppose you read that an artist has an etching in the collection of the Countess Matilda of Lower Stregonia. This sounds significant, but for all you know the Countess may have no taste in art, the artist may have given her the etching free, or her entire "collection" may consist only of that one etching.

Auction and other price records: Briefly, finding any price results whatsoever for an artist is good and the higher those prices are, the better. Interpreting price records will be discussed at length in Part IV.

When you're just starting out, always double-check your final evaluations with experts. Get the consensus opinion from "those in the know." Make sure you're reading and interpreting the data correctly and are not jumping to any erroneous conclusions.

What to Do When You Come Up Empty-Handed

Suppose that, after all your research, you come up empty-handed. You find absolutely no data on the artist you are researching, and all you have to go on is what the seller has told you. This is never good, and whenever you find yourself in this type of situation, you've got a problem – and several possible solutions.

The most common reason why people come up empty-handed is that either they shortcut their research by not checking enough references or they research only at small local libraries or other institutions with inadequate art reference resources. The solution: Try at least two more large libraries in major cities and check more references. Also, explain your situation to specialist librarians or curators, and ask them for advice in case you've overlooked something.

If you still find no information, the problem could be that you are researching a very minor artist who is not accomplished enough to be listed in references. This doesn't necessarily mean you should forget about buying the art. You can, of course, buy whatever you want, regardless of how little-known the artist is. What a lack of data does mean, though, is that you probably shouldn't be paying too much for that artist's work.

You have three possible options in any circumstance where research yields nothing:

- If the art is inexpensive and you like it, go ahead and buy it. You're not risking anything.

Alan Bamberger

- If the piece of art is expensive, if you enjoy taking risks, and if you don't care how you spend your money, go ahead and buy it. (This is not a particularly popular option.)

- Forget about buying the art, no matter what the price, but especially if it's expensive. Look for another artist who's work you like just as much and who has a documented and researchable track record.

Example 1:

Imagine you are considering buying a painting by John James Burton and find this listing in a standard art reference book:

Burton, John James
Painter
Born: Roundtree, Virginia; May 22, 1957. Studied: University of Texas, BA; Oregon Art Institute, MFA. Works Held: Smithville Art Museum, Municipal Museum, International Farm Equipment Company collection. Exhibited: Modern Art Museum, St. Louis, 1985; National Art Association, Wash. D.C., 1988; Municipal Museum (one-man), San Francisco, 1992; Boston Art Museum Spring Show, 1998. Awards: Second Prize, Boston Art Museum, 1998. Member: American Art Association. Mailing address: 2345 Main St., Wildflower, AZ 11111.

You see from reading this that Burton is a relatively young artist who has achieved some recognition. In art business lingo, he would be described as an *emerging* artist. So far, he has an impressive track record. He has exhibited nationally and has work in several significant collections. He has had a one-man museum show and won an award. Assuming you want to know more, here's how you can follow up on this data:

- Contact the two museums and one business that own his art. Find out the circumstances of the purchases or donations, whether the art hangs on a permanent basis, whether they can supply you with additional biographical information, and so on.

- Contact the Municipal Museum for further information on Burton and details on the one-man show. Maybe they published a catalogue of that show and they can send it to you.

- Find out how important the Boston Art Museum Spring Show is and how important the award is that Burton received at that show.

- Find out how important the American Art Association is and what its membership requirements are.

- Contact Burton himself and see whether he can supply you with a complete resume of his career.

Example 2:

Not all art galleries rely on standard reference listings and traditional measures of artistic accomplishment to sell their artists to the public. Some try to distract you from the facts. I can think of several instances where galleries use well-known public figures to promote artists in much the same way that advertising agencies use athletes or entertainers to endorse athletic equipment, automobiles, candy bars, breakfast cereals, and other consumer products. Rather than offer legitimate data about their artists, these galleries show you pictures of the artists in the company of well-known personalities, give you the names of famous people (again of the non-art expert or non-collector variety) who own their art, or use other celebrity-related tactics to convince you to buy.

Know that celebrity endorsements mean nothing unless those celebrities also happen to be accomplished art experts or collectors. No matter how glamorous or important a gallery makes an artist look, standard art references give you the straight story on fame and accomplishment.

Example 3:

Researching and finding out nothing about an artist can be just as telling as finding pages of information. I have visited a number of galleries that exhibit works by artists whom the gallery owners claim are nationally known or even world famous – and who also happen to be artists I have never heard of. The art is frequently accompanied by impressive-looking certificates, documents, or brochures that make claims about how famous the artists are. I sometimes research these artists out of curiosity, mainly because I'm surprised I've never heard of them and suspect that they're not as well-known as the galleries say they are.

Some turn out to be listed in few, if any, standard reference books or other publications where "famous" artists are normally written about. Others are virtually unknown outside the galleries selling their art. The truth is that some artists are misrepresented by their dealers as being far more important than they actually are. Always corroborate dealer claims with your own independent research.

Example 4:

Some "art references," especially those published by special interests, have a tendency to bend the truth or misstate facts. I recall an occasion where I met with an artist who gave me her promotional brochure. She had written it herself, paid for it herself, and designed it to promote her art and her art only. On top of that, she was great at promoting herself in person. She regularly sold her sculptures at what I considered to be impressively high prices.

Her brochure contained color illustrations of her art, laudatory information about her career, and names of private and public collectors who owned her work. It also listed several museums as owning sculptures. I did not bother to check whether any of these claims were true because I did not plan on doing any business with this artist. I filed the brochure away and forgot about it.

Several months later, while speaking with another dealer, this artist's name came up. I told him about her brochure and mentioned that her work was apparently in several important museum collections. He laughed, told me that no museums owned her work, and went on to explain what the truth really was.

According to him, she had mailed sculptures free of charge to these museums as donations. The museums had accepted them, but not for their collections. They were probably sold at white elephant sales or other fundraising events, the proceeds of which were used to finance museum operations. Works by this artist were not recorded in official museum records as being in any of their permanent collections.

Example 5:

Sometimes gallery owners are the ones who neglect to research artists and other dealers or collectors are the ones who profit. I once made a great bargain buy out of a high-profile gallery that normally sells art at top retail prices. The owner had hung and priced a small painting by an important Midwestern artist, apparently without researching it. I recognized it to be worth about $5,000. He had it priced at just under $1,000, and I bought it on the spot.

While I was paying for the picture, I asked this dealer what he knew about the artist. He said he had found small bits of information here and there, but nothing substantial. I asked him what reference books he had checked and he told me. He had only researched briefly, and the books he had used were not the best references for that artist. If he had checked more thoroughly, he would have discovered that an entire book had been written about this artist and several other books contained entire chapters on the painter's illustrious career.

A Look Ahead

Assembling biographical data about an artist is your first step in research. Assuming the artist remains under consideration after you evaluate your findings, you must now turn your attention to the particular work of art that you have selected. The next chapter explains the procedures for researching and evaluating a specific work of art.

CHAPTER 14

Research the Art

Imagine two different works of art by the same artist. One is priced at $500 and the other weighs in at a hefty $50,000. This may sound absurd – that the same artist could have produced both – but it's a relatively common occurrence. The difference in price between an artist's least and most expensive art is often huge.

How can this be? The answer is simple. The same artist can produce great art, good art, average art, terrible art, big art, little art, one-of-a-kind art, limited-edition art, and so on. The range and variety of art that the average artist produces during his or her lifetime can be astonishing.

Unfortunately, you cannot easily tell what works by an artist deserve to sell for a lot of money and what works should be selling for just a little. No standard grading or rating system exists for labeling significance, excellence, quality, or inferiority of all this art. You cannot instantly tell by seeing a quality control label or stamp on a work of art whether it is Class A, Four Star, Extra Fine, Grade A, a second, or an irregular, but you can make these distinctions if you know how. *Methods exist for determining the relative importance of any art piece in terms of the total output of the artist who created it.*

Many novice art buyers never even think about relative importance or significance. They make the mistake of viewing a work of art as an isolated entity and neglect to relate it to anything else the artist has ever produced. As long as it's by the artist, they reason, that's good enough for them. A Picasso is a Picasso is a Picasso. In art dealer jargon, they buy the name and not the art. A common result of this oversight is that these buyers often end up overpaying for inferior art.

For example, I once met a man who was interested in buying a painting by a collectible American artist. He had seen the artist's work at several galleries, liked it, and was aware that it usually sold in the $3,000 to $5,000 range. He decided to shop around until he found just the right picture.

One day at a gallery, he saw a painting by this artist for only $900. It looked similar to some of the more expensive ones he'd seen at other galleries, and it was about the same size. He decided he'd discovered a major bargain and bought it instantly. He now owned the painting that he always wanted.

Unfortunately, this story does not end happily ever after. He brought me the painting and proudly showed me what a great buy he had made. I took one look at it and had to inform him that his treasure was indeed by the artist, but that was the only positive thing I could say about it. I told him that not only was it an inferior example of the artist's work, but it was probably the worst example I'd ever seen. His "bargain" was overpriced even at $900 and was worth only $300-$500 at best.

This collector made two common errors. First, he assumed that as long as the artist had painted it, it had to be good. Second, he believed that all paintings by the artist were worth about the same amount of money – $3,000 to $5,000 each. If he had known how to compare his $900 special to other paintings by the artist instead of briefly looking at name, size, subject matter, and price, chances are good he never would have bought it.

The important point to remember is that when you purchase a work of art, you do not buy an isolated item; you buy a portion of an artist's total output and you have to evaluate it in terms of that output. You want that portion, small as it is, to be a good representative example of the artist's work, not a poor one.

Let's assume you are in the process of researching one of your selections for possible purchase. You assemble biographical data according to the guidelines laid out in the previous chapter and decide that art by this artist is worth buying. Now you have to evaluate the art.

1. *Begin by reviewing the results of your biographical research and look for clues about what the artist does best.* Note any statements relating specifically to the artist's art. Perhaps she won an award for an oil painting of a New York City street scene. Maybe you'll see a sentence describing her as a well-known animal sculptor. Note any information regarding what this artist creates that is most recognized by those in the art community.

2. *Familiarize yourself with the artist's total output.* Find out what she has produced so far in her career, when she did it, what it looks like, how her style has changed over the years, and so on. You have to know and understand the whole in order to properly evaluate the individual parts.

3. *Study as many examples of the artist's art as you can.* See them at galleries; in exhibits; in books, magazines or catalogues; online; and wherever else you can locate them. Note characteristics of the most expensive examples you can find; note characteristics of the least expensive ones. See what the price differences are between the high-end and low-end art done by the artist.

4. *Ask dealers, collectors, and other experts familiar with the artist's work to tell you what the artist is best (and least) known for.* Have them describe the qualities of those works. Whenever possible, view and discuss actual examples in the company of these experts.

Combine the results of research, repeated viewings, and conversations with experts with your answers to the questions detailed below. Keep in mind when researching the relative importance of a work of art that you will occasionally find exceptions to these general rules and tendencies. They do, however, hold true in the great majority of cases.

Is the art an original work of art executed by the artist whose signature it bears or is it a type of reproduction? Many art galleries, for example, sell limited edition copy-prints or reproductions of works of art that are signed and sometimes numbered by the artists who created the originals (as you read about in Chapter 2); some galleries sell them without even the pencil signatures. *No matter how beautiful they look, these copy-prints are not created by the artists whose signatures they bear.* They are produced by computer technicians who scan the original works of art or photographers who photograph them, and printing companies that then print the results as serigraphs, lithographs, giclees, or whatever. All the artists do is spend several seconds pencil-signing (and sometimes numbering) the finished copy-prints.

Reproductions (whether they are prints, photographs, sculptures, or copies of originals made in any other mediums) are *not* original works of art and, as such, are insignificant in terms of an artist's total output. In fact, it is debatable whether they should even be classified as part of an artist's total output. If you have any doubts about art you are looking at, ask one simple question: "Is this an original work of art produced by the artist or a reproduction or copy of an original work of art produced by a publishing company?" Get the answer in writing. Also review Chapter 2 which addresses the differences between originals and copies.

Assuming your selection is an original work of art created by the artist whose signature it bears, continue with the questions listed here.

Is the art major or minor? The terms *major* and *minor* refer to the scope and complexity of individual works of art. A major work is often better composed, more original, more detailed, better executed, more complex, and larger in size than a minor work. Important major pieces display an artist's total range of talents. A major work takes more time and effort to conceive and produce than a minor one and, consequently, major works cost more than minor ones.

Many collectors make two common and often costly mistakes of oversimplifying the differences between major and minor, so before going any further, two warnings: First, don't confuse major with "good" and minor with "bad." Minor works can be just as well executed as major ones. They're simply not as broad in scope or as complex on certain levels.

Second, don't confuse major with "bigger" and minor with "smaller." Bigger is not necessarily better, more important, or worth more money. A well-known art professor of the 1940's and 50's (the time when large abstract paintings were coming into fashion) used to put in his two cents on the size issue by telling his students, "If you can't paint good, paint big." Never judge works of art based on size alone.

Alan Bamberger

Enough warnings – now for a pop quiz. Consider two paintings by an artist known for his farm scenes. Let's say they are equal in size and painted equally well. One shows a red barn and silo surrounded by a field of corn. The other shows the same red barn and silo, but it also shows a house, three children playing on the front porch, two pickup trucks in the driveway, a chicken coop with chickens, several different fields of crops, an adjacent field being plowed by a farmer on a tractor, the next-door-neighbor's farmhouse and barn in the distance, and an approaching thunderstorm. Which one has more characteristics of a major piece?

Now imagine that the first painting measures 8 by 10 inches and the second measures 30 by 50 inches. Assuming again that they are equally well painted, which one is more worthy of being called major?

Lastly, imagine that the first painting measures 30 by 40 inches and the second measures 20 by 30 inches. Once again, assuming equal quality, which one would be considered more major?

In all three cases, if you answered the second, you're absolutely right. The second is far more detailed, and the composition is much more complex. In terms of labor alone, the artist would have had to spend many more hours conceiving and executing the second than the first.

The best examples of any artist's work are referred to as "major" and no matter what artist you are interested in, you should tend towards major examples in your collecting whenever possible and avoid very minor ones. This does not mean that you zero in on the most monumental work an artist has ever produced, but that you at least look for art that has some characteristics of what major pieces look like. If all you can afford is a minor work, you may wish to move on to a more affordable artist. Owning a minor example by a big-name artist is not necessarily better than owning a major example by a lesser-known artist.

You don't always have to buy major, though, or even close to it. If you love the art and it happens to be minor, at least make sure that it's competently executed and fairly priced. Then go ahead and buy it.

As an aside, you'll find minor works overpriced much more often than you'll find major works to be overpriced. Too many people – dealers and collectors alike – either promote or subscribe to the myth that the signature is more important than the art and that anything with the right name on it has to be expensive. The truth is that even the greatest artists produce minor, inferior, and just plain bad works of art that should be priced far below what their best efforts sell for.

Is the art typical or atypical of the artist's work? All artists are known for producing certain types of art. To begin with, most artists are best known for specializing in a particular medium. One may be a sculptor in bronze, the next a painter in oils, and another a lithographer. Getting more specific, each artist is known for producing certain subject matters within their recognized mediums. Our bronze sculptor may be known for his depictions of wild game animals, the painter in oils for her abstracts, and the lithographer

128

for his Los Angeles city scenes. These works of art would be considered "typical" of these artists.

If you're a beginning buyer, play conservative and lean toward purchasing typical works, that is, the art that artists are best known for producing. In the above three cases, these would be a bronze wild animal sculpture, an abstract oil painting, or a lithographed Los Angeles city scene. In general, focus on typical works and avoid atypical, experimental, off beat, or unusual works of art that artists do not have reputations for producing. Continuing with the above examples, avoid a floral still-life painting done by our animal sculptor, a landscape etching by the abstract painter, or a watercolor coastal scene by the lithographer. Even though the quality of these items may be good or their prices substantially less than those of the typical works (as is often the case), they do not ordinarily make good buys. At worst, you could get stuck with a one-of-a-kind experiment that an artist tried, failed at, and decided never to attempt again.

When knowledgeable dealers and collectors think of a particular artist, they tend to think of that artist in terms of what he or she is best known for producing. When they buy that artist, they buy in those terms also. Take the animal sculptor who works in bronze, for example. Because the art community identifies him as a bronze sculptor who depicts animals, that floral still-life painting he did will be considered an oddity and have little appeal for collectors of his work.

Atypical works are not always to be ignored, however. Experienced collectors, for example, sometimes recognize atypical works as being outstanding and worth owning no matter who created them. Advanced collectors who are in the process of forming definitive collections of particular artists' works also buy atypical pieces from time to time in order to complete their collections.

A final note is in order here. Some artists work in more than one medium or are competent in more than one subject matter. In these cases, find out what they are the most proficient in as well as what they don't do all that well. For example, an artist who paints, sculpts and etches may be best known for her sculptures of famous people, reasonably well-respected for her paintings of New England hills, and not particularly well-thought-of for her etchings, no matter what their subjects are.

When does the art date from? *Art from certain periods in artists' careers is often more collectible than the art from other periods.* For instance, Paul Gauguin's Tahitian period is known to be his most brilliant creatively. Career high points can happen at any time – some early, some in the middle, some late – but works of art produced earlier in artists' careers are generally more collectible than later pieces. Grandma Moses, of course, is an obvious exception to this rule.

When researching an artist, determine these peaks from biographical data and by speaking with experts. Get to know when the best periods are and what art from those periods looks like. Art from the best periods is often the most important, the most collectible, and commands the highest prices.

Artists also experience career low points – difficult times, times of change, times when whatever they produce just doesn't quite work. Work from less productive periods is worth substantially less than work from peak periods. Sometimes, for instance, you find art that at first seems relatively inexpensive, but once you start researching it, you discover that it doesn't cost much because it has that "low-point look" that no collectors are interested in owning.

How original is the art? *Original compositions, techniques, and subject matters in art are more significant and collectible than repeats of things that have already been done.* Here we're talking about art that the art community recognizes as a step forward in an artist's career or, even more so, works that advance the evolution of art as a whole. The example below helps to clarify what the term *original* means.

Suppose an artist devotes all his creative energies to producing twenty sculptures for a gallery show. They're like nothing he's ever made before. He agonizes over them for months, experimenting and trying dozens of different compositional options before settling on just the right look.

He shows them at an art gallery and they receive instant acclaim from prominent members of art community. Collectors also love what they see and the show sells out within three weeks. The artist decides that since this work sold so well, he's going to produce the same sculptures over again. This time, he makes forty pieces and within several months they sell out, too. By now, the artist feels he has found a formula for producing art that he can sell regularly and decides to make nothing but these sculptures for the rest of his life.

When dealers, collectors, and other experts look back on this artist's career, they will regard the sculptures from that very first show and those produced shortly after as being the most original – and thus the most significant, collectible, and valuable. Ones produced five or ten or twenty years later, even though they look the same as the earlier ones, will not be as desirable because they are basically reenactments or repeats of creative moments that the artist experienced years before. They lack the originality, risk-taking, and vibrancy of the earliest pieces.

The ultimate repeats are works of art produced by artists who do nothing original, but rather copy what other artists have already done. Continuing with our sculpture example, suppose another sculptor sees how successful the first sculptor is and decides to produce similar sculptures. He rides the first artist's coattails and attempts to cash in on the collecting frenzy. His sculptures completely lack originality, are purely decorative, and are nothing more than knock-offs.

With respect to price, the most original art should cost the most; repeats by the artist who first conceived those originals should cost less; repeats by other artists who copy the original artist should cost the least.

Watch out for galleries that price any types of repeats close to what originals sell for. These galleries are attempting to victimize inexperienced collectors who don't know enough about art and art history to tell the difference. When you're just starting out, rely on the advice of experts and consult biographical data whenever you have questions about the degree of originality.

How well done is the art? Determining quality in art is important. It's also difficult to do when you've been buying for only a short while. *The only way you learn to recognize quality is through experience – by looking at all the art you possibly can, learning about the artists, discussing the strengths and weaknesses of particular works of art with experts, and learning what makes any given piece good, better, or best.* A work of art may be typical, original, from the right period, and so on, but if the quality isn't there, it's not worth buying. When you're starting out, protect yourself on the quality issue by consulting experts and dealing with respected galleries that have experience selling the type of art you want.

Example 1:

Early in my career, an art dealer offered me a darkish, misty sunset scene by a well-known American artist. He wanted $2,000 for the painting and told me that it was a great bargain at that price. He backed up his claim by telling me that two paintings by the artist, approximately the same size as mine, had recently sold at auction for over $10,000 each. He intimated that I would have no trouble doubling or even tripling my money. I believed him and bought the picture.

Several days later, I discovered that the seller had misrepresented the painting by not giving me the full auction story, and, unfortunately, my "bargain" was worth nowhere near what he had told me it was. Yes, the impressive sales had taken place, but both auction prices were for snow scenes, the scenes the artist was most famous for painting. My painting was atypical, nothing like what collectors wanted, difficult to sell, and worth only about $2,000 at the most.

If I had known more about typical versus atypical subject matters at that time, I could have saved myself a couple of thousand dollars as well as the headache of trying to resell that painting. I took time to learn how to make this distinction, however, immediately after realizing what a very poor buy I had made. I also decided never to do business with that dealer again.

Example 2:

Suppose that you are thinking about buying a watercolor of the Rocky Mountains by an artist named Marla Mathews, and you discover certain facts about her career. Here are those facts followed by explanations of how you should respond to that information:

- *She is best known for her watercolors of Rocky Mountain scenes.* This is a point in favor of your buying the watercolor you are considering. Now you have to educate yourself about these mountain watercolors, look at as many as you can, find out what the best and worst ones look like, and compare them to the one you are interested in.

- *She did some of her finest work between 1970 and 1980 and worst work between 1955 and 1960.* Find out when the watercolor was painted, and act accordingly. If she didn't date her watercolors, find out what characteristics identify her high- and low-point pieces.

- *She tried oil painting for several years, but gave it up because she never quite mastered the medium.* You're lucky you aren't considering an oil. If someone offers you one, you should probably pass on it.

- *She had success selling her views of Mt. Ardmore in the mid-1970's, but mass produced them during the early 1980's.* If the work you're considering is of Mt. Ardmore and was done in the early 1980's, either pass on it or pay less for it than you would for a more original piece – one that was done before 1980.

- *Mathews paints best in the 20 by 24 inch size range. Her watercolors that measure larger than 25 by 30 inches are not as well done.* Measure the watercolor you like, compare it to others that size range and to others of different sizes, and act accordingly. If the watercolor you are evaluating is very large, think about shopping for a smaller one.

A Look Ahead

A work of art is often accompanied by either a certificate of authenticity (abbreviated COA), an appraisal, or both. In the art business, specific requirements must be met in order for these documents to be considered accurate, valid, and appropriate to the circumstances in which they're presented. In Chapter 15 you will learn to tell the difference between valid COA's and appraisals and problematic or meaningless ones.

CHAPTER 15

Certificates of Authenticity and Appraisals

Two of the most important, least understood, and most abused documents in the art business are the certificate of authenticity (or COA) and the appraisal. By definition, a valid COA conclusively demonstrates and/or attests that a work of art is by the stated artist, and a qualified appraisal states how much a work of art is worth according to a predefined set of conditions. Unfortunately for those new to buying art, telling the difference between a credible COA or appraisal and a meaningless one is not necessarily easy. So in order to avoid tricky situations, let's take a quick crash course on the basics of each. That way, the next time you're presented with either, you'll have a basic understanding of what you're looking at.

The Certificate of Authenticity or COA

No formal standards currently exist for either authorizing or providing certificates of authenticity. COA procedures are not regulated and subject to no oversight or examination by any official agency or organization (assuming no federal, state, or local laws are broken). Pretty much anyone can print up or write a COA and word it however they please, whether they're qualified to do so or not. As if that's not bad enough, unscrupulous individuals forge official looking COA's and use them to either sell outright fakes or to misrepresent existing works of art as being more important than they actually are. To make matters worse, bogus COA's have been issued for decades; one that's dated 1955, for example, can be just as worthless as one written today. The good news is that within the established art community, the form and content of an acceptable COA are well defined by convention, follow set guidelines, and satisfy specific requirements.

The most important requirement for a COA to be valid is that the individual who authors and signs it is qualified to do so. He must be a recognized and respected authority on the art and artist he certifies as being authentic, and he must have the credentials and acceptance throughout the art community and among his peers for his conclusions to be considered definitive. Qualified authorities include academicians, curators, or historians who have authored books, catalogues, magazine articles, scholarly papers, or who have organized museum or major gallery shows about the artists in question. Qualified authorities may also be artists (in the case of authenticating their own art); publishers (in the case of authenticating limited editions that they publish); respected and established dealers or agents of an artist who receive art either directly from that artist or from her estate (not third party dealers or resellers); direct descendents, informed relatives, spouses, longstanding employees, or heirs of artists; or individuals who have legal, formal, or estate-granted entitlements or sanctions to pass judgment on works of art by specific artists.

A valid COA must be an original document, NOT A COPY, and must be hand signed or otherwise certified by the authority responsible for composing it. It must also include or make reference to that individual's qualifications to authenticate the art, and her FULL CURRENT CONTACT INFORMATION. A COA cannot be considered valid if either the contact information is untraceable or the qualifications are unverifiable.

A valid COA must specifically describe the work of art in question. This prevents the same COA from being misused to "authenticate" more than one work of art. A valid description must include:

- the medium of the art (painting, print, lithograph, giclee, etc.),
- its exact dimensions,
- its title (when known),
- the edition size (when applicable),
- and other distinguishing features or relevant specifics.

Additional details, when known, must also be included such as:

- the date of the art,
- its condition,
- its publisher,
- names of dealers who sold it (when relevant to substantiating the authenticity of the art),
- names of previous owners of the art (when relevant to substantiating the authenticity of the art),
- and the names of reference books or similar resources that specifically mention the art.

For example, ALL limited edition prints by Picasso, Chagall, and Miro are documented in books called catalogue raisonnés (a catalogue raisonné lists ALL KNOWN WORKS OF ART in a particular medium or mediums by a particular artist). In fact, many well-known artists have catalogue raisonnés, and whenever a catalogue raisonné exists for an artist, the corresponding catalogue number or entry for the work of art in question MUST be included in the COA. (If a work of art is supposed to be in a catalogue raisonné, but isn't, and it has a COA anyway, this is very likely a problematic, and the COA may be fraudulent.)

COA's authored by anyone other than recognized authorities on artists are WORTHLESS, no matter how important or official they look. These documents have no credibility in the art community, and no opinions, assertions, or conclusions made in those COA's can be taken seriously. Here are some examples of meaningless statements commonly found in worthless COA's authored by unqualified individuals:

- The art is by the artist because either all or part of it looks like the work of that artist.

- The art is by the artist because it looks like illustrations in books about the artist.

- The art is by the artist based on independent research performed by an individual who is NOT a recognized authority on the artist. (The findings of such research are often accompanied by long convoluted hypothetical explanations that supposedly support the "researcher's" conclusions.)

- The art is by the artist because it bears the signature of that artist. The more important an artist, the more outside proof is required to substantiate the genuineness of any signature on any work of art supposedly by that artist. As difficult as this may be to believe, a signature alone is NEVER enough to conclusively prove authenticity.

- The art is by the artist because "that's what the last person who owned it said."

- The art is by the artist because it was bought in Paris (or some other major city).

- The art is by the artist because it was bought at a gallery with a fancy sounding name.

- The art is by the artist because a collector with a fancy sounding name once owned it.

- The art is by the artist because a rich collector formerly owned it and/or it came from a great big house on top of a hill and/or everything in the estate it came from was valuable, and so on and so forth.

- The art is by the artist because the last owner it bought it a long time ago.

- The art is by the artist because it says so in an appraisal. ART APPRAISALS ONLY STATE DOLLAR VALUES ACCORDING TO THE CONDITIONS DEFINED IN THOSE APPRAISALS. ART APPRAISALS ARE NOT COA'S; THEY DO NOT

AUTHENTICATE ART (unless the appraiser is also a recognized authority on the art being appraised). Appraisals and COA's are two entirely different entities; NEVER CONFUSE THEM.

A formal COA is not necessarily required to prove that a work of art is genuine. Any valid receipt, bill of sale, or proof of purchase from either the artist herself or from a confirmed and established dealer, publisher, or agent of the artist will do. An appraisal from a recognized authority on the artist is also acceptable. Always remember, though, that only documents from QUALIFIED individuals are acceptable. Here are some additional pointers to keep in mind whenever a work of art you are considering buying comes with a COA:

- Read and review the full text of that COA and the qualifications of the individual who authored it **BEFORE** you buy the art to make sure that it meets adequate requirements to be considered valid.

- Never buy art based on a promise that a COA will be provided at some point in the future. Never buy art based on a promise that the COA exists but will only be provided to the buyer and only after the sale is completed.

- If the art is for sale online, request a copy, either by fax or digital image, of the **complete COA** and not just portions of it. Most importantly, verify in writing from the seller that the COA in his possession is an original document and not a reproduction or photocopy.

- Any conditional statements found in a COA such as "in our considered opinion..." or "we believe that..." are warning signs that the art may not be genuine or is problematic in some way. A valid COA conclusively states that the art is by the artist in question.

- A valid COA must present documented proof or evidence in one form or another as that the art is genuine. (This proof may be as simple as signed statement from a respected authority on the artist.)

- If you have any questions about the content of a COA, contact the authority who is responsible for it **BEFORE** you buy the art.

- When the contact information on a COA is no longer valid or out-of-date, confirm that the information corresponds to where the authority actually lived or worked on the date of completion of the COA.

- A COA with only a signature, legible or not, is NEVER valid.

- Names of previous owners, names of dealers or galleries that once sold the art, or information about auctions where the art once sold are only relevant if they speak directly to the authenticity of the art. All names and contact information for such individuals or businesses must be verified in order to confirm that the sales transactions actually took place.

A Word About "Attributed" Art

Works of art are sometimes presented as "attributed" to certain artists in order to justify higher selling prices. In most cases, these so-called attributions are meaningless. By definition, an attribution means little more than in the best opinion of **A QUALIFIED AUTHORITY** on a particular artist, the art in question **MAY BE** by that artist. In other words, not even the authority is sure (the exception being when he clearly states that the art is very likely by the hand of the artist, and provides a detailed and comprehensive explanation to go with it). And if an authority isn't sure, how can anyone else be sure? So basically, the attribution has no value. Either it is or it isn't – what good is "maybe?"

To make matters worse, all kinds of unqualified individuals attribute all kinds of art to all kinds of artists all the time, and 100% of those attributions are worthless. In the art world, the only legitimate attributions are those made by known recognized authorities on the artists in question. And to repeat, all those authorities are saying in the great majority of cases is that maybe the art is by the artist in question, and then again, maybe it isn't. In other words, who cares?

Art Appraisals and How to Evaluate Them

An art appraisal states, in the opinion of a qualified professional appraiser, how much a work of art is worth according to a predefined set of conditions. As with COA's, the only appraisals worth the paper they're printed on are those performed by qualified appraisers, or in other words, professionals who know how to value art and have the credentials to prove it. People who are not qualified to appraise art conjecture about what art may or may not be worth all the time. But when real money is at stake, relying on casual opinions is never a good idea. Not only can an appraiser tell you how much the art is worth, but he can also explain why, put it in writing, and sign it.

The tricky part about appraisals is that the same work of art can be "worth" different amounts depending on specific conditions stated in the appraisal. There are several types of appraisals, so whenever you're handed one, you have to make sure it's appropriate to your situation. Sound confusing? Well, it is – but not so confusing that we can't sort things out right here and now.

The most common and widely accepted type of appraisal is called a "fair market value" or FMV appraisal. This is the appraisal required by the Internal Revenue Service (IRS) in any taxable instance where art must be valued for inheritance, donation, barter, or gift purposes. **A FMV appraisal is also the most relevant and realistic appraisal for people who buy art – and that includes you.** Fair market value as defined in IRS Publication 561 is "the price that property would sell for on the open market. It is the price that would be agreed on between a willing buyer and a willing seller, with neither being required to act, and both having reasonable knowledge of the relevant facts." In other words, you're familiar with the market for the art that you're buying, the seller knows what he's selling, and neither of you are under any pressure to either buy or sell.

In the art world, FMV generally refers to what a work of art would sell for at auction (see Chapter 21 to learn about approximating a work of art's auction value), not at a retail gallery. However, depending on the artist and the conditions of the appraisal, retail gallery prices may also be considered. Auction selling prices are significant because at auction, potential buyers bid against each other with the art selling to the highest bidder. The art is not offered at a fixed price, no one is compelled to bid, the auction house typically knows what they're selling, competing bidders typically know what they're bidding on, and the high bid or selling price is essentially considered to represent an agreement of sorts among bidders as to what the art is fairly worth. This pretty much matches the FMV definition as stated in IRS Publication 561.

Retail gallery prices are not typically used to determine FMV in tax appraisals because in the closed, controlled environments of galleries, prices may reflect gallery policies and costs of doing business more than they do open market forces (including the fair market value of the art). The asking price for a particular work of art may vary considerably from gallery to gallery and may depend more on factors like a gallery's typical mark up over cost, overhead, commissions, location, the owner's beliefs about what art is "worth," buying habits of the gallery's client base, and the ability of the gallery staff to sell art, than it does on the art's FMV. In extreme instances, art priced at gallery retail can be many times the amount it would sell for at auction or what would be considered its fair market value.

The IRS additionally prohibits an appraiser from being "a party to the transaction in which the donor acquired the property," or in other words, an individual who either sells or is involved in the sale of a work of art is disqualified from appraising it for IRS purposes (for possible conflict-of-interest reasons). This point is important for you to keep in mind when evaluating any appraisal. An essential question to ask whenever you're unclear about who appraised the art is: **Does the "appraiser" have any personal or business interest in the artist, in galleries or dealers that sell the art, or any other interest in appraising the art at a certain value?** If yes, then you cannot assume the appraisal represents a fair assessment of what the art is worth. The most obvious example of this is when a gallery provides their own "appraisals" to go with the art they sell. I can assure you that a gallery will never "appraise" their art for less than the sale price; however, they frequently "appraise" it at higher than the sale price. When is an appraisal not an appraisal? When the seller and the appraiser are the same person (or people).

Ready to get practical and learn about the other kinds of appraisals? Good. Suppose you see a piece of art you like, the seller says it's been appraised for a certain amount, and that's what he's selling it for. If you're like most people, you're inclined to believe that since the art's been appraised, it's worth that amount, and it's OK to buy. But as you've probably already guessed, this is not necessarily the case. Art appraisals may or may not have any relation to the art's FMV (the most relevant value for you).

If a seller says a work of art's been appraised or that he knows its appraised value, the first thing you do is ask is to see the appraisal. If the seller says he doesn't have an actual appraisal, but rather that an appraiser looked at the art and gave a dollar value, THIS IS NOT AN APPRAISAL. If the seller tells you he hasn't actually had the art appraised, but that's what he's seen the art sell for elsewhere, THIS IS NOT AN APPRAISAL. No document that you can hold in your hands and read means only one thing – the seller does not have an appraisal.

Let's say the seller does have an appraisal, and he hands it to you. **Pay attention to two things – the qualifications of the appraiser and the conditions of the appraisal.** Regarding qualifications, the person appraising the art must be a professional appraiser with experience appraising this type of art and have no conflict of interest regarding the art, the artist, or any dealer or gallery that sells the art. The appraisal should contain contact information for the appraiser, a conflict of interest disclaimer, and a statement of how the appraised value was determined.

Regarding the conditions of the appraisal, if it simply states what the art sells for at a particular gallery, this is generally referred to as a **retail value appraisal.** A retail value appraisal is almost always higher than an FMV appraisal; it represents what a work of art sells for at a particular gallery, not on the open market. A legitimate FMV appraisal must reflect what the art sells for on the open market, not at one specific gallery. Often, a retail value appraisal is simply a statement from the gallery that it sold the art for the sale price (obvious conflict of interest and, as mentioned above, not technically an appraisal at all). Remember, the appraisal that is most relevant to you is one that states FMV – what the art sells for in general – not at one specific gallery.

A similarly irrelevant appraisal (and potentially the most deleterious to your pocketbook) is a **replacement value appraisal for insurance purposes.** This is the amount of money an insurance company is generally asked to pay when a work of art is either damaged beyond repair, stolen, or destroyed. It represents the **full retail price of the art plus**

139

whatever additional expenses may be incurred to either repair the art or replace it with an exact or approximate duplicate. Unfortunately, there is considerable abuse with respect to replacement or insurance value appraisals, particularly when galleries do them in-house (a conflict of interest) and then represent them to buyers as being what the art is realistically worth on the open market (FMV). Another problem with replacement or insurance appraisals is that the dollar amounts they state can be entirely arbitrary and have little or no basis in fact. Anytime you see the words "replacement value," "insurance value," or "insurance purposes," in an appraisal for art that you're thinking about buying, watch out. This is about as far from a FMV appraisal as you can get. Best procedure when buying art is to disregard any replacement value appraisal and to instead request a FMV appraisal from a qualified appraiser with no conflicts of interest.

Additional Pointers for Evaluating Appraisals

- The amount of money someone paid for a work of art IS NOT AN APPRAISAL. What art sold for yesterday is not necessarily what it sells for today. What someone pays for a work of art is not automatically what that art is worth. People overpay for art all the time and you, as a buyer, are not required to compensate them for their mistakes if they try to sell that art to you.

- A work of art that's "been appraised" for $5,000, but is priced for sale at $2,500, is not automatically a bargain. As discussed above, if the $5,000 appraisal is a retail, replacement, or insurance appraisal, that figure may well exceed the art's FMV.

- Make sure any appraisal you are presented with is current, certainly no older than a couple of years. Art prices fluctuate over time. An appraisal dating from the art boom of the late 1980's, for instance, may still state a dollar amount greater than what the art currently sells for.

- Beware of free appraisals (especially if you are thinking about selling your art). People who offer free appraisals almost always have ulterior motives including trying to buy your art for much less than it's worth, giving your contact information to third parties who will try to buy your art for much less than it's worth (and then pay the "free appraiser" a finder's fee if they succeed in buying it), or talking you into paying for "better" appraisals than the "free" ones you're getting. Also keep in mind that auction houses offering "free appraisals" do not really appraise your art. They give you estimates of what they think your art will sell for at their sales.

Can Anybody Appraise Art?

A surprising number of people believe that they can appraise art just as well as qualified appraisers. They take whatever advice they can get for free (we all know what that's worth), maybe go online, maybe look in a couple of books, maybe find a few lists of art prices, and think that's all they need to price art accurately. But you know what? They have no idea whether the values they end up with are anywhere near the fair market values of that art.

More often than not, they end up with casual ballpark figures, and that's fine for casual situations. But when real money is at stake and you still have questions, whether you're on the buy end or the sell end, whether you've been shown an appraisal or not, consult a qualified appraiser **before** you act, not after. Qualified art appraisers are neutral professionals with no conflicts of interest who value art for a living and who work on your behalf to make sure you have the facts you need to make informed, intelligent decisions about art.

A Look Ahead

An additional question to help you evaluate a piece of art is, "*What other interesting facts can you find out about the art?*" The answer to this question deserves its own chapter – the next one. When evaluating your selections, you need to know as many facts as possible about them, some of which may not be evident from simply researching the artist or viewing and evaluating the art. Particular works of art often stand out above others because of interesting incidental information and are more sought-after by collectors than pieces that lack such information. In Chapter 16 you will learn what kind of information this is and how to go about acquiring it.

CHAPTER 16

Provenance is Profit

What Provenance Means

You're standing in the Triple-A Fine Arts Gallery considering a Vincent Picasso landscape painting for possible purchase. You have researched the artist, you know the milestones in his career and what his most popular subject matters are, and you have decided that his art is worth collecting. You've studied a number of his paintings and have concluded that Triple-A's painting is a significant example of his art. You're done with your research. Right?

Not quite.

Additional facts about a work of art – facts that are not obvious from simply viewing the art, viewing other examples of that artist's work, or researching the artist – can significantly impact its value and collectibility. This information is called *provenance* and includes printed, verbal, or other forms of data relating specifically to that work of art's ownership history. Particularly with important art pieces, provenance looms as a major factor in determining dollar value and marketability. Though not always obtainable or necessary to possess, when you do have it, you must understand what it means, how to interpret it, and how it influences value.

Provenance can be many things:

- *A signed certificate or statement of authenticity from an art gallery*

- *An exhibition or gallery sticker attached to the art*

- *A sales receipt*

- *A film or recording of the artist talking about the art*

- *An appraisal from a recognized authority*

- *Names of previous owners*

- *Letters or papers discussing the art*

- *Newspaper or magazine articles mentioning or illustrating the art*

- *A mention or illustration of the art in a book or exhibit catalogue*

- *Verbal information related by someone familiar with the art or who knows the artist*

- *Any data, in any form, relating directly to the art*

Provenance almost always increases the value and desirability of an art piece, because with it, more exists than the art itself. Let's say you own a

143

painting that was originally commissioned by famous art patrons and hung in their personal collection. You own not just another picture, but rather the one that was commissioned by the renowned Mr. and Mrs. So and So and hung on the living room wall of their mansion on Main Street. The fact that your painting was commissioned, owned, and maintained in an exclusive setting makes it, in a sense, a blue blood among paintings.

Proof that your art was actually executed by the artist who signed it is the most basic function of provenance. Even though the art is signed and looks authentic, additional documentation provides conclusive evidence that all is right. With the proliferation of forgeries these days, the fact that the art is signed and looks like a recognizable example of an artist's work does not always place it above suspicion. But having good provenance does. For example, you can't dispute a painting's authenticity when you have an exhibit catalogue illustrating the piece or a newspaper article showing the artist standing next to that very painting.

Artists often generate provenance on their own and, as a result, influence the futures of individual works of art. Suppose a painter writes in his memoirs, or in a letter to a friend, that his "View of Slattersby Park" is one of his finest compositions. Even though some art critics may disagree, the Slattersby Park painting becomes exceptional among that artist's output because of the artist's documented opinion.

More unusual examples of provenance include documented incidents of controversy or intrigue. A work of art may have been stolen and recovered fifty years later, or have traveled across country in a stagecoach in 1856, or had other adventures befall it. Any revelations that separate an art piece from all others on the market and make it more than just another painting or sculpture or etching or watercolor are what provenance is all about.

Art galleries are well-aware of the value of provenance. Given two comparable works by the same artist, one with good provenance and one without, the one with provenance will invariably cost more than the one without. Your task is figuring out what good provenance is and how much additional value you should ascribe to what amount and what kind of provenance. You can overpay for inferior provenance the same way you can overpay for inferior art.

Let's examine and then analyze four hypothetical provenances that Triple-A Fine Arts could give you on their Vincent Picasso landscape.

Provenance 1: "We bought the painting privately from a local collector who wishes to remain anonymous."

Provenance 2: "This painting hung in an American Art League show at the Boston Museum in 1889, where it won the Hubert D. Thorp prize for excellence in landscape. It was purchased in 1890 by Peter J. Richard, an important New York art collector in his day, and has remained in the Richard family until now. Accompanying the painting is a letter to Peter Richard from

Vincent Picasso, dated July 18, 1891, stating that the picture is 'the best landscape I have painted to date.' "

Provenance 3: "The woman who sold us this painting said that the elderly man she bought it from told her that the painting originally belonged to one of Teddy Roosevelt's best friends, a well-known art collector. According to the elderly man, the woman went on to say, it was supposedly one of Teddy's favorite paintings, and he always remarked on it when he visited that friend's home."

Provenance 4: "This painting once hung in the Presidential Suite of the Mayflower Arms Hotel, Detroit's finest accommodation from the 1940's through the early 1970's. From June 14th to the 16th, 1968, during their notorious *Rock The Solar System Tour*, the Purple Oranges, Britain's premier psychedelic rock band, stayed in the Presidential Suite. On the night of June 15th, 1968, a wild all-night party convened two hours after the concert resulting in damage to the suite that exceeded $20,000. The Vincent Picasso did not escape unharmed. It received a minor tear when Bottomly Scrimpton, lead singer for the Oranges, threw a reproduction Ming table lamp at a cute, but obnoxious groupie, and missed. The tear has long since been expertly repaired. Accompanying the painting is a signed statement from the hotel security guard who was stationed outside the door during the party, as well as photocopies of Scrimpton's letter of apology to the hotel manager for destroying the room and of the Purple Orange's check for the painting's repair."

How do you as a collector evaluate these four provenances in relation to what you are being asked to pay for the painting? Let's say that a good-quality Vincent Picasso, similar in size, subject matter and condition to this one, is worth $10,000 with no provenance. Now for the analysis:

Provenance 1: This is essentially no provenance at all, and as long as the painting is average-to-good quality and in good condition, the asking price should be $10,000. What you should get with your purchase is a signed statement from Triple-A Fine Arts affirming that the painting is an authentic Vincent Picasso. You should also receive a statement of full money-back guarantee should the authenticity of the painting ever be doubted by a qualified expert on the artist. These documents will become the painting's provenance.

Provenance 2: You've got an impressive history here. Vincent Picasso considered this painting to be one of his best, a jury of his peers concurred by awarding him a prestigious award at a national show, and a major private collector agreed by purchasing the piece. That sort of provenance should add at least several thousand dollars to the base price of $10,000 and possibly as much as $8,000 to $10,000 or even more, depending on how many other Vincent Picasso's have those sorts of qualifications. On the high end, if experts believe that this picture is one of

Vincent Picasso's greatest efforts, an asking price somewhat in excess of $20,000 wouldn't be at all out of the question.

Provenance 3: What you're dealing with here is verbal hearsay. This provenance is valid only if the allegations can be investigated and confirmed. Otherwise, assume no provenance – and no increase in price above $10,000 – at all.

Unless Triple-A Fine Arts can give you specific names, dates, places, or any other concrete information in support of the woman's contentions, all you have is gossip that may or may not be true. You need the name of that woman, the name of the elderly man who gave her the information, and the name of Roosevelt's best friend and supposed well-known collector. As for Teddy's liking the painting, his preferences in art are basically irrelevant because he was a politician, not an art expert.

Be especially careful when presented with gossip or hearsay provenance. Sellers sometimes state it as though it's true and then charge more for the art because of it. No matter how good it sounds or how much of it there is, it's not valid unless you can prove it.

Provenance 4: This is a good story. If you buy the Vincent Picasso and hang it in your living room, being able to relate that bizarre incident while showing it off to your friends does have a dollar value attached to it. Your friends would certainly be more entertained hearing about this moment in rock history than hearing the statement, "Look at this wonderful Vincent Picasso landscape I just bought."

Be careful how much you pay for this story, though, because it does not relate to the painting as a work of art, but only to the event, albeit a glamorous one. Assuming the object of Bottomly's indiscretion is average to good-quality, in good condition and that the inflicted damage was minor as stated, asking price should be increased by a modest amount, perhaps $500 to $1,500 at the very most, above the $10,000 base (unless, of course, your mission is to form the definitive collection of paintings damaged by famous rock stars, you're the major expert on the subject, and you couldn't care less who Vincent Picasso is).

Acquiring and Maintaining Provenance

Make every effort to acquire and maintain provenance on all art you own. At the very least, be sure sellers give you signed statements of authenticity, and whatever other relevant data they have in their files, whenever you buy works of art. Keep individual folders on each work of art you own, and save all pertinent receipts, guarantees, statements by the artists, exhibition catalogues, and anything else relating directly to that art (for additional information about building folders, see Chapter 23). Each folder becomes a part of the art it represents and should remain with that art for all time.

Take what the galleries give you, but at the same time, be aware that they have not necessarily had the time to uncover every single fact about every work of art that they sell. Depending on how fascinated you are with certain artists or art pieces and how industrious you feel, you may want to continue the job of acquiring provenance on your own. The more you find out, the better you understand the history of what you buy, the more sophisticated you become as an art buyer, and the more your art is worth.

Those of you who truly enjoy ferreting out facts should think of yourselves as detectives out to acquire the complete history of your art from the day it was created right up to the present moment. Trace its existence as far back as you can.

If you are buying contemporary art, the detective work is simple. Get a statement from the gallery and, whenever possible, a statement from the artist specifically relating to the piece in question, and you're done. Add to your file as new developments take place.

You have to work a little harder on older pieces of art with vague histories. For art by artists who are still living, contact the artists directly. Send them photographs of what you own, and ask them to comment on it. Request that they supply you with general biographical information about themselves and their careers and, most importantly, any data relating directly to your art. Ask them any additional questions you have about the art and its origins.

When an artist is no longer living, speak with or write to anyone you know to have been associated with them or their art and specifically with the art that you own. Locating these people is not always easy. Some collectors use techniques as sophisticated as researching family genealogies, internet databases, death certificates, property records, probate files, and so on. When you've got the spare time to check these sorts of resources, do so. It's a fascinating procedure, and you never know where you'll end up or what you'll find out.

Previous owners are another great source of provenance. Some galleries will give you the names of these people and allow you to contact them. When dealers won't name names (which is often the case), request that they contact those owners themselves, get whatever statements they can, and relate them to you.

A sad commentary on the business of acquiring and documenting provenance on older art is that, in many cases, dealers would rather protect their sources than name names of previous owners or tell you what they know about the histories of the art. This dealer reticence comes about, in part, because of less scrupulous collectors who learn sellers' names and sometimes attempt to contact those sources themselves. They then buy from the sellers' directly, thereby cutting the original galleries out of the profit picture. Thus, unfortunately, keeping provenance a secret is sometimes just good business sense for the galleries.

At other times, families who sell their art wish to remain anonymous. The dealers whom they work with are not at liberty to reveal names because that was part of the selling arrangement. In any event, you still may be able to locate these people and acquire provenance. Your job is just going to be tougher.

When you are fortunate enough to personally contact a previous owner, an individual who knew the artist well, a retired dealer who used to represent the artist, or anyone else who may have information you need, be aware that they sometimes overlook significant details about the art or never mention them simply because no one has ever asked – so ask. By the way, these are also questions you should ask any dealer selling you art. Sample provenance gathering questions include the following:

- *Where did you purchase this art?*

- *How long have you owned it?*

- *Do you know the names of any previous owners?*

- *Can you identify the subject matter, event, location, what it represents, or relate any other information about the piece?*

- *Do you know anything about when, where, why, or how it was produced?*

- *Do you have or know of any printed materials relating directly to this piece?*

- *Was it ever in a public exhibition?*

- *Has anyone ever told you anything interesting about it?*

- *Do you or did you know the artist personally, and if so, what was his or her opinion of the art?*

- *Do you know anyone else who can tell me more?* (You take these names and repeat the procedure.)

Additional, more-specific questions often arise as you pursue your investigations, but these will get you started.

Researching and acquiring provenance is rewarding in the long run because every discovery you make influences a work of art's value upwards. In the same vein, lacking crucial information always results in art being undervalued. Many art dealers have sad tales to tell about selling artwork and then later discovering important, relevant information. You are fortunate indeed when you uncover something about an art piece that the person who sold it to you unwittingly overlooked; and the better you get at locating provenance, the greater the probability will be of that happening.

Example 1:

Provenance can be conveyed verbally, as well as in writing, which is how I acquired information about a painting by Frederick Judd Waugh, the famous American painter of coastal scenes. The painting's subject, a camouflaged merchant ship on the high seas circa World War I, is not exactly a composition Waugh is famous for and, being atypical, not exactly a composition collectors seek out for their collections. His fans prefer dramatic coastal scenes with waves crashing over rocks.

The written provenance consisted of the original owner's name and various lifetime addresses on the painting's back. Since I purchased the painting directly from this owner's estate, I had the opportunity to receive its complete verbal history firsthand from the executor who had been a long-time friend of the family.

According to her, Waugh and the original owner, also an artist, both worked for the U.S. government during World War I. Together they researched and developed camouflage configurations for military and merchant ships. While working with Waugh, this artist invented the color, "Battleship Gray." The painting had been a gift from Waugh commemorating their relationship.

The unusual subject matter was now understandable and no longer a maverick, unexplainable composition. It fit perfectly into Waugh's career as a historically significant work of art.

I subsequently sent a photograph of the painting to a curator of a maritime museum for further information. In his reply, he stated that it was one of the few extant full-color examples of ship camouflage surviving from that time period. This meant that the painting had historic naval significance also. The curator was so impressed by it that he requested it be donated to the museum and stated that, if donated, it would be prominently displayed in their World War I collection.

What initially appeared to be an atypical and, therefore, relatively unpopular picture with collectors, took on a whole new meaning with complete provenance. Because of the painting's significance with respect to Waugh's artistic career, as well as to World War I naval history, the tale accompanying the painting made the piece much more attractive to collectors than it would have otherwise been. Without this information, I would have been hard-pressed to place it in any collection.

Example 2:

I own a painting by a well-known American artist who was active from the late 1920's through the 1950's. I liked it the moment I saw it, and I decided to buy it for my own collection. The only provenance the painting had was in the form of two pieces of paper glued to the painting's back, a museum accession sticker and the remains of another art exhibition tag.

The complete sticker was from a local museum. The museum had apparently purchased the painting for its collection in the early 1930's, but had de-accessed the painting several decades later when it decided to go a different direction with its collecting. The fact that a museum once owned a work of art is always a plus point, but what I discovered several years after buying the painting was an even bigger plus point.

One day I was looking through an old handbook of this particular museum's collection, one that had been published in the early 1940's, and found, to my delight, that my painting was one of only several American pictures illustrated. I could conclude from this that the museum held my painting in special high regard while they owned it. Not only had they considered it good enough to purchase, but they had also felt that it was one of only a few paintings good enough to be prominently illustrated in the museum's handbook.

I continued to puzzle over the remains of the second tag for several more years trying to figure out what specific exhibit it was from. I eventually identified the show from the few words remaining on the sticker and, again to my delight, it turned out to be from a major international art exhibition that had been held in the late 1930's. My painting had enjoyed a much more distinguished history than I had initially thought when I bought it. Dollarwise, the painting has also turned out to be worth a lot more than I had initially thought when I bought it.

A Look Ahead

Suppose you have selected a work of art that, on the surface, appears to qualify for inclusion in your collection and that, according to the research guidelines you have been reading about so far, looks pretty good. Suppose, however, that it has either been damaged in the past, is prone to damage in the future, or worse yet, is an outright fake. In either of the first two instances, there's a distinct possibility that you won't want to purchase the piece. That possibility becomes a certainty if the art happens to be a forgery.

The next two research chapters concern the topics of damage and forgeries. They are not topics that members of the art community – especially art dealers – enjoy talking about, but they cannot be ignored. Inspecting any selection you make for damage and the possibility that it could be a forgery are the last two steps in your research before you address money issues and, ultimately, decide whether or not to buy.

CHAPTER 17

Art and Damage

Just about all art you see on display in galleries looks to be in perfect condition and looks as though it will last forever. Galleries make every effort to present their art to the public in top viewing condition. But what condition is it really in, and will you have problems with it after you buy it? These are important questions that must be answered before you spend your money.

Think of how long you expect the art you buy to last. A work of art is not like a car, a television, or other disposable consumer product that, after a few years, you throw away or trade in and replace with the latest model. You keep art much longer than you keep other possessions. You may decide to sell it twenty or thirty years down the road. You may own it for fifty years and then pass it down to your children. They may pass it down to their children and so on. Whatever you do with it, you always want it to look its best.

Art dealers and galleries, unfortunately, don't do nearly enough to inform and educate their customers about condition, damage, and the consequences of damage. Only at the highest levels of collecting do dealers regularly discuss these topics with their clients. The average art gallery is in business to sell art. Since conversations relating to damage and condition problems are not usually conducive to making sales, such conversations don't usually happen unless they have to. Consequently, you have to arm yourself with appropriate knowledge in order to avoid problem art.

A substantial amount of older works of art, for instance, have been subjected to various degrees of wear and tear over the years and been repaired or altered at various points during their lifetimes. Even though they appear to be in original perfect condition, underneath the gloss may be histories of damage, condition problems, and repairs.

Contemporary art can have problems too. Just because you buy it brand new does not mean you'll never have to worry about it. Some pieces are not very well constructed and are predisposed to wearing poorly over time. Dealers in contemporary art can document cases of art that substantially deteriorated after only a few years in existence.

For example, several decades ago, artists were attracted to certain brands of water-based markers or "water crayons" when they first came onto the market and used them in their art. Within five to ten years, the water crayon portions of that art began to fade, and after ten years or so, they had faded so seriously that they had either totally changed color or had almost completely disappeared. Artists now know to avoid these crayons.

Contemporary art can also have damage repair, even though the art has only been in existence a short while. A gallery employee may have dropped the art on its corner while transporting it from the artist's studio to the gallery, it may have had coffee spilled on it, and so on. Artists can even damage their art in the process of creating it and, rather than start all over, repair the problems themselves.

Whatever the situation and whatever the art, if what you are considering buying has either had problems in the past or has weaknesses in the present that will lead to problems in the future, you have to know about them. The reason is that damage decreases value. Art that has damage, is prone to damage, or has suffered damage that has been repaired is worth less than art in perfect condition. It's that simple.

Damage reduces value in another way, also: you must pay to have it fixed. Art that develops problems over time or is damaged while you own it must be repaired, and those repairs cost money. Not only do they cost money, but they often cost a lot of money. Art restoration and conservation is a highly specialized profession, and spending several thousand dollars to restore an art piece is not unusual.

You should not automatically refuse to buy a work of art because it has damage, however. Damaged art is not worthless as many people believe. For example, I once bought an old, torn, rolled-up canvas at a Texas junk shop for $7.50. The piece looked totally worthless to the shop's owner, but I had no trouble selling it several days later in "as-is" condition for $2,500.

The bottom line is this: *Anyone can learn how to evaluate the condition of any work of art on his or her own.* Whether damage has already happened or is yet to come, whether the art looks beyond hope or in pristine condition, the better you are at assessing the art's condition history and, when necessary, its prognosis for successful restoration, the fewer problems and added expenses you will have to contend with in the course of your buying.

Learning About Types of Damage

No matter what kind of art you buy – oil paintings, etchings, bronze sculptures, watercolors, wood carvings, whatever – you need to learn what specific problems are associated with that type of art. You'll find that for every art form, an entire terminology exists for identifying and evaluating damage. For example, oil paintings can rip, tear, lose paint, or accumulate dirt. Repair procedures include replacing areas of missing paint, closing rips and tears, and removing surface dirt. (The respective technical terms for these repairs are *inpainting, lining,* and *cleaning.*)

If you're getting a little nervous and thinking that the subject of damage might be too difficult to understand, relax. You can get a good sense of the basics after only several hours of instruction. Then, after learning the basics, all you need to do is practice, practice, and practice by looking at art and learning to spot problems.

The best teachers you can find are repair specialists called "fine art conservators." No matter what you collect, when it breaks, fades, dents, rips, cracks, or anything else, an art conservator exists who knows exactly how to fix it. These people are trained experts in their particular fields of restoration.

You can find out much of what you need to know by visiting and speaking with a conservator or two.

Locate fine-art conservators in your area by checking the Yellow Pages under the heading "Art Restoring." Get additional names by asking art dealers or contacting art museums. Museum references are especially good and, in fact, many museums operate their own full-time conservation facilities. Some of these institutions even provide formal instruction on the subject through occasional seminars or lectures. Also write to the *American Institute for Conservation of Historic and Artistic Works* to request its membership roster and see whether any of their members are active in your area. The Institute's address is: 1717 K St. NW, Suite 200, Washington, D.C. 20036, or visit its website online at *http://aic.stanford.edu/*.

Assemble names from these various sources, and speak with the conservators over the phone. Tell them what you collect, and make sure they are experts at restoring it. Anyone with which you decide to work should have years of experience and be able to provide you with adequate references. Assuming they are qualified, tell them you are interested in learning about damage and its treatment, and ask whether you can visit them at their studios. Most are happy to spend at least some time with you and show you firsthand how they work.

While at conservation studios, make sure you do the following:

- See photographs of art in its "before" and "after" condition (you'll quickly realize that expert conservators can truly work miracles).

- See restorations in progress.

- Have conservators show you how to identify and diagnose existing damage as well as damage that has already been repaired.

- Have them show you specific problems that you could encounter with your art.

- Find out how much each of those problems costs to repair (being able to approximate repair costs comes in very handy if you are ever offered a work of art that is not in perfect condition).

- Learn what types of damage are easy to repair, which are difficult, and which are impossible.

- Pay special attention to learning how to recognize permanent damage. For example, paintings or bronzes that have been cleaned with excessively harsh solvents can have irreplaceable amounts of paint or patinas stripped off their surfaces. The better conservators can hide these sorts of problems, but they can never bring the art back to the original look that the artist intended it to have. Irreversible damage seriously reduces dollar value and collectibility; avoid it at all costs.

Another way to learn about damage and condition problems, especially if you want to buy contemporary art, is from artists themselves. Have art galleries, art associations, or museum sale and rental galleries recommend the names of artists who can teach you. As with conservators, speak on the phone first, make appointments, and then visit these artists at their studios. Have them show what characteristics to look for in well-made art and how to avoid inferior pieces. Learn the difference between poorly constructed art and art that has been put together with quality materials by artists who know how to use them.

One important warning: Never confuse artists with art conservators. Never ask artists to assess or repair damaged art, even if it is their own (artists who "repair" their own art tend to rework it the way they think it should look now rather than reconstruct the way it originally looked). They are totally untrained in proper conservation techniques and procedures. Artists and art conservators are two entirely different professions. Artists create art; art conservators restore, preserve, and maintain it.

How Much Damage is Considered Acceptable?

Experienced art dealers and collectors generally avoid art that has been damaged beyond a certain point. The most serious, investment-oriented collectors avoid damage at all costs and prefer to buy art that is in its original, unaltered condition only. The logic is clear: the more damage repair a work of art has, the less it is as the original artist intended it to be, and the more it is as the conservator has reconstructed it. In the extreme instance, some art you find for sale has had such severe damage that it is now primarily the work of the repair person and no longer that of the original artist.

Depending on the type of art, certain amounts of damage are considered minor and acceptable by most collectors; larger amounts become increasingly unacceptable and either significantly reduce or totally destroy the value of the art. What those precise amounts are vary according to factors such as the age of the art, rarity, importance of the artist, and so on. For example, collectors of fifteenth-century Gothic panel paintings are more liberal in the amount of damage they consider acceptable than are collectors of contemporary watercolors.

Have art dealers – not conservators – teach you what amounts and types of damage are acceptable and not acceptable, how they affect collectibility, and how they affect dollar value. Conservators want to restore art no matter how bad the damage is and are especially eager to get going when damage is severe. Repairing major damage is not only challenging to conservators, but also financially well worth their while. As a result, conservators tend to downplay the effects of moderate to severe damage on collectibility. Dealers, on the other hand, have substantially less conflict of interest here and give you more realistic assessments.

Two general rules can help you determine how the extent of damage affects the value of any given art piece:

1. *The greater the percentage of damage, the more value is reduced.* With most art, no damage is best, five percent is minor, but beyond that point, things begin to get a little touchy (unless you happen to be collecting great rarities). Ordinarily, ten percent is about the maximum acceptable amount.

2 *The location of the damage is equally as important as the percentage.* A small amount of damage in the wrong place can destroy a work of art's value.

Consider, for example, a portrait painting of a figure against a black background. Let's say it's in perfect condition except for severe damage to one eye. Eyes are usually the most important details in a portrait and are crucial to understanding and appreciating the picture as a whole. When one eye has to be entirely repainted by a conservator, the essence of the painting is substantially altered and possibly even lost. That new eye will never look the same as the original and, thus, the painting's value is markedly decreased. If, however, that same percentage of damage is to the plain black background behind the figure and the rest of the painting is perfect, overall value is reduced only slightly.

Inspecting Condition Before You Buy

For every type of art that exists, a system also exists for inspecting and determining the condition of that art. You inspect oil paintings a certain way, watercolors a certain way, sculptures a certain way, and so on. Whether you buy period or contemporary art, learn proper inspection procedures for that art and always follow them before you buy. No matter what you collect, the general pointers given below will be of help.

Begin any condition inspection by asking the seller for a full condition report. When repairs have been made in the past, have the seller show you exactly where they are located and how extensive they are. Sometimes – not nearly often enough, but the practice is becoming more common – conservators attach descriptions of their completed work to the art. This information includes what repairs have been made, how they were made, what chemicals or other materials were used in the process, and photographs of the art in its "before" condition.

Inspect the art using the techniques you learn from art conservators, artists, and dealers. Always do this yourself, no matter how much information the seller gives you. You are the buyer; you deserve to examine all selections fully before buying.

How do you inspect for damage? Very closely. If you need a magnifying glass, buy one. Don't be embarrassed to study the most minute details of an art piece. That scratch, chip, or dent may be small, and that repaired tear may not be visible from more than two feet away, but they are there just the same, and they affect the value of the art.

Buy any specialized tools you may need to help check for damage. For example, a hand-held ultraviolet light is often used to inspect for damage repairs on old oil paintings, textiles, works on paper, glass, and ceramics. Make sure you know how to use whatever equipment you buy before you try to use it to examine art you are considering buying. As always, it is best to have fine art conservators, art dealers, or other experts train you in proper use and inspection techniques.

Whenever you see any aspect of an artwork that you don't fully understand or that looks suspicious, ask about it. Whether it turns out to be damage repair or structural weakness or the way the artist intended the art to be, satisfy yourself fully before buying. If you have any doubts whatsoever about a piece, have a conservator independently examine it *before you buy*.

Be wary of sellers who give vague answers to your questions regarding condition or, worse yet, discourage condition examinations altogether. Your best option is not to patronize galleries where you have experienced such treatment. Unless you are skilled at inspecting condition yourself and are willing to take the necessary risks, do your buying elsewhere.

Whenever possible, get a written condition report and an accompanying guarantee that if the condition is not as it has been represented, you receive a complete refund of the purchase price. This guarantee protects you from sellers who deliberately misrepresent the condition of their art. Misrepresentation doesn't happen often, but it does happen.

Maintaining Your Art

Few people ever think of asking how to care for their art once they own it. They hang it on the wall or place it on its pedestal and forget about it. Years later, they discover problems and end up having to pay costly repair or cleaning bills.

Art has care and maintenance instructions just like anything else. Have dealers and conservators show you the best way to maintain yours. For additional instruction, read *Collecting and Care of Fine Art,* by Carl David (New York, Crown Publishers, 1981). Also write to The American Institute for Conservation of Historic and Artistic Works for advice and ask if the institute can recommend any additional publications (the Institute's address was provided earlier in this chapter).

General rules for proper care and maintenance of fine art are as follows:

- *Avoid excess dryness or humidity.*

- *Avoid exposure to direct sunlight.*

- *Avoid temperature extremes.* Average room temperature in the low- to mid- 70's is best.

- *Avoid exposure to smoke from fireplaces, stoves, or tobacco.* If you have a problem with smoke, protect your art under glass or Plexiglas to save costly cleaning bills later.

- *Protect art that has many intricate exposed edges or surfaces under glass or Plexiglas.* Years of dirt and dust accumulation on highly detailed surfaces can be costly, time consuming, and sometimes even impossible to remove. Regular dusting does not necessarily keep dirt from accumulating on this type of art.

- *Frame art using only top-quality materials, and have professional framers perform the work.* Inferior frames, mats and other mountings can damage art over time.

- *Never alter your art in any way for either protection or display purposes.* For example, never cut down a painting in order to fit it into a smaller frame, never drill holes in a sculpture in order to mount a nameplate, and so on. Alterations such as these severely reduce collectibility and dollar value.

- *Inspect your art closely from time to time to make sure no problems are developing.* Catch things early, before they get too serious, in order to avoid expensive repair bills.

- *Never clean art using any chemicals (bleach, ammonia, window cleaner, paint thinner, furniture polish, and so on).* Use nothing more than a feather duster or a light-dry cloth (unless you are instructed otherwise by a dealer or conservator). Clean on a regular basis to prevent dust and dirt buildup.

- *Never attempt to repair art yourself.* Art dealers and art conservators can tell you horror stories of amateur repair attempts that reduced valuable art to worthless junk.

- *Employ only qualified fine art conservators to treat your art – not artists, not your next door neighbor who happens to be handy at repairing things, not any other amateurs who think they know how to fix it.* If you damage your art or it becomes dirty with age, take it to at least two conservators, compare opinions on what needs to be done, on how treatment will be performed, and how much it will cost; then get the work done. Cutting corners by employing semiprofessionals or amateurs may save you a few dollars in the short run, but such an approach could jeopardize the value of your art in the long run.

Example 1:

I once attended an art opening for an artist who, at that time, had been painting about ten years. He was showing a series of large paintings, priced between $3,000 and $5,000 each, done using a new technique he had recently developed. What was on the canvases was not really paint, but rather a heavily textured malleable substance that felt more like soft putty. The art looked great, but I had several strong reactions to it, all negative.

First, the paintings were unprotected. The slightest touch made an impression in the surface texture. Second, keeping the art clean would be extremely difficult. Even a light dusting would alter the putty-like surface. These problems could at least be avoided by protecting the paintings under glass or Plexiglas, but what if these paintings ever got damaged? Would conservators have the technology to repair them? Could they even be repaired or would conservators never be able to reconstruct damaged areas?

As if those worries weren't enough, I looked into the future and tried to imagine what would become of these pictures. Would gravity take its toll and eventually pull this substance down and off the canvases? Would it dry in five or ten or one hundred years and leave great cracks or shrunken areas?

The artist had apparently not considered any of these potential outcomes. To me, spending thousands of dollars on one of these pictures seemed like something between an incredible risk and a complete waste of money. Sure, the art looked great at the moment of the opening, but more goes into creating art than producing temporary good looks. It must be made to permanently survive intact and retain the characteristics it was originally meant to have.

Example 2:

Even standard household cleaners and polishes can destroy works of art. A collector I know completely removed the finish from a $1,500 metal sculpture simply by dusting it several times a month with a nationally advertised spray furniture polish and dust remover. The dustings gradually removed the finish along with the dust in a process which occurred so slowly that he did not realize what he had done until it was too late. The sculpture is now worth only several hundred dollars.

Example 3:

Early in my career, I bought a landscape painting that I thought was in perfect condition. It was a little dirty, so I decided to have my conservator do a light surface cleaning. He took one look at it and immediately told me that something about it was not quite right.

At first, he wasn't sure what the problem was, but after studying the painting for a few minutes, he said he thought the sky looked a little funny. To him, it was painted in a style different from of the rest of the painting. He proceeded to chemically remove a small area of the sky and sure enough, the painting's original sky was underneath. Someone other than the original artist had completely painted it over.

My painting now needed to have the entire false sky removed in addition to the light surface cleaning. The surface cleaning would have cost two hundred dollars at most. Just to remove the sky would cost an additional $1,500, and once it was off, any damage to the original sky, if it was not in perfect condition, would cost more hundreds of dollars to repair. My painting was not worth restoring, and I ended up selling it for less than what I had paid. I now know how to recognize when portions of paintings have been painted over by people other than the original artists, believe me.

A Look Ahead

Related to condition inspection is forgery detection. Both involve close physical examination of art and both are often performed simultaneously. Now more than ever, it is necessary for collectors to be fluent about the nature and detection of forgeries – the darkest side of art research. Chapter 18 will introduce you to the forger's art.

CHAPTER 18

Forgers, Fakes, and Scams

Ask any art dealer whether he or she has ever been taken advantage of by art forgers, and you will find that the answer is almost always yes. Art is faked on a constant basis; anyone can be victimized at anytime. The best forgers are skilled enough to fool even experienced professionals.

Forgers provide whatever collectors are looking for. They know which artists sell well in the marketplace, what their art looks like, and how they sign. After carefully selecting works of art that have just the right look, forgers give those pieces fake signatures or documentations and the deception begins.

Art collecting is more popular than ever, and as a result, forgers are enjoying a great deal of success. These criminals have risen to the occasion and are hard at work keeping up with the increased demand. Now more than ever, you take your chances when you assume that just because a piece of art is signed or otherwise stated to be a given artist's work, all is in order. You've got to "look under the hood" and confirm for yourself that the art is being truthfully represented.

This does not mean that you should run around paranoid, never believing a single word dealers tell you. The great majority of art is authentic; the great majority of sellers are honest. Fakes, however, are a fact of the art business, and the less you know about them, the more likely you are to end up with one.

No matter where you buy art, you should be concerned about forgeries. Whether you shop exclusively at established galleries and are protected by money-back arrangements or you decide to explore alternative avenues for acquiring art, you could end up purchasing a forgery. However, adventurers who get the urge to wander outside established gallery settings, as many art buyers do once they get their feet wet, are particularly vulnerable. Flea markets, estate sales, traditional auctions, online auctions, antique shops, online antique collectives, traveling art shows, and less-established galleries are great places to look for art bargains, but they are also places where you're likely to come into contact with art forgeries.

No matter what your budget, you should be concerned about forgeries. You've probably heard occasional news stories about collectors being taken for millions of dollars by forgery rings or about a valuable original being removed from the wall of a museum and a worthless copy hung in its place. Tales like these make great entertainment, but they're not characteristic of the techniques and methods of the average forger – the forger whose work you could well encounter as you shop for art. Art forgery is widespread and routine; forgers fake art in all price ranges, not only at the level of expensive art by famous artists. Don't think you're safe just because you're not buying artwork by Picasso or Van Gogh.

Be aware of the following three truths about forgers and forgeries:

- *Forgeries are everywhere.*

- *Forgers fake all types of art.*

- *Forgers forge and sell art in all price ranges.*

You or anyone else can take certain precautions to help identify and avoid questionable works of art, but a strong word of warning is in order here. *As long as you're unsure of your ability to spot fakes, stick with established dealers who provide money-back guarantees of authenticity.* Buying art on your own without expert advice is always a risky proposition. Regardless of those risks, however, some of you are going to take chances anyway, so the balance of this chapter offers some tips and hints that might help you avoid getting had.

Know Your Artists

No matter where you buy or what you are buying, the number-one rule is to know your artists. An artist's style, subject matters, colors, favorite media, signature, and other qualities of his or her art are as unique and individual as fingerprints or handwriting. Knowing what an artist's work looks like, how it is constructed, and how and where that artist customarily signs can protect you from buying a fake that happens to have his or her name on it.

The great majority of transactions involving forgeries could be instantly eliminated if only buyers took time to learn more than artists' names before heading out into the open market. Whenever you are offered art by an artist whose work you don't know all that well, get the advice of experts, locate known examples by that artist, and compare them to what you are being offered. Always do this *before* you buy.

How Forgers Sell

Forgers have to sell what they produce, and they do so in a variety of ways. They victimize art dealers, private collectors, antique shop owners, flea marketers, art gallery owners, estate liquidators, online venues, and other outlets. Some even hawk their wares through the classified ads of local papers. The most innocent-looking sale can have forgeries in it. Don't think you're safe just because you are buying from a little old lady who lives out in the country, far from big-city evils.

You, or anyone else, can come face to face with someone intentionally selling fakes. These people know how to back you into a corner and limit your options in terms of deciding whether or not to buy. Here are several ways they work:

- *They prevent you from doing research by claiming that they don't have time to wait.*

- *They insist that the art has been handed down in their families or that it was purchased directly from the artists, but don't allow you any time for verification.*

- *They fabricate various forms of provenance or certificates of authenticity.*

- *They distract you from normal research procedures by making you think you're getting great bargains.*

- *They tell you they have other buyers just waiting to buy if you don't.*

- *They claim to be reputable and established dealers who have been in business for many years.*

Forgers say whatever is necessary to fool you. Watch out when any aspect of a selling situation seems out of the ordinary.

Forgers also consign to auctions. They usually victimize local or regional houses that don't employ full-time art experts, but even major houses get fooled from time to time. Online auctions are another place where forgers ply their trade. At sites where sales take place between private parties without supervision by specialists, for example, the forgers – not the online auctions – have total control over how their fakes are represented.

As with art dealers and antique shops that inadvertently buy and then sell occasional forgeries, auctions also innocently pass them on to private collectors. Auctions protect themselves with disclaimers, though – everything is sold "as is," buyer beware. This situation makes auction buying, especially at small, transient, less-established firms or at online venues a risky venture for novice collectors. Unsupervised online auctions are particularly treacherous places for inexperienced buyers to shop. If you make a mistake buying art at any type if auction, *you* are responsible and not the auction house. (You can read more about auction buying in Chapter 24, "Buying Art at Traditional Auctions," and Chapter 25, "Buying Art at Internet Auctions.")

Learning to Detect Forgeries

Learning to inspect art for signs of tampering is similar to learning how to evaluate it for damage, condition, and durability problems. You should contact the appropriate experts – namely dealers, curators, experienced collectors, and conservators – and ask them to teach you what to look for. Each specific type of art has a specific system of checking for authenticity, and you learn that system from experts in those fields.

In order to distinguish a work that is totally original from one that has been manipulated in some way, you have to become familiar with every aspect of the art, not just the subject matter and the signature. You have to know it from top to bottom; inside and out; back, front, and sides. With a painting, for example, you not only look at the composition and signature, but also at the framing, the back of the picture, the sides, the gallery stickers, the labels, writings or markings on any other parts of the painting or the frame, and so on. Every detail about a work of art is a clue to whether or not it is right.

Finding authentic originals to study and learn from is never a problem. The hard part (and the important part) is finding forgeries to compare with those originals. Dealers are sometimes reluctant to show forged works, but many have one or two put away in the back rooms of their galleries or can tell you where to go to see them. Examine forgeries firsthand whenever possible and see exactly how and where the tampering has taken place. Encourage dealers to show you examples and explain them to you at every opportunity.

Other ways to learn about forgeries include attending seminars sponsored by art galleries or museums and reading about famous forgers and how they operate. For example, several major American museums have exhibited various types of forgeries next to originals so that patrons and collectors were able to compare and contrast the different qualities of each. The Antiques Roadshow television series on PBS is another good resource for watching experts speak about forgeries. For you forgery fans who are intrigued by the topic and would like to do some further reading, two good books on the subject are *The Art of the Forger* by Christopher Wright (New York, Dodd Mead, 1984) and *The Forger's Art* edited by Denis Dutton (Berkeley, University of California Press, 1983).

Also contact the *International Foundation for Art Research*. This non-profit organization is dedicated to integrity in the visual arts and deals extensively with art theft, fraud, fakes, and ownership issues. If you want up-to-the-minute news on the state of the art world's underbelly, subscribe to their publication, *The IFAR Journal*. Write to: International Foundation for Art Research, 500 Fifth Avenue, Suite 935, New York, NY 10110. You can also phone them at (212) 391-6234 or visit their website at *www.ifar.org*.

Spotting the Art and Craft of Forgery

The great majority of forgeries involve manipulation of a signature. An old signature is altered or removed, and a new signature is added. Or, if the art is unsigned to begin with, a new signature is simply added. Sometimes the art is actually by the artist whose signature has been added – it was originally unsigned and was then signed by a third party to increase its value – but this makes no difference. It's still a faked signature, and whenever someone other than the original artist signs a work of art without revealing that they have done so, you are dealing with a forgery.

Correct signatures should look natural and unforced, be located where the artist customarily signs, be in the color or manner the artist customarily signs in, and match in other particulars such as how T's are crossed and I's are dotted. Checking a signature against an example in a reference book or signature dictionary sometimes helps, but just because the two look identical doesn't mean you automatically assume the one you're checking is right. The forger could have copied from the exact same reference you're using. You've got to go further and study multiple examples firsthand from a variety of sources, including book, magazine, and online illustrations. Preferably you should study the artworks themselves.

Beware of pencil or pen signatures on paintings, works on paper, or sculptures (unless this is how the artists ordinarily signed). Forgers who are not very good at using brushes and paints sign signatures this way. With sculptures, for instance, writing fake signatures is much easier than carving or casting them. Even when such signatures are authentic, serious dealers and collectors still tend to avoid them. They prefer signatures in the medium of the composition: oil on oil, watercolor on watercolor, gouache on gouache, wood carved into wood, metal sculpture signatures cast in the metal, and so on.

Make sure pencil or ink drawings are signed in the identical pencil or ink used to make the drawings. Sometimes a discrepancy between inks or leads is obvious; other times it is only visible under a magnifying glass or jeweler's loupe. The slightest difference between the ink or lead used on the signature and that used on the drawing usually means trouble. Settle for nothing less than a perfect match.

Suspect signatures scratched into dried paint or sculpted surfaces. In these cases you notice small chips or other irregularities around the lines forming the names. Usually, these are visible with the naked eye, but once again, magnifying names is a good idea. Scratched names are frequently added well after the art has been completed, not immediately after as is the normal procedure for any artist.

Check to see that names blend naturally with the rest of the art. Signatures that look out of place may have been added recently. For example, a name on an older painting or sculpture may look fresh and new, a name may be in a color that seems out of place with the rest of the colors in the art, and so on.

Sometimes original signatures are erased or painted out and replaced with different ones. Examine places where artists sign (usually the lower corners of pictures, bases of sculptures, margins of graphic works, and so on) and see whether attempts have been made to alter or remove old names. Small areas differing in brush stroke, color, or texture give this away.

Make sure names are spelled correctly. Surprisingly, this does happen! Artists themselves have been known to misspell, but you will most likely be dealing with a forger's error.

Watch out for paintings, watercolors, and prints that are unsigned on the front, but signed elsewhere – perhaps on the back of the canvas, artist board, paper, or stretcher bars. These pictures may be genuine, but once again, unless an artist is known for signing in locations other than on the front, watch out.

Art that is only initialed, as opposed to fully signed, can present problems. For one thing, forging initials is easier than forging entire names. For another, art executed and initialed by minor artists can be misrepresented as being by famous artists who just happen to have the same initials. Here, the forger leaves the art exactly as it is. All he does is find a good, collectible name to match with the initials on the art and then claim that the work was done by the more collectible artist. Unless an artist is known for signing with initials only, exercise caution. (In similar manner, forgers also misrepresent art that is signed only with common surnames like "Smith" or "Jones" and claim that it is by well-known artists who happen to have those same last names.)

Certain artists have names that are easily copied and often faked. Find out who those artists are from dealers and fellow collectors. Be especially careful when you are presented with art signed by those artists.

Some dealers have reputations for handling forgeries or forging art themselves. You'll learn who to watch out for only after you get well-involved with collecting. Art dealers and other art business insiders do not name names and incriminate people until after they get to know and trust you.

Some forgers do not sign names, but instead photocopy artist listings from reference books or take old newspaper or magazine articles and attach them to the backs of unsigned pictures, to the bases of unsigned sculptures, and so on. The presentation may look official and indisputable, but no signature is no signature, and that's that. Additional proof of authenticity is required.

A variation on the photocopied listing ruse is the fabrication of official looking documents or certificates that appear to authenticate unsigned works of art. Once again, the art is still unsigned, and unless these authentications are from respected experts or authorities, be very careful (of course, these documents and names can be forged, too). If you have any doubts, get the art reevaluated by experts you know and trust before you decide to buy.

Don't assume that provenance automatically makes a work of art genuine. Some forgers list names of auction houses or galleries as previous owners with the insinuation being that because these establishments owned or handled the art, it is genuine. This is not necessarily the case, especially when these previous owners or sellers are not authorities on the art or artists in question. A fake is a fake no matter how many previous owners or sellers it's had.

Beware of unsigned works of art which identify the artists only by nameplates on the frames of paintings, the bases of sculptures, and so on. Anyone can purchase beautiful, custom-brass, antiqued nameplates and have them engraved in any manner and with any artist's name. No matter how impressive the plate, the art is still unsigned, and you need more proof.

Framing, backing, glass, or special mountings and display cases are sometimes used to disguise forgeries and make close inspection difficult. Sealing the back of a picture, for example, may hide a new canvas that has been painted to look old. Enclosing a bronze in a Plexiglas case may make it difficult to tell whether it is an original or a recast. If you have questions, request permission to remove the art from its frame or case and examine it up close.

Pay attention to the asking price. Forgers often entice victims by offering big name art at extremely cheap prices. When the price seems to be a bargain and the seller is well-aware of this, the reason could be that the art is a forgery. Sellers are rarely inclined to give art away at bargain prices unless something is seriously wrong with it.

Watch out for "verbal" forgeries. This is the easiest way of all to fake authenticity. All a seller has to do is show you an unsigned work of art and insist that a particular artist did it or that it looks remarkably like the work of that artist. Unless that seller is a recognized and accepted authority on the artist and is willing to put all statements into writing along with an unconditional money-back guarantee, avoid the art.

Watch out when unsigned art is "attributed" to well-known artists. Phrases like "attributed to," "school of," "manner of," and "style of" are sometimes used to describe works of art, particularly at auctions. No matter which of these phrases a seller uses, the art is *not* by the artist in question. It only looks like it could possibly be by the artist in question. Always pay substantially less for an attributed work of art than you would for a genuine one (unless you know something that the seller doesn't). Also make sure that the person doing the attributing is a recognized authority on the artist because, otherwise, the attribution is meaningless. Many dealers and experienced collectors avoid attributed works of art altogether.

In extreme cases, everything is faked. A nameplate is added, a special pedestal or frame is constructed, a signature forged, fake gallery or exhibition stickers are added, and a date or title or inscription is written or glued to the back or base. Do not assume that just because so many details point to the authorship of a particular artist that the art is automatically genuine.

Watch out for forgeries that were faked decades ago and have been on and off the market ever since. Forgers have faked art by a surprising number of artists for many, many decades. In certain cases, particularly with more famous artists, forgers began faking their art even while they were still living (as they now do with some of today's most recognizable names). Be aware that older forgeries are among the most difficult to detect. Learn from galleries and dealers who specialize in the art you buy, which artists' works you should be the most cautious about buying. As always, if you have any doubts about any work of art you are thinking about buying, consult a recognized professional who is knowledgeable about the life and work of the artist.

As you can see, forgers manipulate in many ways, so thoroughly inspect all details for any art for which you are unsure. Never shortcut the inspection procedure; get outside expert opinions whenever you have questions. And don't try to be too clever, especially when you're buying out there in the wilds. That bargain you think you are sneaking past some unsuspecting dealer may well be bogus.

Some Methods for Inspecting Paintings

Inspecting signatures on paintings in darkened surroundings under ultraviolet light is a relatively common practice. Forged signatures sometimes "fluoresce" or appear to float above the rest of the composition. Art dealers, conservators, and other experts can teach you how to examine art under ultraviolet light.

Infrared rays are also used to inspect paintings. This technique, known as *infrared reflectometry*, involves the use of a special video camera that transmits pictures of an infrared exposed painting onto a television screen. Infrared reflectometry can detect previous restorations, paint inconsistencies, and sometimes even act like an x-ray to identify paintings under paintings.

Pocket microscopes (those that enlarge details in the range of 32 times) sometimes come in handy when examining paintings. As paintings age, the paint tends to shrink and surface cracks eventually appear. Many cracks are so small that they are not visible to the naked eye. These "hairline cracks" are visible under microscopes, however, and studying the cracks around a signature helps to determine whether that name is as old as the painting itself or has been recently added (forged). Old original signatures hairline-crack right along with the rest of the paint. Newly added names, on the other hand, do not show cracks and appear to rest over the original hairline cracks. The paint of a faked signature can also "bleed" into adjacent hairline cracks. Have professionals show you how to use a hand-held microscope to recognize these and other signature problems before you go out diagnosing paintings on your own.

Chemical detection and examination techniques also exist for identifying forged or tampered-with paintings. Solubility tests, for example, have to do with how quickly paint dissolves in certain chemical solutions. Basically, paint that dissolves quickly in mild solvents tends to be new. Paint that dissolves slowly is older. For example, if a paint sample from a signature that is supposed to be 100 years old dissolves easily, that signature could be fake. *Never* do any sort of solubility testing on your own – only expert conservators and similarly qualified investigators know how to do it properly.

Pigment identification is another test conservators and investigators use to identify problem art. Usually, this is done using a technique called *polarizing microscopy*, which involves studying the way paint samples look under a microscope when exposed to polarized light. If a painting is signed and dated 1889, for example, but polarizing microscopy reveals that the signature contains a pigment that wasn't invented until 1930, something's obviously not quite right. Another situation where authenticity could be questioned is when signature pigments don't match those of the rest of the painting. Once again, this sort of testing must be performed only by qualified professionals.

Forged Limited Edition Prints

Prints are easier to doctor than most other works of art because only pencil signatures need to be added. Forged signatures on prints are also more difficult to detect than those on other types of art because just about anyone with writing skills and larcenous intent can practice signing a particular name 500 or 1,000 times and get pretty good at it. Forgers who forge print signatures do not have to worry about mixing special paint colors, camouflaging existing signatures, matching special pencil leads, and so on. A few seconds with an ordinary everyday pencil is all that's necessary.

Forgers manipulate prints in several ways, the main one being that they add signatures to unsigned prints. Unlike paintings and other works of art, prints with fake signatures are usually the work of the artists whose names they bear; the print is authentic, but the signature is not. So don't automatically believe, for example, that just because an authentic Picasso, Chagall, or Dali lithograph happens to have what appears to be Picasso's, Chagall's, or Dali's signature on it that these artists actually signed them. You may need to consult an expert.

One of the more common techniques of print forgery is for forgers to remove (or excise) unsigned original lithographs by famous artists from deluxe books, magazines, or portfolios and then fraudulently sign them. Some forgers even cut worthless illustrations out of ordinary books, magazines, or portfolios, forge signatures on them, and offer them for sale as original hand-signed limited edition prints or lithographs. Sometimes these prints are even accompanied by bogus certificates of authenticity. Book, magazine, and portfolio prints are usually smaller in size (about the size of book or magazine pages) and usually have no margins. If you are offered such a print that is signed by a famous artist, ask the seller whether the print was originally published as a stand-alone, signed, limited edition or was instead part of a book, magazine, or portfolio. If he answers the latter, watch out.

Copy-print reproductions (see Chapter 2) of original prints by famous artists are sometimes marketed as hand-printed originals. Here, the prints are either hand-signed by forgers and sold as originals, or they are left unsigned, "verbally" doctored, and sold as originals. Copy-print reproductions of prints are worth only a few dollars each at best, no matter how famous the artists are and whether or not they're hand-signed. For example, a signed original Chagall lithograph might be worth $30,000. That same lithograph unsigned might be worth anywhere from $200 - $2,000. A copy-print reproduction or illustration of that lithograph cut out of a book or issued as an unlimited mass-market print would be worth about $2 - $20.

Have print experts show you how to recognize the difference between reproductions or copy-prints and originals. One way to tell an original is to look for the "plate impression" around the image of the print. When the plate containing the original image is pressed onto the paper by an artist's printmaking press, the pressure is so great that the paper under the plate is compressed, thereby leaving a border line, visible to the naked eye, in the shape of the plate. Copy-prints and book illustrations are rarely pressure-printed with plates and, therefore, lack plate impressions.

The great majority of reproductions are also composed of dot-matrix or ink jet printer patterns – much like newspaper illustrations – while originals are not. When you magnify reproductions, you see series of dots or dot patterns. When you magnify originals, you don't. Certain digitally-reproduced prints, however, do not show dot-matrix patterns and can be more difficult to detect (but they won't show plate impressions either). Whenever you have any doubts, check with outside experts, in addition to the sellers, *before buying*. An excellent resource for locating reputable print experts is the *International Fine Art Print Dealers Association* or IFPDA. For information about the organization and a list of their members, go to *www.ifpda.org* or *www.printdealers.com*.

Problem prints are especially pervasive online, particularly on eBay. The most faked signatures are those of Picasso, Chagall, Miro, Dali, and Matisse, but the problems extend well beyond that. eBay is an exceptionally risky place to shop for art by famous artists, but for those of you who insist on doing so or who like to beat the bushes at other risky venues like flea markets or estate sales, here are some additional problem print pointers to keep in mind:

- The most common sources of excised prints are Derriere Le Miroir (portfolio), Verve (periodical), XX Siecle (periodical), and books called catalogues raisonnés that list and show the complete prints of famous artists like those of Chagall and Miro. If you see names like these in descriptions of prints, this very likely means that they have been removed from those books or portfolios and signed with fake signatures. Most knowledgeable dealers will tell you that famous artists like those mentioned above rarely signed prints that were originally published in books, periodicals, or portfolios.

- Beware of vague explanations like the print came "from a major estate," or "from a well-known collector," or "was purchased in a bulk lot from the publisher" or came from "a Beverly Hills (or other impressive location) gallery." Claims such as these are not adequate proof that a signature is genuine.

- Sometimes prints are removed from art gallery exhibit catalogues and signed. These may be even smaller than prints cut from books.

- Prints that are described as being heliogravures or photogravures are **not** original prints but rather reproductions of originals. The two names my sound impressive, but they are nothing more than photoreproduction techniques. Furthermore, artists rarely hand signed them.

- Double-page prints, particularly those removed from Derriere Le Miroir portfolios, often have visible creases or folds down their centers, although sometimes these creases have been pressed out and are difficult to detect unless you look closely. Other multiple-page prints may have as many as three of four creases. Always check prints for creases as this is generally a good indication that they have been removed from books or portfolios and signed with fake signatures.

- Signatures on excised prints and lithographs are often in the compositions themselves (since the images were printed without margins). Be wary of any hand signatures in the compositions themselves as this is atypical; the overwhelming majority of genuine limited edition prints are published with margins and then signed in those margins.

- Sometimes a seller represents a print as being "signed in the plate." This does not mean that the print is hand signed, but only that it was printed with a signature already on it. Do not confuse hand signed with "signed in the plate." Prints that are sold only as being "signed in the plate" are nowhere near as valuable as those that have been signed by hand.

- Some prints are posthumous impressions, or ones printed after the artist is dead. These are also commonly referred to as "restrikes." For example, a recent impression of a Rembrandt etching made from an original plate has nothing to do with Rembrandt. Rembrandt died in 1669 – over 300 year ago – and has no involvement whatsoever with this restrike. And of course, a posthumous impression hand signed by the artist (not all forgers check artist death dates before they fake the signatures) would be proof of life after death.

- Some prints are created by other artists "after" the original artists. In other words, another artist makes a copy of a print, drawing, or painting by a famous artist. Copies or reproductions of art by famous artists have only decorative value and are almost never signed by those original artists.

- Prints removed from books, magazines, or portfolios may be painted, colored, or otherwise embellished by hand as well as signed with fake signatures. This is not a common occurrence, but it does happen.

- Exhibition posters from museum or gallery shows of art by famous artists may have signatures that are not authentic. Beware of any poster that was originally published unsigned and is now signed.

Forged Sculptures

The most common problem encountered when buying sculptures is identifying whether you are being offered a reproduction or an original. Most art dealers tell you when they are offering reproductions, also known as "restrikes," but others simply say nothing. If you don't ask, they won't volunteer the information.

Another problem with sculptures is known as "posthumous casting." This means that a sculpture is cast from an artist's prototype after the artist has died. Often this is done without skilled supervision and without the knowledge of the artist's descendants or estate executors. As with reproductions, these castings are then marketed as originals.

A relatively recent development in sculpture forgery is the replacing of minor names on sculptures with those of major artists during an actual casting process. In this type of forgery, bronzes by minor sculptors are recast from old castings. But before the recasting, original signatures are covered over or filled in and replaced with more important names. This used to happen only on rare occasions but is now becoming more prevalent.

Learn how to evaluate sculptures from sculpture dealers. They can show you how to recognize differences between later castings and originals. The evaluation techniques that dealers can teach you include ways to tell the difference between new and old patinas, ways to compare variations in detail between originals and restrikes, and how to spot other tricks that forgers use to make new bronzes look old.

Example 1:

I've bought forgeries. In fact, I've bought them on several different occasions, each time under different circumstances. I'll recount three incidents of who took me, what I bought, and how I got taken, or, as I prefer to think of it, how I took myself.

First incident

Who took me: The owner of a small-town antiques shop.

What I bought: Two paintings by well-known American artists.

How I got taken: The paintings were way under-priced, and I was more interested in getting bargains and maximizing my profit than examining the paintings and requesting provenance. I asked the seller no questions about the art because I didn't want him to suspect that he was selling so cheaply (clever me). I figured I was safe because this fellow was way out in the country, he appeared to know little about art, and he seemed like an innocent antiques dealer who just happened to have a couple of paintings hanging on his walls. He turned out to know a lot more than he let on. He was a crack forger who had sold many fakes during his career. I did not discover that my paintings had forged signatures until well after this dealer had closed up his shop and moved on. He left no forwarding address.

Second incident

Who took me: A local art dealer.

What I bought: A small painting by a well-known American artist.

How I got taken: I was familiar with the style and signature of this artist. At a glance, all looked right. The painting matched perfectly in both respects, so I felt no need to examine it in depth. When I got home, I realized that the artist's name was spelled wrong. I then took a look at the name under ultraviolet light, and it "floated," as some fake signatures do. I returned the painting the next day, and the dealer gladly refunded my money. I later found out that he had a long-standing reputation for forging signatures. This was an excellent forgery, by the way; I still think about how good it was except for that minor spelling error.

Third incident

Who took me: A vendor at a local flea market.

What I bought: Three small paintings by an early twentieth-century Dutch artist.

How I got taken: I was unfamiliar with this artist and had never seen any examples of his work. I asked the seller how he knew the paintings were authentic. He gave me a detailed story about how he had purchased them in Europe from a reputable dealer and assured me that they were absolutely genuine. I believed him and bought the paintings. I soon offered them to a major art gallery and was immediately told that they were fakes and that a European dealer/forger had recently been selling them throughout the area. The next day, while relating the incident to another gallery owner, he told me that he had bought the same three paintings from the same flea marketer several months earlier and had returned them after discovering that they were not authentic. I did the same, and I'm sure this flea marketer continued reselling those paintings until he found a victim who kept them.

Example 2:

Several years ago, word was out among dealers that a certain art restorer was faking signatures. His primary outlet was a small local auction house where he would put as many as five to ten forgeries through every sale. Dealers and experienced collectors knew which pictures to avoid, but no one had enough evidence to accuse the man directly and inform the auction house owner about what was happening. In the meantime, plenty of unsuspecting "bargain hunters" with no idea what they were bidding on were getting taken for hundreds, and sometimes thousands, of dollars per forgery.

I did occasional business with this restorer and, on one occasion, sold him a pleasant nineteenth-century landscape signed indistinctly in the lower right corner of the canvas. Some months later, the picture appeared for sale at the local auction house. The original signature had been removed and replaced with a new and more important one in the opposite corner. I saw the painting at the auction preview and had all the proof I needed to inform the auction house about what was going on.

The good news is that this restorer was permanently barred from consigning to that auction. The bad news is that he remained active as a forger for years afterwards. His work continued to show up at other local auctions and antique shops, but he got better at covering his tracks. He no longer consigned items himself but instead had others do it for him; also, he never consigned too many items to one place.

Accusing, arresting, and convicting forgers is almost impossible. In order to prosecute someone for producing forgeries, that person must literally be caught in the act of forging; that is, a third party must actually *witness* the signings firsthand. Keeping forged art off the market is harder yet. Works of art have been forged for hundreds of years; art forgery will never end and, in fact, art fakes will most likely become even more of a problem with the passing of time. The responsibility for detecting and avoiding bogus art lies with you, the buyer. Make sure you protect yourself.

A Look Ahead

This completes your basic course in art and artist research. At this point, assuming the initial selections you made during the course of your Part II art gallery and artist explorations are still under consideration, you have only one additional detail to evaluate: the asking prices. If you're like the great majority of art buyers, you want to pay fair and reasonable prices for whatever art you buy. Part IV, the final part of this book, shows you how to determine what those fair prices are and explains how to go about buying the art once you have made those determinations.

Part IV: Buy

The relationship between art and money has become much more of a science in recent years than it's been in the past. An ever-increasing number of art prices are determined not arbitrarily, but according to documented happenings in the fine art marketplace. An increasing number of people buy the art that they do for more than purely decorative purposes and, these days, whenever the word "art" is mentioned, you can bet that the word "investment" won't be far behind. Unfortunately, a good number of people take their art buying to extremes and buy it the same way that they buy stocks, bonds, and pork bellies. But that does not mean that you must blindly follow suit. You can still approach buying art with love, passion, common sense, *and* the wisdom to pay fair prices for the art that thrills you the most.

The final and, in many ways, most important step in buying art is understanding the selections that you are considering for purchase in terms of what you are being asked to pay for them and, in the end, buying them if they seem acceptable according to all other guidelines laid out in this book. Do not confuse this process with procuring art for "investment" purposes. The goal of Part IV is merely to assure your fair treatment in the marketplace, nothing more. You accomplish this by acquiring a working knowledge of the general relationship of art to money, getting instruction in evaluating specific asking prices, and learning how to properly consummate art business transactions.

CHAPTER 19

The Economics of Art: An Introduction

Art is a commodity. This statement may sound crude, but it's the truth. Art is bought, sold, and traded in the marketplace much like all other articles of commerce. The fact that money changes hands as art moves between artists and dealers and collectors requires that it be examined, at least in part, from a purely economic standpoint.

Fine art never starts out as just another thing to buy and sell. Its creation is one of the most personal and individual forms of expression known to humankind. It is the product of an artist's confrontation with, reaction to, and interpretation of life and the specific reality in which he or she lives. But the moment a work of art is completed and leaves the artist's studio, it becomes subject to many of the same laws of buy and sell, and supply and demand, as do other hard goods.

To begin, let's examine two fundamental truths about the art economy:

1. *Some art is worth more than other art.* Certain works of art provide us with more to look at and think about than other art. These works may be historically significant, unique in special ways, technically superior, the products of pure genius, masterworks by great artists, and so on. Collectors pay more for art with such distinguished characteristics than they do for art that does not possess such levels of depth, significance, or quality.

2. *Art prices can fluctuate over time.* The values of works of art do not necessarily remain constant over time. Changes in value can be the result of general outside forces such as taste, fashion, or overall economic climate. They can also be the consequence of progressions of events within particular artists' careers or within the scholarly art community.

Dealers and collectors respond to these two phenomena by evaluating dollars and cents, as well as aesthetics, when they buy. Beauty, visual appeal, and critical acceptance are considered in varying degrees right alongside asking price, demand in the marketplace, and projected financial performance over time. Dealers, of course, must seriously consider financial implications of all art that they sell because they have to stay in business.

Some collectors place a similar emphasis on the money aspects of art; others collect primarily because they love art and don't care that much about the money. No buying pattern is right or wrong, better or worse. There are pure speculators and pure art lovers – and everything in between – buying, selling, trading, and otherwise manipulating art according to their own personal feelings and beliefs about art and dollars.

The total of all of this transacting results in what can be called the art economy or art market. Whether the art involved ends up in a museum, in a private collection, in an historical society, in a dusty attic or damp basement, or in the garbage, anytime it transfers from owner to owner, dollar values are assessed according to certain criteria, and money in some form or other – cash, trade, tax-deductible donation, gift tax, etc. – changes hands. But before learning what these criteria are and how to apply them to what you want to buy, you need to know some basic facts about the relationship of art to money.

The Liquidity of Art

The first, foremost, and number one important truth about art and its relation to money is that art is not immediately liquid. Repeat: Art is not immediately liquid. You cannot simply cash in the art that you own like stocks, bonds or other investments whenever you feel like having money. Selling art takes time, sometimes months, sometimes years, and that's longer than many people who want quick cash are able to wait.

Art is more like real estate in terms of liquidity. If, for example, you put your house up for sale at a certain price, you have to wait until the right person comes along and buys it. You may get lucky and sell it quickly; it may remain on the market unsold for months.

Certain art dealers and art galleries would like to make you think that art is instantly convertible to cash. But no matter what sort of profit-laden tales they tell, you take your financial life into your hands when you "invest" non-discretionary capital in art with the idea that you can convert it back to cash at any given moment.

Many people are not aware of how *il*liquid art is. They don't realize that art galleries have to wait quite a while for customers to come in and buy what they have for sale. A small percentage of art does sell immediately, but the great majority takes weeks, months, and sometimes even years to sell. Art galleries will tell you that, on the average, a work of art takes between two and eight months to sell.

As for auctions, the art sales you read about in the papers may seem immediate – as if sellers are cashing in their art instantly – but that's not true at all. With auctions, you often have to wait six months or longer between the time you notify the auction house that you're interested in selling and the day you finally get your check in the mail. At worst, your art may not sell at all, in which case the auction house returns it to you and you have to try and sell it all over again somewhere else. Online auctions have considerably shortened the time period necessary to consummate art sales, but the prices that you net when selling art online tend to be unpredictable, uneven, and frequently less than those you can net when selling through established galleries or at traditional auction sales.

Art is immediately liquid in one sense, though not a pleasant one. Most art is convertible to cash within a week or so, but, unfortunately, you have to accept whatever buyers are willing to pay you at the moment you decide to sell. If you need money fast, you have no time to solicit or wait for acceptable offers. For example, if you have one week to sell a sculpture you paid $5,000 for and the best offer you get is $750, that's it. Either sell the sculpture or keep it.

The bottom line: *Spend only discretionary capital on art.* Never tie up emergency funds or money you need for day-to-day expenses to buy art. That's an extremely high-risk proposition.

Unique Aspects of the Art Economy

The art economy may resemble other economies in how sales are transacted and how works of art change hands, but it is very different in several important ways.

With art, no obvious relationship exists between price and product. Suppose you have three paintings that are identical in size, quality, subject matter, cost of materials, amount of time they took to paint, and all other physical characteristics. The only dissimilarity is that each was produced by a different artist. Even though all else is equal, one painting may be priced at $200, one at $2,000, and the last at $200,000. Whereas the price differential between a Hyundai and a Rolls Royce, for example, is based on concrete variables like manufacturing time, amount of labor involved in production, quality of materials, and end-product performance, with art, this is not necessarily the case.

No formal laws, standards, or regulations exist for pricing art. People selling art can price it as high or low as they want, for whatever reasons they want, and change their asking prices whenever they feel like changing them. A seller can ask $100 for a work of art or $100,000 for it. Any price is legal as long as the seller makes no intentionally false claims about that art and does not misrepresent it in any way.

Art is not subject to quality controls. No law requires artists to have produced art for a certain period of time, to be licensed, or to have reached a certain level of accomplishment before being allowed to sell their art (at whatever price they decide to sell it for). Anyone can claim to be an artist, anyone can create anything and call it art, and anyone can sell it.

What does all this mean? It means that you've got to be aware of the unique aspects of the art market and take them into consideration every time you evaluate art asking prices. Explaining price differences between Painting A and Painting B, for instance, may not be as straightforward as explaining price differences between a Rolls Royce and a Hyundai, but the differences can, without question, be explained and understood by anyone – including you!

Art as Investment

Buy art because you like it, not for investment purposes. *Again: Never buy art purely for investment.* Artists do not sit in their studios deliberating about how to create commodities that will compete well with stocks, bonds, oil futures, or other artists' art. Monet did not wonder, for example, about how his Giverny canvases would perform financially over time or how they would compete against works of the Munich School. Don't insult artists or art dealers and trivialize their art by viewing it as currency.

Far too many buyers are attracted to art because they have either heard, read, or otherwise become aware that certain works of art have substantially increased in value over time. They don't know much about art, but they do know that they would like to make some money by owning it. The most unfortunate of these speculators end up paying highly inflated prices to charlatan dealers who talk only money and speak of art as the path to riches.

We are all aware that some art does increase in value over time and that many art experts and advanced collectors consider the financial ramifications of their purchases. But if you ask these people what attracts them to art above all else, money is always far down the list. If you also ask these people what percentage of art increases in value over time, their unanimous answer will be, "Not very much." The great majority of art produced on this planet fades slowly into obscurity. You'll have a much easier time, for example, finding a $2,000 work of art that will be worth $500 in ten years than you will have finding a $2,000 work of art that will be worth $4,000 after that same period of time.

And don't forget those pesky commissions that you almost always pay when you either buy or sell art. When transacting in stocks or bonds, commissions rarely exceed 2 percent. When buying or selling real estate, commissions are usually in the range of 3 to 6 percent. With art, paying a commission under 10% to either buy or sell is rare (this sort of commission structure applies only to extremely valuable works of art). Commissions to sell art at auction normally range from 15 to 30 percent; commissions to buy art at auction generally range from 10 to 15 percent; commissions to either buy or sell art through galleries usually range anywhere from 20 to 60 percent.

O.K. math hounds – are you ready for a story problem? Mr. Jones buys a painting at Joan's Art House for $1,000, 30 percent of which is Joan's commission for selling the painting. ($300 is Joan's profit; the remainder, or $700, is what Mr. Jones pays for the painting.) Explained in another way, if Mr. Jones were to return to Joan's Art House several months after purchasing the painting and ask Joan to resell it for him, she would again price the painting at $1,000, take her standard 30 percent commission, and pay Mr. Jones $700 when it sold.

Several years later, Mr. Jones decides to sell the painting at Joe's Auction Company and to pay Joe a 20 percent commission for making the sale. Buyers at Joe's Auction Company pay Joe a 10 percent commission above and beyond the hammer price. So here's the question: What percentage does Mr. Jones's painting have to increase in value, beyond its original value of $700, so that it sells for enough money at Joe's Auction Company for Mr. Jones to break even, that is, for him to recoup his initial $1,000 "investment"?

Time's up... It has to increase in value over 90 percent!! It has to be hammered down at $1,250 plus the buyer's premium of 10 percent ($125) or $1,375 total ($125 to Joe from the buyer, $250 to Joe from Mr. Jones, with the remaining $1,000 going to Mr. Jones, thereby netting him his original purchase price). In other words, the painting has to increase in real dollars from $700 to $1,325!

Without exception, reputable dealers agree that if the art that you buy happens to go up in value, that's great and you're fortunate. If it doesn't, that's fine too because it will continue to beautify and enrich your environment and provide you with pleasure for as long as you own it.

Why Some Art Increases in Value

Only the very best art is destined for fame, fortune, and financial stardom. When you read in the newspapers or hear on the news, for example, that "art" has increased in value by a certain amount per year over the past so many years, know that the best works of art by the world's best artists are what they are referring to. They do not mean every piece of art that has ever been produced.

Art that increases in value does so because acknowledged art experts such as museum curators, established art dealers, and art scholars view it as significant in some way and agree that it should be recognized, honored, or distinguished above all other art. For example, when a major museum decides to put on a one-person show of a particular artist's work, anything that artist has done in the past or will produce in the future tends to increase in value. The museum show focuses attention on the artist, legitimizes the art in the eyes of the art-buying community, attracts new collectors, and in general, increases demand for the artist's work. Art that is "worth more" in the opinion of the experts also tends to be worth more in dollars and cents.

A distinction must be made here between real and artificial increases in value. Real increases, as stated above, have to do with general consensus among experts in the art community that certain art has merit above and beyond most other art. Artificial increases have to do with art galleries arbitrarily raising their asking prices or making claims regarding the collectibility of their art, either for no apparent reason or for reasons they concoct on their own, independent of what the scholarly art community thinks.

Alan Bamberger

For example, suppose you walk into Triple-A Fine Arts Gallery and see a limited edition print. The asking price is $3,500. The gallery owner tells you that only last year, the print could be purchased for $1,750. When the edition sells out, she adds, the price will go even higher, and that art by the artist is on its way to becoming highly collectible in the future.

Assume that the rise in price is artificial – not real – and that the claims are meaningless if the artist has not accomplished anything significant over the past year, if there has been no dramatic increase in demand for his art, if no experts have recently commended the artist for outstanding achievements, and if no other outside evidence can be presented to substantiate the owner's statements. Assume instead that the she has simply decided to increase her profit margin by attempting to manipulate the artist's market on her own. She may totally believe every word she tells you, but unless the art community agrees, she's doing little more than dreaming.

Sooner or later, art that has been artificially inflated in price or marketed as collectible when, in fact, it's not, deflates back down to realistic levels. Art that legitimately increases in value, on the other hand, usually maintains its value or continues to increase in value. Only the passage of time combined with continual reassessments by art experts, not hype or declaration, determine what is great in art, what increases in value, and what is destined to be forever forgotten.

A Look Ahead

Individual works of art can be categorized in terms of how old they are, how well-known the artists are, how early or late they were produced in the artists' careers, how long the artists have been producing art, how much art the artists have yet to produce, and how much art the artists have already produced. All of these variables influence art values. The next chapter takes a more in-depth look at the relationship between art and money.

CHAPTER 20

More Facts About Art and Money

On the most fundamental level, a work of art can be categorized in terms of its age. Older art is generally referred to as period art; newer art is referred to as contemporary art. Period art is associated with artists who are either no longer alive or with living artists who have completed substantial portions of their careers. Contemporary art is associated with living artists who have significant percentages of their careers still ahead of them. An artist who has either completed, or is close to completing, his or her career has basically produced all of the art that he or she will ever produce. Contemporary artists, on the other hand, have yet to produce dozens, hundreds, or even thousands of works of art, depending on the artist, the rate at which he or she produces art, and the number of productive years remaining in his or her career.

Period art, because it exists more or less in fixed quantities and is older, is evaluated differently from a financial standpoint than is contemporary art, which is newer and steadily increases in quantity. Additional factors such as expert opinions, fame of the artists, fashions and trends, and tastes of collectors also affect the way art is evaluated from a financial standpoint, but a significant degree of art-market activity can be explained directly as a function of the age of the art and the passage of time. Suppose, for example, that two career artists, Bruce and Sharon, are equally well-respected in the art community, their art is equally in demand by collectors, and art by both artists sells at the same rate. Let's say that Bruce and Sharon have each produced 1,000 works of art, but Bruce is retired – 1,000 works of art is all that he will ever produce – and Sharon is in mid-career and will continue to produce art for several decades to come.

Each time a collector buys a work of art by Bruce, the total number of his artworks remaining in the marketplace decreases by one. This is not the case with Sharon, however. Assuming that she produces at least one work of art for each one that she sells, the total number of her works on the market during her active career either remains constant or increases. Bruce's art becomes scarcer with the passage of time; Sharon's art does not. As a result, collectors must become increasingly competitive to own Bruce's art whereas with Sharon's art, all they have to do is wait for newly produced pieces to come onto the market. In dollars-and-cents terms, selling prices of Bruce's art tend to escalate more, due to the dwindling supply and resulting competition than do selling prices for Sharon's art which are inclined to hold more steady because supply remains constant – she replaces her sold art with new art.

As Sharon approaches the end of her career as an artist, however, the values of her art begin to fluctuate in much the same way that the values of Bruce's art have fluctuated. Her earliest pieces, which are also her oldest, and, in a sense, constant in number (that is, she can never produce her early pieces again, but only brand new ones), begin to increase in value with the passage of time. As collectors buy up her early works, those pieces become increasingly scarce in the marketplace and, as a result, competition to own becomes greater. Once Sharon completes her career, all of her art becomes subject to increasing scarcity and resulting price rises in the same way that Bruce's art has.

I'm now going to take a big leap and, for the benefit of all of you readers who understand the Wall Street Journal better than you understand art periodicals like those listed in Appendix I, further elaborate on relationships between art and money by making several modest analogies to the stock market. Art and stocks are somewhat similar to one another in terms of how old or new they are and how they tend to fluctuate in value over time. Art and stocks are also very different, however, in terms of their liquidity and in the percentage commissions that people pay dealers to buy and sell them, as you saw in the last chapter. Hopefully, you will not misinterpret the following comparisons to mean that art is the same as stocks and that you can go out and buy art in much the same way as you buy stocks.

Established dealers, experienced collectors, and members of the scholarly arts community, of course, frown on analyzing art from a strictly financial standpoint (as do I), but doing so provides a fundamental insight into how the art business works for people who don't know much about art, but do know something about money. And money must certainly be addressed because, although no one knows the total dollar value and number of artworks sold worldwide on an annual basis, that dollar amount certainly ranges into the billions, and the number of pieces sold easily ranges into the low millions.

Before we get started with the art-to-stocks comparisons, let's lay out the ground rules. The only art that can fairly be compared to stocks is art produced by artists who are recognized within the art community as having talent and as showing potential to become well-known at one stage or another during their careers. The better recognized and more significant an artist becomes, the more the following analogies apply to that artist's art. Art by artists who remain unknown, amateurs, minor, hobbyists, or are in any other way casual about their art and who do not get involved with the established arts community, is not particularly relevant to the following comparisons. And remember: *Never buy art for money reasons alone. You'll end up disappointed far more often than not.*

THE ART OF BUYING ART

The Speculative Growth Stocks of the Art World

A speculative growth stock is that of a company that exists based primarily on a concept, such as an internet start-up firm. From a time standpoint, that company is brand new and their ideas about how to make money remain unproven. A business model is in place and employees of the company work to turn the company's concept into reality, but the company is most likely operating on borrowed capital and has yet to turn a profit. From an investment standpoint, buying a speculative growth stock is an extremely high-risk proposition. The company may go bankrupt, as happened to hundreds of businesses during the dot-com crash, in which case you lose your investment. Or it may one day become part of the Fortune 500 – a far less likely outcome – in which case you're in line for early retirement when you decide to sell your stock.

The "speculative growth stocks" of the art world are works of art by artists who are either fresh out of art school or who are otherwise just starting out in their careers, but who manage to attract the attention of small segments of the art community very shortly after beginning to show their work. These artists have progressive ideas about art, their art engages viewers, and they attract attention with what they create. Whether they can consistently bring those ideas to fruition in ways that ultimately resonate with the established art community over significant periods of time remains to be seen.

At present, these artists are totally unproven, they've made little or no money-producing art, they do not make their livings producing art, and nobody knows whether they'll ever become career artists. Very few will ever become well-known; far fewer than that will ever become famous. Over time, the large majority will either stop creating art altogether, or will approach it as more of a hobby or pastime, and go into other professions – some art-related, some not.

From a purely financial standpoint, art by these artists tends to be inexpensive and, in terms of financial gain, a very high-risk proposition. If you buy art by a relatively unknown artist who eventually succeeds, you usually do very well financially; if the artist fades into obscurity, so does the dollar value of your art. From a pure entertainment standpoint, however, buying art from artists who are just starting out is often great fun and a wonderful adventure. Another upside, of course, is that no matter how the art fares financially, you bought it because you like, it enriches your life, and it gives you joy when you look at it.

The Aggressive Growth Stocks of the Art World

The two most important characteristics of an aggressive growth stock are that the company is growing rapidly and, at the same time, showing a healthy profit. Such a company tends to be smaller, younger, and growing at a rate in the area of 20-50% annually. From a time standpoint, the company's business model has not yet been proven over the long run, and the company's ultimate survival is still somewhat in doubt. From an investment standpoint, buying an aggressive growth stock is a relatively risky proposition. Growth may suddenly go flat or even negative, in which case you either break even or lose money. On the flip side, the company may continue its high rate of expansion for years in which case you get to buy a larger house when you sell your stock. Overall, chances that the company will survive and that you'll retain and eventually profit from your investment are better than with speculative growth stocks.

The "aggressive growth stocks" of the art world are works of art by emerging artists. These artists tend to be younger and relatively early in their careers, but have survived beyond being total unknowns. Most have either garnered gallery representation, participated in significant group shows, or been otherwise recognized within the art community as having the talent and potential to perhaps one day go on to bigger and better things. Selling prices of art by these artists tend to be reasonable but can also be on the rise, due to their increasing exposure in the art community. The price rises are based on excitement within the art community and belief among collectors that the artists have talent, but those rises tend to be more rational and predictable than those of artists who are just starting out.

From a purely financial standpoint, the jury will be out on these artists for years to come, and the chances that they'll become well-known or famous and sell their art for big prices are still relatively small. Dollar values will depend on how consistently they perform in their careers and how well their work is received by the art community. Unless they become famous, their selling prices will ultimately level off and then fluctuate modestly – sometimes up, sometimes down – with the passage of time. From an entertainment standpoint, the emerging artist sector of the art community is a vibrant and exciting one where things can happen fast. And, as always, the perennial upside to owning any type of art is that no matter how it fares financially, you bought it because you like, it enriches your life, and it gives you joy when you look at it.

The Classic Growth Stocks of the Art World

Classic growth stocks are those of well-known companies with established track records. These stocks tend to steadily increase in value, but not as fast as speculative growth or aggressive growth stocks can potentially increase in value. Return on investment is generally good as these companies tend to have quasi-monopolies and, therefore, substantial control over their markets. Classic growth stocks are not particularly dependent on product cycles and are not affected that much by overall economic conditions.

The "classic growth stocks" of the art world are the best works of art by artists who are established, well known, and famous. For the most part, these artists are either no longer living or have completed substantial portions of their careers and have been recognized as significant, influential or important by the art community for anywhere from decades to centuries. Like classic growth stocks, art by these artists also has quasi-monopolies in the marketplace. The art of Picasso or Da Vinci, for example, will never lose its place in art history, be displaced from museums and replaced with different art by newly determined famous artists that the scholarly art community one day decides are more important.

The best, most-significant artists may or may not be household names, but their reputations – whether regional, national, or international in nature – are well-established within their respective areas of the art community and will remain so for all time. Their art is the art that you see at museums, historical societies, and at other public institutions; their names are the names that you read about in art books. On those occasions when this art comes up for sale, it sells at the best galleries and at the major auction houses around the world.

From a purely financial standpoint, art by these artists tends to be the most expensive art of all and also tends to steadily increase in value over time. The amount of this art in the marketplace is constantly decreasing because, as mentioned above, many of the artists who created it are either no longer alive or are approaching the ends of their artistic careers and are, therefore, producing either little or no art. Since the art is not replenished when it is sold or donated into public or institutional collections, this segment of the art business is basically a sellers' market.

Resale values of the best art are well documented in art price references like those that you'll learn about in the next chapter. When a collector decides to sell such a piece, he's generally able to locate a willing buyer, most likely through an art gallery or an auction house, without too much trouble. That buyer, in turn, often pays more than the collector paid for the art. At the risk of sounding boring, remember, once again, that collectors buy great art not because it tends to increase in value, but because it's beautiful to look at, superbly executed, is among humankind's greatest achievements, and it enriches lives.

The Cyclical Nature of Art Prices

Art in general is similar to cyclical growth stocks in that both are sensitive to the performance of the overall economy. Art prices tend to fall when the economy slumps, bottom out and start to rise when the economy begins to recover, and continue to rise steadily during healthy periods of growth. The simple explanation for the cyclical nature of art is that it's one of the last things that people need in order to survive and, therefore, it's one of the first things to get cut out of the budget when money gets tight or the economic going gets tough. With few exceptions, fine art is the ultimate discretionary expenditure, which means that most people buy art only after they feel very financially healthy.

When the economy turns down, virtually no art is immune from devaluation. However, different types of art lose value at different rates. As mentioned above, the great art by the most famous artists is the most resistant to bumps in the economy, tends to drop in value the least, and recover the fastest. This relative invulnerability is related to the size, strength, and wealth of its collector base. The wealthiest collectors almost always have adequate funds available and are prepared to compete and buy when the right work of art comes up for sale. After all, this may be the one chance they ever have to compete for a particular work of great quality or rarity – weak economy or not.

Art by artists who are just starting out or who are not that well-established in their careers fares less well in a poor economy. The more unknown an artist is and the greater the uncertainty surrounding his or her future as an artist, the more that artist's prices tend to fall. In general, less well-known artists have weaker collector bases, not only with respect to solvency, but also with respect to commitment.

Mediocre works of art, no matter who the artists are, do not fare well in a poor economy. In general, mediocre works of art tend to be owned by less experienced collectors who buy more by name than by quality and are not particularly committed to collecting. These collectors also tend to be more speculative, impulsive, and fickle than are experienced collectors who know how to recognize quality art, are willing to wait for it, and hold onto it once they have it.

The Myth About How an Artist's Death Affects Prices

Many people believe that when an artist passes on, his or her prices skyrocket. This a myth perpetrated by less-than-scrupulous art dealers who say anything to make a sale. The worst way to buy or sell art is based on financial considerations alone, and for a dealer to infer that an art sale or purchase should be based on an artist's age or health status is not only misleading, but also disgusting.

The truth is, in the overwhelming majority of cases, an artist's death has little or no impact on the value of his or her art. Most artists die of old age; all changes in the markets for their art have taken place slowly, sensibly, and in an orderly manner for decades. Death comes as not much of a surprise to anyone and, consequently, supply, demand, and prices of the artist's art remain relatively unchanged.

The rare instances when death significantly impacts artist price structures occur when artists are relatively famous, their art is higher priced, they're in demand and collectible, and, most importantly, they die suddenly and unexpectedly. During the time periods immediately following the deaths of Warhol and Basquiat, for example, the markets for their art became unstable and inflationary. Dealers and collectors were caught off-guard, they scrambled to buy up art that they had perhaps been only thinking about purchasing when the artists were still alive, a temporary buying panic set in, and prices spiked in the upward direction. As time passed, however, panic buying subsided, and prices gradually fell back to more realistic levels.

In some instances, an artist's prices can actually drop on the occasion of his or her death. For example, an executor or family member may mismanage an artist's estate by dumping all of the art on the market at once and, in doing so, temporarily flood the market and depress prices. Prices can also decline when the market for an artist's art is based more on the artist's personality, media profile, flamboyance, social contacts, or sales skills than on the quality of his or her art. With the artist's number one promoter gone (namely the artist herself), art values fall flat.

Speculative Art Market "Bubbles"

Every once in a while, an uncontrolled, uninformed, speculative art buying frenzy results in a "bubble," or rapid and unjustified rise, in art prices. In the late 1980's, for example, credit was cheap, the economy was strong (particularly in Japan), record art sales were being reported almost daily in the news media, and, consequently, a large number of speculators jumped into the market to make some "easy money." Unfortunately, many of these buyers lacked the knowledge and perspective necessary to understand what was going on, and when the art party ended, they lost plenty of money.

As usually happens during these inflationary spirals, too many people who don't know what they're doing chase after too little art, and not only does the best-quality art spike upwards in price, but so does art of mediocre and even poor quality. Inexperienced speculators jump into the market and buy indiscriminately thinking that just because a piece of art has the "right" signature on it, they'll have no problem selling it at some point down the road for more than they paid – similar to the progression of a chain letter. Sooner or later, though, the economy turns down, the money supply dries up, and, as mentioned above, art is one of the first extravagances to get cut out of the budget. The speculators attempt to cash out of their art and suddenly realize that no new speculators are waiting in line to perpetuate the myth.

The art price inflation of the mid- to late-1980's, for example, was extremely intense, and the fallback in prices in the early 1990's was equally drastic. Mediocre art by famous artists, as well as large percentages of art by many secondary artists, still sells for less than what it was selling for over a decade ago. The good news is that prices of the best-quality art have recovered for the most part and even exceeded their dizzying 1980's heights in a number of instances. The really good news is that the speculators have pretty much evaporated, prices have stabilized, and the serious dealers and collectors are no longer being held hostage by fine art Philistines. Sooner or later, though, people will forget what happened in the eighties and another speculative wave will wash over the art market.

Smaller speculative price run-ups happen in the art market with some frequency. Individual artists get hot, dealers and collectors buy in advance of major museum shows hoping that prices will surge upward once the shows open, art of particular geographic regions suddenly becomes all the rage, and so on. Unless you can buy, sell, or collect on the level of the professionals, your best approach to any inflationary situation is to sit back and wait until the dust settles.

All Art Pays Dividends

No matter what happens to art prices or what happens to the artists whose art you buy, if you buy art because you like it, you're already experiencing benefits that will continue to accrue for as long you own it. It's all yours, it beautifies your environment, you learn from it, it enriches your life, and no one can ever take those positives away. No matter what a work of art is worth on the open market, it pays dividends in ways that no other material possessions can.

Example 1:

Collectors often ask me whether they should buy particular works of art. I ask them whether they like the art and, of course, they all answer yes. But on further questioning, that "yes" is sometimes based on beliefs unrelated to the art itself like how much they think it's going to appreciate in value, how much of a deal they think they're getting, or how famous they think the artists are. If you find yourself in the position of trying to decide whether or not to buy a work of art that you honestly believe you like, ask yourself a few questions like those below.

- Would I like this art as much if the artist was virtually unknown and just starting out in her career?

- Would I like this art as much if the artist's prices haven't gone up in 15 years and aren't expected to rise anytime soon?

- Would I like this art as much if I found out that I was paying a full retail price for it and not getting any special discounts?

- Did I start liking this art more when the seller began telling me how important it is and how famous the artist is?

Be careful whenever considerations unrelated to how you experience a work of art when you look at it begin to influence your decision of whether or not to buy. It's what you feel that's important, not so much what you think.

A Look Ahead

With these basic art and money facts in mind, let's move on to the specifics – namely, evaluating the asking prices of whatever works of art you have selected for possible purchase. Being able to understand a given work of art in terms of a set dollar value is the final goal of buying art intelligently. How much art are you getting for how much money? That's the question you will learn how to answer in Chapter 21.

CHAPTER 21

Evaluate the Asking Price

Any work of art you see for sale and are interested in owning has a price attached to it. If you're like most people who buy art, you're not looking to make a financial killing, but you do want to make sure that the asking price is fair and reasonable before you pay it. You make that determination by evaluating that price.

You may wonder how you can possibly determine on your own whether or not art asking prices are fair, but it's really not that difficult once you know how. In fact, evaluating art prices is much like evaluating the price of any consumer product you are considering buying – you find out what you want to know from the firm representing the product, and then you check independently to make sure that what they tell you is true.

Unfortunately, not all art dealers appreciate people who know how to evaluate art prices. They resent buyers who ask too many questions and would rather sell to clients who believe that dollar values are set according to mystical procedures that only art dealers can understand. Know right now that that's simply not the case!

The single most important truth about art prices is that they are deliberately set according to methods that you or anyone else can understand. Furthermore, they may be verified as reasonable or unreasonable just as deliberately. You need a certain amount of knowledge to reach those conclusions, of course, but once you've acquired it, you'll be capable of making them entirely on your own. Never let anyone tell you otherwise.

Before going any further, be advised that procedures for evaluating art prices are not meant to take the place of the art research described in Part III of this book. Buying art based on financial considerations alone without any understanding of the artists, the art, or the history behind the art falls into the category of pure speculation and is an extremely high-risk proposition. You cannot intelligently evaluate an asking price without first researching and evaluating the art, the artist, and the provenance.

Many novice art buyers don't fully understand what price evaluation entails. They ask what few price questions come to them at the galleries selling the art, blindly accept everything they are told, and assume that no further investigation is necessary. They believe that they achieve adequate insight into asking prices when, in fact, they accomplish nothing of the sort. Galleries are, of course, more than happy to answer money questions about their art, but in the great majority of cases, you have an obvious conflict of interest.

What gallery do you know that believes their asking prices are anything but fair? What gallery do you know that will advise you not to buy their art because they think it's overpriced? The answer to both questions is none. Buyers don't necessarily get taken advantage of when their complete price research consists of asking sellers price questions, but at the very best, they get biased opinions.

Comprehensive art-price evaluation means more than having a quick chat with the seller. You've got to accumulate a variety of data from throughout the art community in order to get a balanced overview of the value of any art you are considering. You acquire this data from three primary sources:

- *The seller.* When evaluating asking prices, acquiring information from the seller is the only sensible way to begin. They are experts at what they sell and can provide extensive data about asking prices.

- *Art auctions.* By studying price results of art that has sold at auction – specifically, art that is comparable to what you are considering buying – you can get an idea of what your art would be worth outside of its gallery setting and of the overall strength of the market for that art.

- *Resources that do not have conflicts of interest.* By consulting independent art experts who have no vested interest in whatever art you are considering, you can get informed, unbiased opinions on the prices you are being asked to pay.

This check and balance system protects you from overpaying for art. Learn how to use it and profit.

Asking the Seller

As mentioned above, art price research always begins with the seller. The single most important and only absolutely necessary question to ask any seller, no matter what you are being offered, is this: "*How did you arrive at your asking price?*"

A satisfactory answer – that is, the type of answer you want – is one that explains and justifies the price you are being asked to pay in terms of specific, current-market information about the art and its artist. Without exception, a satisfactory answer must include concrete data about other works of art by that artist that have already been sold, the circumstances under which they sold, and how much they sold for.

You want facts here, actual sales results – persons, places, dates, dollar amounts – and the more you get, the better. You want proof that work by the artist is changing hands on a regular basis at prices comparable to those that you are being asked to pay. And you want information about where the art is selling *in addition to* the gallery that you are doing business with – auction houses, other art galleries, and so on. When you get these sorts of detailed responses to that most important price question, you know you're dealing with reputable dealers.

An unsatisfactory answer to the big question – one that may appear to justify an asking price, but actually does not – is when you are told that other dealers' asking prices are comparable to what you are being asked to pay. This information gets you nowhere. Asking price alone is never an indication of market strength or fair market value. Asking price is not relevant until someone actually pays it. To repeat: *The amount of money a work of art is being offered for by an art gallery is not how much that art is worth.* It's only how much the gallery hopes to sell it for.

Another unsatisfactory answer is one that only relates price information about sales that have been made at the gallery trying to sell you the art. Price records solely from the seller's gallery are never adequate proof that what you are being asked to pay is fair or that a market exists for the art outside of that gallery's doors. Even when a gallery has sold numerous works of art at prices comparable to what you are being asked to pay, this could mean nothing more than that the gallery personnel are experts at talking people into buying that art or that they sell primarily to clients who neglect to evaluate the prices of what they buy before they buy it. You need additional information about what level of recognition (in dollars and cents terms) the artist is receiving in other sectors of the market.

Whatever answer you get to the big question, record every single detail of it. You are then ready to continue your price evaluation outside of the gallery selling the art and see what the rest of the art community has to say.

Checking Art Auction Prices

The amount of money a work of art sells for at auction is an excellent indicator of how liquid that art is, how strong its market is, and what it is worth when it has to sell immediately for cash. High auction prices indicate that a healthy, no-hype market exists for an artist. Low auction prices, on the other hand, indicate a weak or unstable market. It's that simple.

A major goal of your price evaluation is to approximate how much any work of art you are interested in buying would sell for at auction and then to compare that value to the price you are being asked to pay. You need to make this comparison not because you intend to sell the art, but as a person who buys art intelligently, you want it to have some degree of financial strength on the open market, outside of its biased retail environment, and in the neutral auction setting. In other words, you don't want your art to be worthless the moment you take it out the gallery door.

Art auctions continually take place around the world. Several hundred thousand significant works of art are auctioned annually. Auction houses sell everything from Old Masters to contemporary art and an average sale consists of between 100 and 300 pieces. All major international auction houses and a number of regional ones publish catalogues of every art sale they conduct.

Learning how to read auction catalogues is an essential part of art price evaluation. These publications are the most important source of art price information in the art business. A single catalogue can supply you with comprehensive sales data on several hundred works of art.

Almost all art dealers have auction catalogues in their libraries and will be happy to teach you how to read them. A few minutes is all it takes. For our purposes now, what you need to know is explained below.

Auction catalogues individually list each work of art to be sold along with basic facts about it. An average catalogue entry for a work of art includes the lot number of the art in the sale; the name and nationality of the artist; the artist's birth and death dates (when applicable); the title, medium and dimensions of the art; the location and spelling of the signature as it appears on the art; relevant incidental information (a previous owner's name, where the art was exhibited, etc.); and the amount of money the auction house believes the piece will sell for. Entries also note whether the art is illustrated in the catalogue. The better houses illustrate many of the works of art that they sell either in color or black and white.

Let's imagine you are studying an auction catalogue entry for a painting by an artist named Blake Stoneman and that it provides the following information:

Lot Number: 4027
Artist: Blake Stoneman; American (1912-1981)
Title: Northern Coast on a Stormy Day
Signature and location: B. Stoneman in the lower left corner
Medium: Oil on canvas
Dimensions: 27 by 36 inches (68.5 by 91.5 centimeters)
Estimated selling price: $1,000-$2,000.
Illustrated in the catalogue.

No matter what auction house is selling this picture, the actual catalogue entry would look something like this:

*4027   BLAKE STONEMAN (1912-1981)
NORTHERN COAST ON A STORMY DAY
Signed lower left: B. Stoneman
Oil on canvas, 27 by 36 inches,
68.5 by 91.5 cm
See illustration   (Est: 1,000/2,000)

After an auction sale is held, all prices realized at that sale become a matter of public record. Anyone can contact the auction house to find out how much any item in that particular sale sold for. Let's say that the Blake Stoneman painting sells for $2,500. You can call the auction house and ask them how much it sold for (this amount is known as the *auction record* for that painting) as well as for auction records of other Stoneman paintings the auction house has handled in the past. The auction house will give you those results.

Supposing you are interested in finding out how much Blake Stoneman paintings have been selling for at auction houses around the world. This would involve contacting auction house after auction house to see whether they have ever sold his art and, if so, how much it has sold for. You can see that this would be a rather difficult, expensive, and time-consuming task. To make matters worse, auction houses are not generally enthusiastic about taking the time to give out price information to people doing art price research.

Fortunately, you don't have to bother auction houses with continual price requests. You or anyone else can locate all the auction records you want simply and easily because several publishers keep track of auction sales for you in books, CD-ROMS, and in online databases known as *auction record compendiums*. These references are published annually (computer databases are updated continually) and contain anywhere from about 150,000 to over 3,000,000 auction records from many hundreds of auction houses throughout the world from sales taking place during periods ranging from a single year to several decades. See Appendix II for a list of the major auction record compendiums and Appendix VII for a list of online auction price databases and brief comments on their respective strong points.

These books, CD-ROMS, and online databases sell from about $100 to nearly $2,000 each, but you don't need to buy them to use them. Most major public library, museum, college, and university art departments have at least some auction-record resources in their art reference sections. Find out which libraries carry which auction records, and when you need information, just call or visit these institutions and ask the art librarians to supply you with whatever auction records you need.

Make sure you have access to most, and preferably all, major compendiums and online databases because they regularly differ in the quality and amount of information they provide. Not every library has them all, and some libraries carry only one or two. If you have to contact more than one library in order to cover all auction records, do so. Art dealers and serious collectors generally have auction records and database access in their galleries, too, but most are reluctant to share them with you unless they know you well.

Auction records are easy to read and understand. Each compendium and database has instructions on how to read results and all list results in basically the same formats. Artists are listed alphabetically and individual price results for any particular artist tend to be grouped together by medium (painting, watercolor, etc.), price (listed from highest to lowest dollar amounts), or by date of sale with the most recent sales first. Under Blake Stoneman, for example, you would find the $2,500 entry and entries for other Stoneman paintings that sold during whatever time period the particular compendium that you're using covers.

The $2,500 Stoneman entry would look something like this in an auction compendium:

> Stoneman, Blake   American (1912-1981)
> $2,500   Northern Coast on a Stormy Day,
> signed lower left, (05/12/07, Smith's-NY, #4027,
>   illus.), 27 by 36 in. (68.5 by 91.5 cm), oil on canvas.

This entry gives the same basic information about Stoneman and his painting that you find in the auction house's sale catalogue. Inside the second set of parentheses are the date of the sale (05/12/07), name of the auction house (Smith's), location of the auction house (New York), the lot number of the painting (#4027), and the notation that it is illustrated in Smith's catalogue of that sale (illus.). Note that auction compendiums in book form do not illustrate paintings, but some online databases and CD-ROM's do. Another way to find out what a particular work of art looks like is to refer to the original sale catalogue.

Approximating a Work of Art's Auction Value

Suppose you have selected a work of art for possible purchase, have reached the point in your research where you are seriously considering buying it, and are ready to determine its approximate auction value. The procedure is the same no matter what type of art or artist you are evaluating, but for our purposes here, let's say you are considering a Blake Stoneman oil on canvas of a mountain scene that measures 24 by 30 inches and has an asking price of $4,500.

Your first step is to locate as many auction records as possible of Stoneman paintings that have sold at auction in recent years. Here's how you do this for any artist:

- *Personally check or have art librarians check hard-copy auction record compendiums, art price CD-ROMS, and online art price databases for price results.* Ask art librarians, experienced collectors, or other experts to work with you until you know what you're doing, and remember to check as many different compendiums as possible, not just one or two.

- *Start with the most recent auction results, and locate all entries under the artist's name.* Repeat the procedure going back through at least three years worth of records (you should preferably check five to ten years worth).

- *Write down, print out, or photocopy full listings of all pieces of the artist's work that have sold during the time period you are checking.*

- *Whenever possible, check actual auction catalogues, CD-ROM's, or online databases when compendiums note that items are illustrated.* You need to visually compare as many pieces as possible to the one whose value you are in the process of approximating. Obtaining specific catalogues usually involves contacting the individual auction houses (unless you happen to be on friendly terms with dealers or collectors who have them in their libraries).

You are now ready to take the auction records you have located and approximate an auction value for your Stoneman painting or whatever art you are evaluating. Below are some general rules that will help you analyze, interpret, and understand those records and apply them to your art.

The most significant auction records for your purposes are those that describe works of art most similar in size, subject matter, medium, date executed, and other particulars to the one you are researching. The amounts of money these works sell for are the best approximations of your art's auction value. In our Blake Stoneman example, since you are researching an oil painting of a mountain scene measuring 24 by 30 inches, pay special attention to auction records of mountain scene oil paintings with similar qualifications. You would not pay much attention, for example, to records of very dissimilar works of art like a painting of ships on the ocean measuring 6 by 9 inches or a floral still-life watercolor. Comparing the selling prices for the ship scene or the still-life to your mountain scene would be like comparing apples to oranges.

Auction prices of art similar to the art you are evaluating should generally be at least 40% to 50% of what the gallery is asking you to pay. The higher the percentage, the greater the art's resale value on the open market. You do not, for example, want to pay a gallery $4,500 for the Stoneman painting you are considering when similar paintings sell at auction for only $300 to $500 each. Remember that auction prices are an excellent indicator of value on the open market and that, in the great majority of cases, records that are consistently far below gallery retail indicate either a weak or unstable market for that art or overly ambitious pricing by the gallery that's selling it.

The works of art that sell for the greatest amounts of money are usually the ones that collectors of that artist prize the most. If, for example, Stoneman mountain scenes fetch the highest prices at auction, assume that they are more sought-after by collectors than any of his other subject matters. The more characteristics a work of art you are researching has of the higher-priced works, the more you should think about buying it.

The works of art that sell for the least amounts of money are usually the least desirable in terms of collectibility. If Stoneman mountain scenes sell for less than all other subject matters, assume they are not in demand by collectors. When art you are researching falls into the low end of the artist's auction-price continuum, think about looking for something a little more collectible.

Pay the most attention to those dollar amounts that the majority of the art in question auctions for, not the minority. For example, if you locate twenty different auction records for Stoneman paintings, nineteen of which are in the $2,000 to $4,000 price range and one for $15,000, assume that Stoneman's art auctions in the low thousands of dollars, not the tens of thousands. Isolated high (or low) price records are not accurate market indicators.

See how auction prices change over time. You want indications that an artist's art is at least holding steady and preferably increasing in value. Watch out when you see decreasing or erratic records.

You need at least half a dozen auction records to establish any meaningful pattern for an artist. One or two isolated records of pieces selling at auction cannot be relied upon to provide any concrete conclusions about a particular artist's market. What you can conclude from one or two auction records, though, is that the artist has at least been through auction and is at least viewed by auction galleries as salable in a public arena. In other words, any auction records are better than no records at all.

Let's return now to our Blake Stoneman mountain scene and analyze it in terms of some hypothetical auction records. Suppose you locate ten auction records of Stoneman oil paintings that have sold over the past five years, with characteristics as follows:

- The selling prices range from a low of $300 to a high of $4,000.

- Two are mountain scenes, five are coastal scenes, and three are landscapes.

- One mountain scene is about the same size as the painting you like; the other is much smaller. They sold for $2,000 and $350 respectively. The $2,000 painting sold four years ago.

- The three highest records, $4,000, $3,500, and $3,000 are all coastal scenes and all about the same size as your mountain scene.

- The remaining records are for landscapes with no mountains, the smallest selling for $300, the largest for $900.

- In general, Stoneman's prices have been slowly increasing over the past five years.

Based on this data, you can make certain assumptions about Stoneman's market, determine an approximate auction value for your mountain scene painting, and compare it to the gallery's $4,500 asking price. The following interpretations and conclusions would be considered reasonable by the great majority of art experts:

- Stoneman collectors prefer coastal scenes over mountain scenes and landscapes (his three highest auction records are all for coastal scenes).

- Mountain scenes are acceptable to collectors as evidenced by the fact that the larger one fetched a respectable price.

- Stoneman's landscapes without mountains are not that collectible; they all sold low.

- Collectors prefer larger paintings over small ones; the small ones sell inexpensively.

- The auction value of the mountain scene you are thinking about buying would probably be between $2,000 and $2,500 today. This price estimate is based on the similarity in size and composition of yours to the mountain scene that sold for $2,000. The $2,500 high estimate takes into consideration the fact that the $2,000 record is four years old and that the Stoneman market is stable and gradually strengthening.

- Comparing that $2,000 to $2,500 auction approximation to the $4,500 asking price, you could conclude that $4,500 is, at worst, just slightly on the high side, but not overly so. You could call it fair retail because even the lower auction value of $2,000 falls within 40% to 50% of the gallery retail.

Suppose you are evaluating an asking price and find only few low auction records for the artist or, worse yet, none at all? This is not usually a good sign in terms of the artist's resale value on the open market. In most cases, this means that the artist's market is weak, the artist is minor or younger, and that auctions are not interested in handling his or her work because it won't sell for very much money. Exceptions do exist, though. For instance, an artist might be so collectible or rare that collectors hold on to their art, rarely resell it, and when they do, rarely place it up at auction. Art research, as well as conversations with the seller and no-conflict resources, usually indicate whether this is the case or not. Regardless, you're still in the dark as to performance at auction.

No matter what the reason for a lack of auction data, you are by no means at a dead end. You can still approximate an auction value on the art. It's a little different from normal procedure, but not very difficult.

To obtain an approximate auction value in such a case, contact at least several auction houses, both regional and national, that conduct regular art sales. (See Appendix III for a list of significant American auction houses). Ask every specialist you speak with the following two questions:

- Are you familiar with this artist?

- Would you auction his or her work if given the opportunity?

It's good when the auction experts answer yes to both parts of this inquiry, not so good when they say yes to the first and no to the second, and worse yet when they say no to both.

Whenever someone at an auction house gives you at least one yes answer, ask whether that person can give you ballpark estimates on what they think art similar to the art you are considering buying might sell for at one of the auction house's sales. Don't automatically assume that the values you get are the approximate amounts that the art would actually auction for. These dollar figures do come from informed sources, though, and should be given serious consideration. This is especially true when every firm you call gives you the same approximate values. Regardless of the responses you get, always combine them with seller and no-conflict-resource inquiries.

As an aside, don't get into the habit of constantly calling auction houses for this sort of advice, especially when you can locate adequate price information elsewhere. Auction firms are in the business of selling art, not running price-information hotlines.

Consulting No-Conflict-of-Interest Resources

The consulting of no-conflict-of-interest resources is equally as important as auction-price evaluation and is the other procedure you must employ in order to corroborate any price information sellers give you. Here, you solicit the thoughts, feedback, and prognostications of outside experts regarding your selections. This information, combined with auction-price evaluation and with what the seller tells you is, in the great majority of cases, all you need to determine the fairness of an asking price.

No-conflict research becomes all the more important when little or no auction records exist for an artist whose art you are considering. In these cases, no-conflict resources provide the only conclusive price information you have to go on outside of what a seller tells you.

No-conflict-of-interest resources are exactly what they sound like – they are dealers, collectors, and other experts who are independent from and have no vested interest whatsoever in the art or artist you are researching or the gallery you are patronizing. Ideally, they do not sell or collect that art on a regular basis, and profits from any related transactions they may be involved in do not constitute a significant percentage of their incomes. Above all, these resources should be individuals you know and trust.

A no-conflict resource can be anyone you meet in the course of your art-buying activities. Over time, you get to know certain authorities who eventually become friends or acquaintances you can confide in about your buying. The better you know each other, the more they'll be willing to help you by giving you honest advice whenever you need it.

For example, an art dealer you have never done business with before is not likely to comment on a work of art you are considering buying that hangs in another dealer's gallery. To her, you are a stranger asking pointed questions that could involve her taking sides or incriminating the other dealer. But the better she gets to know you, understand your intentions, and do business with you, the more likely she'll be to give you the valued opinion you want.

Be patient about acquiring no-conflict resources. You'll eventually figure out which individuals you work best with and are able to trust as honest, nonbiased resources for consistent and accurate art price information.

Here are the types of questions you should ask every no-conflict resource you have about a piece of art you are considering buying:

- *Have you ever heard of this artist?* The more recognizable the artist's name, the better. No name recognition, on the other hand, is never a good sign. Combined with poor or nonexistent auction records, this could mean that you stop here, forget about the artist, and look for something else to buy. Assuming you get at least some name recognition, proceed with your questions.

- *What do you think about the artist's art and his or her progress as an artist?* You want to hear that no-conflict resources respect the work of the artist and have good things to say about his or her future.

- *What do you think about the market for this artist's work?* In response to this question you want indications that the market is broadly based and increasing. The greater the variety of galleries, experts, and collectors supporting an artist's work, financially as well as critically, the better. Look for signs that prices the art sells for are at least holding steady and preferably increasing.

- *This question is for no-conflict dealers only: Would you handle this artist's work if someone offered it to you for sale and, if so, how much would you charge for it?* This is an important question. The more galleries who answer "yes" and the closer their hypothetical selling prices are to what you are being asked to pay, the better. Also, the more enthusiastic no-conflict galleries are about handling the art, the better.

- *Again, for dealers only: If you are willing to sell this artist's art, how fast do you think you can sell it?* The faster, the better. A month or less selling time is a sign of an active market and a desirable artist. A year is not. In fact, galleries who think a year or more is necessary to sell the art would most likely not be willing to sell it in the first place.

- *For no-conflict collectors and other experts who do not buy and sell art for a living: Do you already own work by this artist or, if you don't, would you consider buying a piece for your collection?* You want "yes" answers; you want enthusiastic answers.

- *Here's what the art I'm thinking about buying looks like, and here's how much I'm being asked to pay for it. What do you think?* This is the most important question because the more no-conflict resources who view your situation as acceptable, the more you should consider buying the art. It's also the most difficult question because anyone who answers it is required to take a position on a dealer and his art. Since it is so direct, ask it only to those no-conflict resources whom you confide in the most. Seriously consider all answers you get here in making your final decision.

Get to know as many no-conflict resources as possible who are qualified to answer your financial – as well as your aesthetic and informational – questions about art. The greater the number of these people you know and consult, the more data you can acquire and the better informed decision you can make regarding whatever art you have selected. Remember to cultivate these relationships gradually and diplomatically so that you can ask sensitive questions like this last one and get truthful, helpful answers.

By the way, you don't need one hundred percent enthusiasm, perfect agreement, and purely positive answers to every question from every authority you consult. A variety of responses is fine – different people have different tastes and opinions. What you should look for, though, is an overall positive response to the art and artist in question.

In summation, when no-conflict resources recognize the name of your artist, you're off to a good start. When they say positive things about the artist, that's better. When they express a willingness to actually tie up gallery space and sell the art or display it in their collections, that's best. When they comment favorably on the asking price of the particular piece you are thinking about buying, that's about all you need to go ahead and buy.

One final note: Just because an asking price turns out to be too high or an artist turns out to be not that well-known throughout the art community, do not automatically refuse to buy the art. If you really love it, go ahead and buy it no matter what it is. *You can buy any art at any time for any price and for whatever reason.* All that price evaluation techniques provide you with is a knowledge of the dollars and cents aspects of that art – not a verdict on what it means to you personally.

Evaluating Art by Younger Artists

Auctions sell art by established artists, that is, artists with healthy collector bases, good name recognition, strong markets, and art that is in short enough supply that bidders will compete to own it. Auctions are not normally interested in selling art by younger, unproven, or less-experienced artists. These artists tend to have minimal name recognition, uncertain or unstable collector bases, modest career accomplishments, and art that is readily available in the marketplace. For most of these artists, years or even decades will have to pass before their work shows up at auction (assuming it ever does so at all).

Evaluate the prices of art by a younger artist by assessing the artist's resume, career accomplishments, exhibition experience, and recent sales history. When the art is for sale at a gallery, ask to see the artist's resume. The resume should list solo shows, group shows the artist has participated in, articles or reviews about the artist, awards the artist has won, collectors or institutions that own the artist's work, and so on. In order to be taken seriously, a resume **must** include names, dates, and places. Watch out when instead of a resume, you're given an essay about the artist, especially if it's peppered with generalities like "the artist has exhibited internationally," or "the artist is world famous." Babble like this means absolutely nothing unless accompanied by facts to back it up.

In addition to the resume, speak with the artist's dealer, no-conflict resources, and, when possible, with the artist in order to best assess the market for the art. And don't be afraid to ask questions including ones about prices. As someone who is considering spending hundreds or thousands of dollars or more on art, you are entitled to ask as many money questions as you want. Below are several factors which tend to indicate that a younger artist's art is priced fairly.

- *At least half of the pieces in the artist's last show sold.* This means that collectors see merit in the art and believe that it is reasonably priced. The greater the percentage of art that sells and the more shows the artist has had with similar results, the better.

- *The artist is represented by multiple galleries.* This indicates not only demand for the art, but also that the artist is capable of satisfying the needs of more than one seller. The greater the number of galleries that represent an artist and the more widespread those galleries are, the better (assuming they sell originals and not repro prints like giclees in either limited or unlimited editions).

- *The artist has been represented by the exhibiting gallery for a significant period of time.* This means that the dealer can consistently sell the art and believes in the artist's future potential. The longer an artist has been with a gallery, the better. If the artist is showing at a new gallery for the first time, he or she should be able to show evidence of extended relationships with other galleries and explain the show with the new gallery in terms of its being a logical career move.

- *The artist's prices have risen in recent years without a decrease in sales.* Increasing prices, even if as little as 10 to 20 percent, and steady or increasing sales indicate a healthy market for the art. (Remember that arbitrary price increases are meaningless; price increases based on increased demand, popularity, critical acclaim, and recognition by the art community are what you're looking for.)

- *The artist's prices compare favorably with those of artists who produce similar art, live in the same geographical area, and have similar career accomplishments.*

- *The artist has had at least one or two significant shows per year in recent years.* This means that the artist is able to consistently produce art and that collectors are consistently buying it. Infrequent or sporadic shows are not generally a sign of a dedicated and productive artist.

- *The artist regularly shows in different parts of the country or better yet, internationally.*

- *The artist has received awards, grants, or other distinctions for his or her art.*

- *The gallery is able to document the artist's current selling prices with records of consistent completed sales at comparable prices.*

- *The gallery can show you at least one or two favorable reviews or comments about the artist from respected critics, critics, academics, or comparably credentialed members of the art community.*

- *The artist has been featured in articles or reviewed in art magazines, on major art websites, or in other respected publications.*

- *Books or exhibition catalogues, other than those that are self-published or printed by vanity presses, have already been or will soon be published about the artist.*

- *The artist has either been or will soon be included in museum shows.*

- *Established or well-known collectors own art by the artist.* Collectors are considered to be established or well-known if they are known and respected for the quality of their art collections, not if they are famous or well-known only for accomplishments unrelated to art collecting (such as actors, actresses, sports figures, monarchy, etc. etc.)

Using Art Price Guides as Research Tools

Art price guides do exist, and they are fast becoming popular as "quick fix" references for evaluating asking prices. They are affordable – the most inexpensive cost about $20 each – as well as easy to obtain and easy to use. However, they also have severe limitations as reference tools, limitations you should be aware of so that you don't place too much emphasis on the information they provide.

Price guides are designed to give brief biographical information about artists in combination with either several sample auction records or low to high price ranges. Price data they provide comes almost exclusively from auction records. A typical price guide listing would look something like this:

STONEMAN, BLAKE; American; (1912-1981)
paintings –   300-4,000

This listing gives you the artist's name, nationality, birth and death dates, and tells you that his paintings auction between $300 and $4,000.

Let's say you're researching that 24 by 30 inch Blake Stoneman mountain scene oil painting from our earlier example by consulting a price guide as opposed to auction records. All you can tell from this listing is that Stoneman paintings have been through auction and have auctioned in the $300 to $4,000 range. That's it. Here's what you cannot tell:

- You cannot tell how many auction sales that price range is based on – it may be two, it may be fifty.

- You cannot tell what type of paintings sell in the $4,000 range and what type sell in the $300 range.

- You cannot tell what subject matters bring the best prices, the worst prices, or the average prices.

- You cannot tell what sizes bring the best and worst prices.

- You cannot tell how price results are grouped. For example, twenty Stoneman paintings may have auctioned for $300-$500 and only one for $4,000.

The bottom line is this: Use art price guides with extreme caution and never make a decision about whether or not to buy a work of art based only on entries in price guides. Price guides are good to check when you need quick, general price information, but that's as far as you should go with them. Note whatever price information you find, but always check auction records and no-conflict resources for the full story on exactly what has sold for how much.

Appendix I lists the most popular price guides and comments about each. If you insist on researching an artist in price guides, check that artist's entry in every guide you can. As with auction-record compendiums, information often varies from one guide to the next.

A Look Ahead

At this point, you should have no trouble deciding how fair or reasonable an asking price is. In other words, you're finally done with all your research and evaluations! Can you believe it? You're ready to buy art.

But wait one last minute. Suppose you could buy that art for less than the seller is asking for it? If you find this possibility appealing, then the next chapter is for you.

CHAPTER 22

Negotiate the Buy

You're ready to write out your check and buy a piece of art except for one small detail: you'd like to pay less for it. Whether you think the price is too high, you have a policy never to pay full retail, or you love to bargain, you're not quite ready to complete the transaction. So where do you stand?

You happen to be in luck. Art dealers have been known to leave room in their asking prices for negotiation or, as it is more commonly called, bargaining. You may just get a break on the money issue if you know how to conduct yourself.

Reasons for flexibility in asking prices vary. Dealers know that certain clients expect "deals" or that they enjoy bargaining; galleries leave room for employee commissions; outside market factors sometimes force dealers to pad asking prices; dealers themselves may accept, or in rare instances, encourage bargaining as part of the art-buying process; and so on. Whatever the situation, art buyers and sellers negotiate final selling prices all the time.

In its most primitive form, bargaining consists of two opposing parties battling against each other for no reason other than money. The seller wants to sell for as much as possible, and the buyer wants to pay as little as possible. Anything goes, and the one who outsmarts the other with the cleverest tactics wins.

Mature bargaining or negotiating, on the other hand, is far from a simple battle over who can make who pay the most or sell for the least amount of money. Good bargaining is a cooperative venture in which both buyer and seller sit down together with the intention of reaching an agreement on how much a particular work of art is worth. Research results are studied, price data is evaluated, arguments from both sides are considered, and value is determined to the satisfaction of both parties. When agreement is reached, the art sells.

Negotiating art prices is not a sport. It is a tool for addressing any situation in which you believe that an asking price is too high. Rather than throwing up your hands and walking out the gallery door, speak with the seller about what you think that price should be. Make an offer. Consider bargaining as a petitioner's process where you request that the person in a position of power (the seller) reconsider his or her decision to price the art at the level that he or she has.

Intelligent bargaining or negotiating begins by your presenting a well-constructed and well-documented case about what you think a particular selling price should be and why. The seller, in turn, either accepts that offer, makes a counter offer, or states that the asking price is firm and refuses to consider any offer. You then respond to the seller, and so the process continues until the two of you either agree or else agree to disagree.

The procedure may sound easy, but negotiating for art is an art in itself. You can do it right, and you can do it wrong. Learn the fine points and etiquette of bargaining in order to get what you want and get it without offending anyone the next time you think you should be paying less than what you are being asked to pay.

How a Negotiating Relationship Evolves

When you first consider the possibility of buying art from a gallery, you have no idea how the owner feels about bargaining, and the owner has no idea how you feel about his asking prices. The moment you begin to find these things out about each other is the moment you decide to negotiate an asking price. At that point, opinions about how high or low prices are begin to emerge from both sides.

This first encounter over money is a difficult time in any dealer-client relationship. At the very least, you have to be diplomatic and sensitive to the seller's feelings. You can easily offend by making an offer, because you are essentially saying that you think the art is worth less than the dealer thinks it's worth. Make mistakes at the outset, and you can seriously damage or even destroy a relationship before it ever begins. Make an intelligent offer, though, and you'll find that the seller will listen to and respect whatever you have to say about the art.

The outcome of a first negotiation affects you in two ways. The obvious one is that a particular asking price is evaluated and agreed upon to the apparent satisfaction of both you and the seller. The not-so-obvious outcome – but much more far-reaching one – is that the two of you begin to discover each other's positions on how art transactions should progress to completion. You set the tone for all future dealings with that seller.

During the next few negotiations, you pretty much determine the course of your business relationship together. Consistent positive outcomes mean that you each come closer and closer to understanding exactly what the other wants, and, as a result, every successive negotiation becomes easier than the last. The seller develops a good idea of the most you are willing to pay, and you get a feel for the least he or she is willing to accept.

The twofold object of successful negotiating is, therefore, to buy art at prices you want to pay and, at the same time, to keep sellers working for you, keep them on your side. Poor bargaining technique may net you a good price on an art piece or two in the short run, but in the long run, your collecting suffers because dealers get put off by your bad buying habits. Knowing how to negotiate means knowing how the art of buying art works.

Proper Bargaining Etiquette: Dos and Don'ts

The first and most important step towards intelligent negotiating is knowing when *not* to negotiate. *When you see art you like and you determine through research that the asking price is fair, buy it without making an offer.* Intelligent collectors respect sellers' abilities to price art accurately and always recognize when those prices are fair to begin with. Sellers, in return, treat those collectors with equivalent respect.

When you honestly believe an asking price is too high, do make an offer. Before you present that offer, though, research and organize evidence to back it up. Take time to build your case. Make sure you can give a solid presentation, and support everything you say with facts. Dealers do not appreciate frivolous offers and can quickly tell whether you have a legitimate concern or are just trying to pay less for the sake of paying less.

Do make your offers reasonable ones that dealers can conceivably accept. Extremely low offers lead to bad feelings much more often than they lead to completed sales. Dealers can only reduce prices so far before they are taking losses on their art, and no dealer is interested in doing that. When the offer you want to make is far below the asking price, think seriously about not making it and buying something else instead. Dealers never appreciate "lowball" offers.

Do be tactful, and pay close attention to sellers' reactions as you go. Sellers should be receptive to what you say at all stages of the negotiations. They love having intelligent discussions about art, even when the end result might mean that they may have to lower their prices. Know when to stop, though, once they begin to lose interest in what you have to say. With experience, you'll be able to tell exactly when that is.

Do base offers on facts about the art, not facts about your personal financial situation. For example, you see a sculpture you like and determine that the $1,000 asking price is fair. If your budget is only $500 per work of art, don't arbitrarily offer the dealer $500 for the sculpture. Either wait until you can afford to buy it, or shop instead for sculptures more in your price range.

Do learn how individual dealers react to your offers. You will find that every dealer has his or her own peculiarities in bargaining situations. Knowing what those quirks are helps reduce friction during negotiations. There is no universally "right" way to negotiate. Tailor your bargaining techniques appropriately for each of the dealers you negotiate with.

Do make an offer only after the seller has had the art for a while and has not been able to sell it. A month is a good minimum waiting time. If you're not sure how long the art has been for sale, ask. If you make an offer on a fresh new arrival before the dealer has a chance to show it to other potential buyers, that dealer will almost certainly take offense.

Do pay close attention to dealers' overall responses to your offers. The best dealers give you positive, constructive responses during negotiations that teach you about art and the art business. Whether or not they accept your offers, they supply you with important information about why they feel their asking prices are fair and how they set them, and thus they continue to educate you at all times. Avoid dealers who are not interested in having price-related discussions or who consistently refuse your offers without giving any reasons why.

Knowing what not to do in a negotiating situation is just as important as knowing what to do. You make offers in hopes that they will be accepted, so you certainly don't want to sabotage yourself during the bargaining process. Avoid certain behaviors and maximize the chances of getting what you want.

The most important don't is this: Don't start talking price the moment you see something you like. This is not only rude, but it also alienates sellers. You give them the impression that all you care about is money, and you're inclined to give as little of it away as possible. Even when you know precisely what you want to offer the moment you see a piece of art and can back that offer with facts, get to know the seller before diving right in and making your offer.

Don't make an offer without carefully thinking it through because the seller just might surprise you and accept it. When a seller accepts your offer, you are obliged to buy the art. Dealers do not appreciate collectors who make offers, have them accepted, and then decide that they are not interested in buying the art after all. This is bad etiquette and will seriously impair future negotiations.

When no price tag is visible on the art and you have to ask how much it costs, don't give the impression that you think it's too high the moment you hear it. Avoid rolling your eyes, groaning, making faces, and that sort of thing. Dealers dislike collectors who have knee-jerk reactions to selling prices.

Don't negotiate for the sport of it or suggest that an asking price is too high on art that you're not really interested in buying. Make offers only when you're serious.

Don't get a reputation as someone who always wants it for less, someone who thinks that the asking price is always too high, no matter what it is. Dealers will stop showing you good salable art, and they will show you only second-rate or hard-to-sell pieces that they don't mind getting rid of at bargain prices – and that's assuming they'll want you around their galleries in the first place.

Don't bargain when you're shown special consideration. For example, when a dealer calls you first to see a piece of art that has just arrived, either buy it or pass on it. Do not bargain. He is showing you special treatment, and you should return the favor. If you think the price is too high, wait until the dealer has had the art for a while, had a chance to show it to other collectors, and has not been able to sell it. Then make your offer.

Don't talk about all the great art bargains you've gotten in the past while in the process of negotiating a price. Not only is this irritating, but it also gives the seller the idea that you only buy art when it's cheap. Why should he bother showing you anything if all you talk about is how little you paid for something similar two years ago or how a dealer across town once sold you a such-and-such for half what it was worth?

Don't beat a seller over the head with an offer. When a dealer tells you he would rather not sell at the price you want to pay, don't continue to give reasons why you should get it for less. Even if the seller does eventually give in, you'll pay for those few saved dollars in future negotiations.

Advanced Negotiating

Gain experience negotiating with dealers by keeping your offers conservative at first and making them only when you feel absolutely justified in doing so. As with any learned and practiced skill, the more offers you make, the better you get at making them. After awhile, you acquire a feel for how far you can go in any given situation, even with dealers you've never met before. You'll not only know more about the art you collect and what it's worth on the open market, but you'll also know more about how to bargain for it.

Expert bargainers can closely approximate how much dealers they've never met before are willing to accept for their art even before negotiations begin. They recognize differences between sellers who are firm on their asking prices and those who are flexible. They know just the right moments to offer just the right amounts. Offers are still based in fact and reason, but in advanced negotiating, a little more strategy comes into play in terms of timing, the way the offer is proposed, and so on.

The ideal situation for you or any buyer is to determine the least amount of money a dealer is willing to accept for an art work without being offended or insulted. The fact is that in any negotiating situation, this "least amount" does exist. The more money you can save without damaging a relationship, the more money you'll have to spend on future acquisitions, and, oddly enough, the more respect you'll get from sellers for your negotiating skills. Being able to determine "least amounts" is not really a skill you can learn through study, so don't start signing up for "How To Get What You Want" seminars or run to the library and read all the books you can on negotiating technique. You learn only through real-life experience.

Another point that advanced negotiators are aware of and take into consideration is that art prices often fluctuate according to sellers' moods, financial situations, frequency of recent sales, feelings about particular works of art, and so on. For example, a dealer who hasn't made a sale in several weeks and needs to pay bills is more willing to consider offers than one who is making regular sales.

Some dealers are more inclined to entertain offers at certain times of the year than at others. For example, the summer months are often slow months for art galleries and, therefore, good times for making offers. On the flip side, fall and late winter/early spring are busy times of the year, times when your offers are less likely to be accepted.

In many instances, the longer a dealer has had a work of art in stock, the more he or she will be open to taking offers on it. Sooner or later, dealers get tired of looking at the same old art, decide to increase available storage space, and so on.

With time, you'll be able to take greater risks when the moment of monetary truth is at hand. For now, play conservative and don't take too many chances too fast. You want negotiations to be cooperative ventures, not combative ones.

Surprisingly, the most advanced and mature form of negotiating is no negotiating at all. Here, you and a seller understand each other so well that selling prices are agreed upon instantly. This goal of complete understanding and total trust is one you should strive for. In the end, the less time you waste bargaining, the more time you can devote to learning about art and forming a meaningful collection.

A Look Ahead

So let's say you make an offer on a work of art, and the seller accepts it. The big moment has arrived. You pull out your check book and get ready to write. Time to buy!

Or isn't it?

Buying art is a little more complicated than simply writing a check and walking out the gallery door with your new acquisition. You've got to follow certain procedures and take a few precautions at the point of purchase in order to assure yourself a lifetime of happiness with your art. The next chapter considers these procedures and precautions.

CHAPTER 23

Make the Buy

When you buy art, you can pay for it, take it home, display it, and forget about it – as many people do – but that would be rather ill-advised. Your purchase is a long-term investment in more ways than one, and you should be concerned about its future. Your relationship with this art is just beginning, and you want it to be a successful one. What you do now could easily affect the art's value – historical value, scholarly value, and dollar value – for generations to come (and for your descendants, in particular).

You must also be concerned about possible negative outcomes of your purchase. Two important points to consider are these: What if the art has been misrepresented to you in some way or, in a worst case scenario, is not even by the artist it's supposed to be by? Obviously, you have to protect yourself. Attend to certain details now in order to maximize your enjoyment of the art, influence its resale value, and save yourself potential complications later.

Paying for Your Art

Before looking to the future, let's deal with the present – the moment at which you actually pay for your art. You have two options here. You can either pay for it all at once, or you can pay for it over a period of time.

Many art galleries are amenable to allowing clients time to pay for their art, especially when the art is expensive. In these cases, collectors sometimes need to pay in several installments or make other special purchase arrangements. Even with moderately priced art, collectors may be given the option of making several payments over time, whether they need to or not.

The best procedure, assuming you can afford it, is to pay the full price at the time of purchase. That way the transaction is complete and clean, you own the art outright, the seller has no further claim to it, and you have an immediate sense of how much money you've just spent. Even when you are offered optional payment plans, if you can afford to pay the total amount at once – which should be almost always – pay it.

Then again, if you are the type who likes to take advantage of terms just because they are available, that's fine too. Never use them as an excuse to overspend, though. A good procedure is not to ask for or insist on terms unless you need them. The best procedure is not to need them at all.

For you first-time buyers who are paying over time, know that art galleries do not charge interest. *Installment payments should never total more than the agreed-upon purchase price of the art, assuming you pay within a reasonable amount of time, usually three months or less.* If you need any longer than three months, you're probably spending too much and should consider tightening your budget and choosing another work of art that you can better afford.

When you buy art in installments, always make your payments on time. Dealers are quite flexible in sitting down with you and deciding how much you should pay by what dates. All you have to do is make those payments when you say you're going to.

Don't get a reputation for dragging things out. If you don't pay when you're supposed to, dealers will lose interest in extending you financial considerations, and, at worst, they may refuse to do any further business with you. They'll also tell other dealers to watch out for you, and that can seriously impair your ability to buy. The art world is small, word travels fast, and no dealer likes doing business with clients who don't pay on time.

Documenting Your Purchases

Formally document every work of art you buy. If problems ever arise with any art you own, proper written documentation leaves no question as to how the art was represented at the time of purchase. Never assume that verbal assurances are all that is necessary.

The first document you need whenever you buy art is a proof of purchase — a receipt. That receipt should accurately describe the art according to size, medium, artist, date executed, and any other pertinent details. It should be fully signed and dated by the seller.

The second document you need is a guarantee or certificate of authenticity signed and dated by either the seller, the artist, or an independent authority qualified to make the determination of authenticity. This is a written statement confirming that the art in question is by the artist that the seller says it is by. Also stated should be any other facts relating to authenticity that have been told to you by the gallery.

The third document you need, especially when you are buying art that is not brand new, is a condition report, that is, a statement of the art's condition at the time you are buying it. This document should either state that the art is in perfect original condition or accurately describe any damage that the art has incurred over the years and specify whatever actions have been taken to repair it.

Along with this documentation, you need one more thing: An unconditional money-back guarantee. Included in or attached to your receipt, authentication, and condition report must be a guarantee by the seller to return your purchase price in full at any point in the future should the art turn out to be other than how it has been represented in any of those three documents. Sellers must take full financial responsibility for all statements they make about the art they sell.

Your receipt, authentication, condition statement, and money-back guarantee are the core of your documentation process (as an aside, they can all be contained in a single document), but they are also just a portion of the records you should keep. Start and maintain a file, beginning with these documents, on every piece of art you buy. Inside that file goes anything relating to that art or artist. Along with the core documents go relevant gallery and artist correspondences, newspaper or magazine articles, exhibition catalogues, invitations to openings, and so on (if you have questions about how to acquire additional data for your files, review Chapter 16, Provenance is Profit).

Never alter or destroy any of your file documents. Some collectors, for instance, throw away their original bills of sale because the art has increased in value since they bought it, and they don't want anyone to know how little they originally paid for it. They believe that the receipt will decrease the art's value, or if they ever decide to sell, buyers will offer less if they find out the original cost. Nothing is further from the truth! The art is worth what it's worth no matter how little it originally sold for.

For example, when you see a Van Gogh painting, do you think about how little it sold for decades ago? Do you think it would be worth less to a collector today because he or she knows that it sold for only a few dollars just after the turn of the century? Would you be interested in seeing an original receipt for a Van Gogh painting dating from the turn of the century? Do you think that receipt would have historical significance and be worth money in and of itself? Of course it would. Case closed.

Summarizing, always include the following in your art files:

- The bill of sale.
- The authentication.
- The condition report.
- A money-back guarantee protecting you if condition, authenticity, or any other data the seller gives you ever turn out to be other than as they were stated.
- Any incidental material that the seller gives you.
- Any pertinent correspondences from the gallery, the artist, relatives of the artist, and so on.
- Two good, clear photographs or digital picture files of the art – one in color and one in black and white (just in case the art ever gets stolen; black and white photographs reproduce better in newspapers, magazines, and other publications where you might want to make the theft known to the general public).
- Any material that you receive at any future date relating to that art or artist.
- A current appraisal of the art (less than three years old).

- Full instructions on what to do with the art should anything ever happen to you.

Each file becomes a record of the art piece that it represents. It protects your investment in case the art gets damaged, destroyed, or stolen. It is a source of information and details that you otherwise might forget. It educates and informs all interested parties. And, at any point in the future, that art's history can be traced right back to the day you bought it – and to an earlier time if you did extra research or were provided with its previous ownership information from the seller.

Above all, a file becomes part of the art itself and can be passed on to all subsequent owners of that art. The truth is that you won't be around forever to provide a verbal explanation of your art and the history behind it. Whoever owns it after you will have the information you accumulated on hand to help explain its value and significance. And should subsequent owners – your descendants in particular – happen to be people who don't care that much about the art and would rather sell or donate it than keep it, they'll have adequate data on hand for income tax purposes or to protect themselves from being taken advantage of by unscrupulous buyers.

Return and Exchange Arrangements

Before beginning any discussion on returning or exchanging art, remember that art is not currency. Art galleries are not banks where you exchange dollars for art and then, at some later date, return that art for any fraction of, either greater than, equal to, or less than, your initial purchase price. Return and exchange arrangements are not convenience services for transforming art into cash whenever you feel like it. You should, however, buy art only after you completely understand the return or exchange policy of the gallery selling it.

Many galleries offer what is called a *short-term return privilege* and provide it in writing. Here, you are allowed to return the art for a full cash refund for a limited period of time immediately following your purchase. This period can range anywhere from one week to a month or so, depending on the gallery, during which time the art is returnable for whatever reason you have for not wanting to keep it, no questions asked. Of course, it is hoped by all involved that you will choose your art wisely and never have to take advantage of this option. Remember that if you have any doubts whatsoever about whether you really want to own a particular work of art, take it home on approval *before you buy it.*

Just about all galleries offer some form of *long-term return/exchange arrangement.* Such policies, which vary from gallery to gallery, concern how your art is to be handled if you decide to bring it back months, years, or even decades after you buy it. The two main options offered under such arrangements are taking your art back on consignment and selling it for you or allowing you to exchange your art for gallery credit equal to your original purchase price. When art has increased in value since you purchased it, terms will have to be worked out with sellers on a piece-by-piece basis.

Almost all galleries agree to take your art back on consignment at any time and sell it for you. This saves you the trouble of having to resell the art yourself. The galleries display your art, offer it to their clients, and assume the responsibility of completing the sales transaction for you.

Not all consignment arrangements are the same. Understand what fees or commissions a gallery charges for reselling your art in this manner. Some galleries attempt to net you your original purchase price, some give you a portion of the profit if they sell your art for more than you paid for it, and others take a set percentage of the selling price no matter what the art sells for. Whatever the arrangement, know what it is, and get it in writing before you buy.

Consignment selling has one major drawback: There is no guarantee your art will sell. Galleries have no problem offering consignment service because it involves no financial risk on their part. They only pay you if and when your art sells, not before.

Some dealers may lead you to believe that all you have to do is bring your art back, and within a short period of time they'll resell it, and you'll have your check, possibly with profit over your original purchase price. Don't believe this for a moment. Selling art on consignment takes time, and you may not recoup anywhere near the amount of money you originally paid. At worst, your art could sit for sale indefinitely without selling, in which case, you recoup nothing.

When galleries make consignment sound like a sure thing – like you can cash in your art at any time (usually with profit) – call them on it. Insist that they put their promises in writing and that they guarantee those returns. How many galleries do you think will be willing to go that far? You guessed it: none. The best approach is not to do business with these sorts of galleries in the first place.

A final note about consignment. Honest and experienced art dealers will tell you that, looking back on their years in business, they have sold some art that they would love to resell and other art that they would just as soon never see again. *No one can predict the financial future of any art or artist.* The passage of time is the ultimate determinant of how easy, difficult, or impossible reselling your art on consignment will be.

Here's a worst-possible-outcome scenario that puts consignment selling into its proper perspective. Suppose you buy a sculpture from a gallery that guarantees in writing to take it back on consignment at any point in the future. Ten years later, you ask the gallery to resell it for you. The gallery owner tells you he'll take the sculpture back on consignment, but he'll have an extremely difficult time selling it, if he can sell it at all, because the sculptor is no longer popular and has totally dropped from public view. He suggests that you'd be better off donating it to charity for a tax deduction. The final outcome here is that you receive none of your original cash outlay, and the consignment agreement is not even worth the piece of paper it's printed on.

Another circumstance where consignment arrangements become worthless is when the gallery from which you bought the art goes out of business. Minimize this outcome by making sure galleries with which you do business have been in operation for years and have good reputations in the art community.

Many galleries allow you the option of exchanging your art at any point in the future for a trade value equal to the full original purchase price. In this instance, a gallery credits that dollar amount toward a new purchase you make from their current stock at the time of the return or after. This gives you the luxury of returning your art effortlessly and at no cash loss should your tastes change or should you decide to upgrade your collection.

Exchange policies vary form gallery to gallery. Some galleries allow exchanges for anything in their stock; others allow exchanges from only certain portions of their stock. The most common arrangement allows you to exchange your art for any art that a gallery owns outright, but not for art that is there on consignment from other owners. If trade on consignments were allowed, a gallery would have to pay a consignor immediately upon receiving your art, which would be basically the same as giving out a cash refund without taking any cash in. With rare exceptions, immediate cash is not issued to anyone when art is exchanged. Cash is paid out only after art sells.

Return or exchange policies at the same gallery can even vary from art piece to art piece, so understand what your options are on each individual work of art you buy. Never assume anything, and, as always, get whatever you are told in writing.

One final word: *Never abuse a return or exchange privilege.* Becoming known among dealers as someone who regularly returns art is bad for your reputation, and galleries will become reluctant to do any further business with you. When you buy art, be pretty sure you like it, pretty sure you can afford it, and pretty sure you're going to keep it.

Art Buys that are Less than Ideal

Not all sellers provide buyers with proofs of authenticity, condition reports, data about the art they sell, consignment or trade-back arrangements, and other amenities. They sell art pretty much "as-is" and have the attitude that once you buy it, you own it, and they want nothing more to do with it. This is their privilege and should not be taken as an indication that the art they sell is inferior in any way to "guaranteed" art.

The fewer assurances you get at the point of purchase, though, the more informed you have to be about what you are buying. When you're just starting out, the best procedure is to avoid buying art that comes with few or no guarantees and protections. Buy only from dealers who stand behind what they sell and who take full responsibility for representing it properly. As you gain experience, however, and learn more about what you're doing, you can become more adventurous in your buying habits.

Whenever you buy art under less-than-ideal circumstances, still record and file whatever information the seller gives you. With no authentication, condition report, or money-back guarantee, at least try to get a receipt that accurately describes the art as to artist, size, subject matter, and other particulars. Ask for a signed statement telling how the art was acquired and whatever additional facts the seller knows about it. If you are shown any documents relating to the art, ask that they be included in your purchase. When that's not possible, borrow them and make copies for your records.

Maintain a file even when you get no written information from a seller. Write a statement yourself recounting the circumstances of your purchase, the purchase price, what the seller told you about the art, where it supposedly came from, and any other interesting details surrounding how the acquisition was made. This sort of documentation can eventually prove to be just as valuable and informative as the official material you get from established galleries.

Example 1:

I once bought a painting from a dealer who gave me no guarantees on it. That was fine with me because I felt sure it was authentic and knew that for the size, subject matter, and quality of work, the price was fair. Several months later, however, another dealer saw the painting and told me she thought it could possibly be a forgery.

I decided to show it to an expert and see whether he would authenticate it for me. He wouldn't. He didn't come right out and say the picture was fake, but I got the idea that it (and I) obviously had problems. I contacted two other experts, and they gave me the same response: no go on the authentication.

I returned to the seller and explained my situation. He told me that although my plight was unfortunate, he was not willing to take the painting back and return my money. He had sold the art "as is"; I had bought it "as is." I was stuck with the painting. I, of course, stopped doing business with this dealer, but only after learning an expensive lesson – do everything possible to get guarantees, no matter how limited they might be. No matter how much you think you know, you can always be fooled.

Example 2:

An art collector told me about a time she tried to return a limited edition print to the gallery from which she had bought it. When she bought the print, the gallery verbally guaranteed that she could have an immediate full cash refund if she returned it within two weeks. However, nothing was put in writing.

About a week after purchase, the collector had second thoughts about the print and decided to return it. She brought it back to the gallery, explained her decision, and was told that the employee in charge of returns and exchanges was on vacation and would be back in several days. The person she was speaking with then attempted to convince her to keep the print. He said that the value was only going up, the artist was on the verge of having a major museum show, and so on. According to him, she was making a terribly wrong decision.

She insisted on returning it, however, and came back to the gallery several days later to complete the process. This time, she was introduced to the gallery owner, who talked to her about exchanging the print for one of equal value rather than taking the cash. She refused, demanded her money, and was finally allowed to "officially" return the print.

At that point, the owner took the print back, but the woman still received no cash as she had been led to believe she would. He told her that restocking forms had to be processed, and she would have her money back within six to eight weeks.

The happy ending is that she did eventually get her money back. The lesson: *Get it in writing and understand the terms.* No matter what you are told and how wonderfully you are treated at the moment you buy your art, know gallery policy, and have it in writing.

A Look Ahead

A unique art-buying and selling situation in which sellers regularly provide little or no guarantees on what they sell happens to be, oddly enough, extremely popular with art buyers. In the great majority of cases, the sellers do their best to properly represent what they have for sale, but in the end, you – the buyer – are the one charged with researching and evaluating any art you are interested in buying. You must decide whether or not it is authentic, what condition it is in, how significant it is, and what you think it's worth, because once you buy it, it's yours for keeps. The next two chapters address the highest profile and highest risk art arena of them all – an arena that no book about collecting art is complete without discussing – *the auction*.

CHAPTER 24

Buying Art at Traditional Auctions

This chapter about buying art at traditional auctions and the following chapter about buying art at online auctions are placed at the end of this book, because that is exactly when novice art buyers should consider buying art at auction. This is not to say that auctions are bad places to buy art, and you should avoid them. Quite the contrary. Auctions are great places to buy art, but only on the condition that you know what you're doing when you buy there.

More people than ever before are excited at the thought of buying art at auction. More people than ever before actually do buy art at auction. The great majority of auction-related publicity, most of it generated by the auction houses themselves, is overwhelmingly pro-auction. In response to all this hype and hubbub, someone has to take the conservative, sober, and sensible approach to action at the auction. We'll do that here.

Anyone can attend auctions for the purpose of buying art; no law prohibits them. Auction houses have no knowledge or skill requirements for people who participate in and buy art at their sales. As far as these establishments are concerned, the more bidders they attract, the better.

Auctions are places where art experts, art dealers, and seasoned collectors go to buy art. Auctions are also places where beginners who aren't too sure about what they are doing go to buy art. In fact, even people who have no idea what they are doing buy art at auction. The less experience buyers have, the more substantial the risks they take when they buy at auction. Unfortunately, many amateur auction patrons don't realize this.

The auctions we are primarily concerned with here are the less-well known, secondary, and regional or local firms. These smaller houses are the ones that conduct the great majority of sales worldwide and are also the ones where you are at the greatest risk when you buy art. In the substantial majority of cases, staffs and owners of small auction houses are not qualified to oversee and accurately evaluate every piece of art that is placed for sale at their establishments.

This chapter is also applicable to some of the major houses, in spite of the fact that they are a great deal more selective in what they sell. Even though they employ qualified experts to carefully examine and screen all art before it is accepted for sale, you still take big chances buying at these establishments if you don't know what you're doing. The very best auction houses (see Appendix VIII) do employ experts who can consult with you about what you're buying, but this is the exception rather than the rule. *No matter what caliber of auction house you patronize, though, the great bulk of the responsibility to know what you are buying and how to go about buying it always lies with you.*

Auctions Versus Art Galleries

Buying art at auction is different from buying at galleries. Sure, the art you see at auction looks basically the same as the art you see at galleries. It is often attractively presented, displayed, and lit, and hangs on the walls and sits on the pedestals just like an art gallery would display it. But that's where the similarities end.

Auctions are less specialized than art galleries. For example, you can find galleries dealing in types of art as specific as Minnesota art and artists, American art from the 1930's and 1940's, contemporary French sculpture, and so on. Specialized galleries are experts at what they sell; they spend all their working hours focusing exclusively on the art that they specialize in and, as a result, are able to provide their clients with the maximum amount of knowledge about that art.

Auctions, on the other hand, do not specialize and, thus, do not provide that level of knowledge and background information about what they sell. The great majority of auction houses accept whatever people bring them, display it all together in the same room, and let the potential buyers figure out what's what. You can see anything from Old Master portraits to contemporary abstracts, from New England coastal scenes to Moroccan landscapes all up for sale at the same auction.

Auction houses do the best they can, with whatever resources they have on hand, to determine whether the art that people consign for sale is authentic and in reasonably good condition. But beyond that, they do not perform the types of in-depth evaluations that private galleries do (such as determining how good the examples are, whether they are typical or atypical of the artists' work, what periods in the artists' developments they represent, whether they are done in the artists' preferred mediums, what condition they're in, and so on).

Because auctions accept such a wide range of art, they generally do not present consistent quality the way galleries do. Galleries pick and choose specific pieces for their clientele. Auctions do this to a certain extent, especially the best houses, but most tend to be less selective. Once again, they throw everything together and let the buyers decide what's great, good, and not so good. After all, auctions are not in the art gallery business, they are in the business of selling as much merchandise as possible for their consignors within set periods of time.

Auction houses rarely invest money in what they sell. This no-risk situation for the auction houses gives them a special advantage over art galleries, many of which routinely buy their art outright and, therefore, stand behind it in terms of quality. Because auction houses do not pay for what they accept on consignment, they can take chances and accept marginal items that may or may not do well at their sales. For example, dealers and collectors regularly use the auction option to dispose of second-rate pieces and other types of inferior quality or problem art that they either can't sell through their galleries or no longer want in their collections. Merchandise that does not sell is simply returned to the consignors, and the auction firms are no worse off for their efforts. In fact, some firms collect fees whether or not the art sells. (Incidentally, some major firms do advance cash on important consignments, but that practice involves only a minute percentage of all art sold at auction.)

You have no return or exchange privileges at auction. Unlike buying at galleries, when you buy art at auction, it's yours for keeps. All sales are final. Make sure you like whatever you bid on before you buy it because if you change your mind, the only way to get your money back is to place it back up for sale and hope for the best.

A most important difference between auction houses and galleries is that the majority of auction houses provide few, if any, guarantees on what they sell. The best houses do offer what amount to limited guarantees of authenticity. Depending on the firm and the state they are located in, they allow you to return merchandise for certain periods of time after it is sold ranging anywhere from thirty days to as long as five years in exceptional cases. In order for an auction firm to take art back, however, you must conclusively prove, based on expert opinions, that it was not properly represented. When a limited guarantee ends, auctions are no longer legally bound to accept returns, although many established firms still may take them back when buyers present strong enough cases and insist on having their money refunded.

Whenever you attend an auction, familiarize yourself with their statements of policy called the "Conditions of Sale." You usually see them at the beginning of auction catalogues or posted on auction house walls. If you can't find them, ask to see them. Read the conditions word for word. Once you become familiar with such conditions, you realize just how cautious you have to be when you buy at auction as opposed to at a gallery. They state exactly what the auction house is responsible for regarding what they sell – which is not too much – and what you are responsible for – which is just about everything.

For example, you are at an auction where the auctioneer states that the next item to go up for bidding is a painting signed "John Doe." The auctioneer means exactly what he says – that he is selling a painting signed "John Doe" – and nothing more. He is not guaranteeing that the painting is by Doe. Maybe it is, maybe it isn't. All he is doing is stating the fact that it happens to have a "John Doe" signature on it. Are the painting and signature authentic? That's for you and fellow bidders to decide.

The average auction sale is the ultimate arena for the policy "Let the buyer beware." Auctions are not retail art galleries that provide fully documented, fully condition-inspected, fully researched, and fully guaranteed products to the public. Never confuse the two.

Mistaken Beliefs that People Have About Auctions

Some of the reasons why so many art buyers find auctions so attractive are not really valid at all. Clearing up a few commonly held misconceptions will help place auction buying in its proper perspective.

The belief that auctions are where you go to find bargains is not necessarily true. The chances of your getting a bona fide bargain at auction are slim, and the lucky few who tend to make bargain buys are usually highly experienced professionals. First of all, auction houses want everything they sell to sell for as much money as possible. When they receive art on consignment that they suspect might have value, they research it. If they don't have the capacity to research it, they do the next best thing, which is publicize the fact that they have it for sale as widely as possible and do whatever is necessary to catch the attention of buyers who do know how to research it. All they have to do is reach two buyers who know how much the art is worth (which is almost always accomplished with ease), and then let the bidding begin. Add to this the fact that fine art professionals monitor all significant art auctions around the world in order to make sure that no better works of art slip through unnoticed. In the end, virtually all quality pieces end up selling for respectable prices.

Another reason for the lack of bargains is that just about the only person who wants to see art auction cheaply is you, the potential buyer. Everyone else wants to see it sell for as much money as possible. The auctioneer wants high prices because that means good profits and good publicity for the auction house. High prices also mean more business for the auction house because potential consignors are encouraged to consign merchandise. Consignors naturally want to get as much money as possible for what they consign. Collectors who already own works by artists whose art is up for sale at auction want that art to sell high, because strong sales increase the value of the art in their collections. And don't forget the rest of the art community. They want high prices because that indicates a healthy and active art market in general. So it's you against the world.

In spite of all this, plenty of people continue to shop auctions for bargains. An ironic consequence of this "bargain-hunting" is that prices of second-rate works of art periodically spiral to ridiculous heights, especially during times of extreme art speculation such as the mid- to late-1980's. Later, after speculation subsides, these inflated prices drop back precipitously. As you read in Chapter 20, this phenomenon is primarily due to inexperienced buyers "buying by name" and not possessing the skills necessary to recognize that the art they think they are getting "so cheaply" is of mediocre quality or problematic in other ways and not worth the "bargain prices" they believe they are paying for it.

The belief that auction prices are always less than art gallery prices is not true. Auction art does not always sell at wholesale or below retail. Some art sells for more money at auction than it does anywhere else. In fact, certain art dealers regularly monitor auctions and cash in on the phenomenon by playing to whatever the current auction buying crazes are. They consign a continuing flow of the exact types of art that bidders are inclined to pay strong prices for at any particular auction.

The belief that art is worth what auction houses think it will sell for is not necessarily true. Many auctions either include estimated selling prices in their sale catalogues or tell you about how much they expect certain items to sell for. Although many such estimates are accurate, some are too high and others are too low. You take your financial life into your own hands when you bid on art based only on auction house estimates.

Why are estimates sometimes too high? There are a number of reasons. An auction house may place an unrealistically high estimate on a certain piece of art as a favor to a client who regularly consigns merchandise, a research error may lead a staff person to overvalue a work of art, the auction house may be fishing for a buyer to pay at or near a deliberately overestimated price, and so on.

Why are estimates sometimes too low? Again, for various reasons. Research errors may be to blame. Other times, auctions purposely put low estimates on art in order to attract buyers to their sales. The theory here (which does seem to work) is that once people are physically at a sale, they tend to buy even if they don't get the art at the low prices they thought they would. Also, the lower the reserve prices that consignors place on their art (the least amounts of money that they're willing to sell it for), the lower the estimates can be, and the greater the likelihood that the art sells and the auction houses make money.

The belief that no one ever overpays for art at auction is not true. One reason why people overpay is that they mistakenly accept pre-sale estimates as gospel. For example, when two or more bidders believe that unrealistically high estimates are realistic or that the quality of a work of art is better than it actually is, the art sells for more than it's worth. Other reasons why people overpay usually involve their bidding for reasons other than wanting to own art (more about that in the next section).

The belief that only people who know nothing about art attend small-town, offbeat, or country auctions is not true. This is a misconception suffered by bargain hunters who fantasize about finding Rembrandts for pennies at backwoods sales. As mentioned above, pros monitor just about every auction, no matter how remote it is. When something good comes up for sale, people who know how much it's worth and are willing to pay good money for it somehow manage to find out about it.

Who Bids at Auction, and Why Do They Bid?

Assuming you know how to evaluate and research a work of art you see at auction, you still have to know what to do next and how to act at the sale itself. A lot more goes on at auction sales, in a psychological sense, than people innocently holding up their bidding cards and buying art. Within the ranks of the bidders, there are many different forces at work. All kinds of people bid on and buy art at auction for all kinds of reasons.

Experienced rational buyers make up the large majority of auction bidders and are also the most predictable. Such buyers research whatever art they are interested in buying and bid in an informed, calculated manner. They know exactly what they want and how much they are willing to pay for it. If they get it, fine. If they don't, they wait until next time.

At the other end of the rationality continuum are those few bidders who go completely wild and are victims of what is often described as "auction fever." They bid as much for thrills, excitement, and victory over the competition as they do for the art itself. For them, nothing quite equals the emotional charge of thrusting their bidding cards skyward in the midst of crowded rooms, beating out fellow buyers, and taking home their "trophies." The most excessive among them decide they must own certain items no matter what the cost.

Other, less-common types of bidders and bidding styles include the following:

- *People who purposely bid art up in order to inflate the value of their own collections.* For example, an individual or gallery that owns a lot of art by one artist places a piece of that art for sale at auction and has friends or acquaintances deliberately bid it up to a higher price than it has ever sold for before. The impressive auction record becomes public knowledge, and people who see it without understanding how it came about mistakenly conclude that the artist's work is increasing in value and collectibility.

- *People who bid because they see an arch rival bidding.* These individuals may not even be interested in owning the art or care how much they have to pay for it. All they care about is competing.

- *People who bid on art only when they see specific dealers or experienced collectors bid on it first.* They respect those dealers or collectors and figure that anything these pros think is worthwhile bidding on must be good. As an aside, dealers and collectors who are victimized by people watching their every move often counter this problem by bidding over the phone or by hiring confederates to bid in their places.

- *People who bid to impress spouses, friends, relatives, or business associates.* The art is always secondary here.

- *People who bid on art they never intend to own and do so only to see how high they can push up the final selling prices before safely dropping out of the action.* The few bidders who do this are usually skilled auction buyers who know just when to quit and rarely, if ever, get stuck with anything they don't want. They could almost be called shills except that they have no connection to auction houses and do what they do entirely for personal thrills and amusement.

You see that plenty goes on at auction besides the simple buying of art. People can bid on whatever they want for whatever reason they want to and pay as much as they feel like paying for it. What does this mean for you? You've got to be absolutely confident of your intentions and your knowledge of what you are bidding on before getting involved.

Auction Plus Points: Why Buy Art at Auction?

In spite of all these cautions and warnings, auctions can be great places to buy art. Any experienced auction buyer will tell you this. *If you know what you are doing, and this is a big "if," you can buy wonderful works of art for reasonable prices at auction.* You can even find bargains if you're really skilled at researching, setting your limits, and bidding.

To begin with, auctions sell a significant amount of better-quality art fresh out of estates or private collections. Private sellers do not always have the time, the inclination, or the know-how to sell their art through galleries and, as a result, choose the easy auction option. Corporations, businesses, museums, historical societies, and other institutions further contribute to the fascinating array of art that auction houses continually place at their public sales.

Auctions are about the only places where you can compete for art directly with art dealers. Auctions are free and open public forums where anyone has the identical opportunity to bid and buy alongside anyone else. Dealers have no strategic advantages over anyone else like they do in many other buying situations (such as special trade discounts, early or exclusive viewing privileges, and so on).

All potential buyers are treated equally at auction. Private galleries, on the other hand, frequently offer their latest arrivals to their longest-standing and best clients first. They sell plenty of art before the general public ever has a chance to see it. At a gallery, as a first-time or second-time buyer, you either have to choose from what's left over or wait until you move up in a gallery owner's customer hierarchy before being able to take first pick of the best new arrivals. At auction, you have that pick immediately.

The fact that auction houses sell art "as is" gives you reason to be cautious in your buying, but the "as is" situation can also work in your favor. Perfectly good-quality art may be placed at auction poorly framed, with minor damage, dirty, or with other easily rectifiable problems. Dealers buy this art at wholesale prices, clean it up, frame it, and mark it up to full retail after providing those services. Like dealers, you can also buy these types of art at reduced prices, have it repaired, cleaned, and framed yourself, and save money over the extra profit margin you would normally pay galleries to do it for you.

The fact that auction houses do not specialize can be viewed as a plus point rather than a drawback. Because auction houses accept a much greater variety of art than galleries do, they provide you with regular opportunities to view different and unusual pieces that you would not ordinarily see for sale anywhere else. You can use these opportunities to broaden your general knowledge of art and possibly even expand your art-buying horizons.

Auction houses tend to be more open with respect to supplying provenance than galleries are. Many auction houses will contact consignors at buyers' requests to see whether they mind revealing their identities, whether they are willing to provide written statements or other information about the art they consigned, and so on. Galleries tend to be more protective about their sources. When private dealers acquire art at bargain prices or are supplied by regularly producing sources, they are especially not interested in naming names.

At auction, you often have a longer time to deliberate over what you see for sale than you do at galleries. Most auction firms announce their sales anywhere from several weeks to a month or more in advance. This gives you ample time to research the art you like, view it repeatedly during the pre-sale period; and decide how much you really like it, whether you want to own it, and how much you are willing to pay for it. Private galleries, on the other hand, often offer brief options to buy, sometimes lasting as little as a day or two, before they resume offering their art to other clients. This sort of pressure situation is never in the buyer's favor.

How to Buy at Auction

Suppose you want to buy art at auction at some point in your art-buying career. First-timers have to start somewhere, and, no matter what type of auction you intend to patronize, the learning procedures are basically the same.

When you're just starting out, stick with established auction houses that have experience selling art. Be wary of traveling auctions, special art auctions conducted by firms that do not regularly handle art, "bargain art" or liquidation auctions, and other out-of-the-ordinary, transient or irregularly held sales. The risks to beginners are simply too great at events like these. Attend offbeat sales without participating in order to broaden your knowledge of what auctions are all about, but as far as actually bidding, wait until you've had more experience bidding at established auctions.

The first step in learning about auctions is to preview and attend as many sales as you can *without bidding*. Research any art that interests you just as though you were actually going to buy it. Do standard artist and art research, inspect the art's condition, research selling prices, and decide the maximum amounts you would be willing to pay if you were actually bidding. Attend the sales themselves, feel the excitement, watch what happens, pay attention to how the auctioneers offer the merchandise and how the buyers respond, get accustomed to the rapid pace at which the lots sell, imagine yourself making bids, and acclimate yourself to the pressurized atmosphere of the sales room. Once you feel reasonably comfortable and familiar with how auctions progress, you're ready to seriously compete against other bidders and buy art.

An essential rule to follow at any auction where you intend to bid is this: Always attend the preview, and spend plenty of time studying the art while you're there. The preview is the most important part of any sale because it is here that you have a chance to view the art firsthand, examine its every detail, inspect it for condition or authenticity problems, and decide how much you like it and whether or not you want to own it. *Never* bid on or buy art that you have not previewed in person beforehand.

At any preview, study all the art for sale. Even if you don't like a piece, spend at least a little time looking at it and learning about it. This exercise will increase your knowledge of art in general. After you've taken a preliminary look around, then start focusing in on the specific works of art that appeal to you the most.

Carefully study your favorites for ten or fifteen minutes each, come back in an hour or two and study them again for ten or fifteen more minutes each, come back the next day and repeat the procedure, and so on. The more you look at your choices, the better you get to know them, understand how strongly you feel about owning them, and assess how they would look on display in your home or place of business. Make sure you like the way they look and that you really want to own them, because once you buy them, they're yours. (You can't take auction art home on approval and take it for a "test drive" like you can with gallery art.)

Determine the condition of any art you intend to bid on. Take it off the wall or remove it from its pedestal, turn it over, lift it up, look at it under a magnifying glass, do whatever you have to do in order to inspect its every detail. Note whatever problems the art has. (At some auctions, particularly the better ones, you need either permission from the management or staff supervision in order to closely examine art.)

Study all information the auction house provides about the art. This may be in the form of a listing in an auction catalogue, it may be on a sheet of paper you are handed as you arrive at the preview, or in some other form. Copy anything you cannot take from the auction house, and keep it on hand for future reference.

Have the auction staff person or persons in charge of art tell you everything they know about the art you are interested in bidding on. See if the staff person is aware of any condition problems. Ask also if that person knows where the art came from, whether any official documents accompany the art, why it was consigned, and any other details you might need to evaluate before you place your bids. Find out everything you can. Write down any pertinent information, and save it for future reference.

After attending the preview and gathering information, research, research, research! Find out everything you possibly can about the art and its artists from sources outside the auction house according to the procedures outlined in Part III of this book. Study biographical information about the artists. Determine the significance of the art. Evaluate the artists' price structures according to procedures outlined in Chapter 21. Never rely solely on the pre-sale estimates the auction house gives you; independently confirm and corroborate any other statements the auction house has made to you either verbally or in the sale catalogue.

Based on your research, decide what your maximum bids will be, and *stay with those bids right through to the close of the bidding*. Whether or not your high bids relate to the auction house estimates or what the art eventually sells for, do not change your mind at the last minute. The moment you reach your limit on any one bid, put your bidding card back in your lap and wait for the next item you're interested in to come up for sale.

Controlling yourself during bidding is especially important if you are an inexperienced bidder. Novices tend to get carried away at the last moment, throw their research results to the wind, and bid just to buy something no matter how much they have to pay for it. In the heat of a crowded, fast-paced auction sale, a few seconds of indiscretion can cost you big dollars. So don't be upset if you come away empty-handed. You'll find plenty more works of art to bid on at future sales.

If you are nervous about buying at auction and want to work your way into it more gradually, hire a no-conflict resource, such as a dealer or an experienced collector, that you know, trust, and can confide in to inspect, research, and even bid on the art for you. Attend the preview together, examine and discuss the art, research it, and decide what to do based primarily on this experienced individual's professional opinion. The best auction houses offer consultation services, but even so, hiring independent unbiased experts makes better sense. Most experts perform this service either for a flat fee or for a percentage of the final selling prices, usually ranging between 4 and 10 percent.

Asking independent experts for their opinions without paying them can sometimes be hazardous to your bidding. Those professionals can conceivably become your adversaries when they are under no obligation to work on your behalf. For example, your innocent questions may call an expert's attention to a work of art that he did not notice initially and would have overlooked entirely if you hadn't asked him about it. The expert might decide you're on to something good and end up bidding against you.

Example 1:

Experienced dealers and collectors know to attend all auctions where art they are interested in bidding on is being sold. They appear at the sales ready to bid regardless of how high the pre-sale estimates are, how much experts expect the art to sell for, and how dim prospects seem for getting that art at the prices they're willing to pay. In the auction business, you never know what's going to sell for what until it actually sells.

A friend of mine likes to relate a story about a painting he saw at an auction preview. It had a pre-sale estimate of $20,000 to $40,000. Interest in the picture was strong and the general word among those in the know was that the final selling price was expected to be somewhere between $40,000 and $50,000. Although this collector was willing to bid as high as $30,000, certainly a respectable amount of money, he had pretty much given up any hope of getting the painting. Nevertheless, he attended the sale.

When he arrived, he found the auction room nearly empty. Even so, the other works of art were still selling at substantial prices – nothing was selling terribly low. He didn't have high hopes for being the winning bidder on his favorite painting, but now he felt that at least he had an outside chance because of the low attendance. When it came up for sale, he sat silently without bidding and prepared to watch it sell for well over $30,000. To his surprise, bidding abruptly stopped at $18,000. He couldn't believe it. He raised his card and got the painting for $19,000 – almost 40 percent less than what he would have gladly paid and less than half of what the experts had expected it to sell for.

He explains his good fortune as follows. Everyone who was interested in the painting was so sure it would sell high that no one left any absentee bids on it, and no one attended the sale. Everyone thought everyone else would be bidding on it when, in fact, they had all psyched each other out. The only person left who was willing to pay any serious money for it was him.

Whether his explanation is right or not, such unexpected turns of events happen all the time at auctions. If you see art you like at a preview, never assume it's out of your reach until the final bid is made, and the hammer falls.

A Look Ahead

Online auctions present an entirely different array of research, bidding, and buying circumstances than do traditional auctions. In fact, the approach to bidding and buying online only vaguely resembles that of bidding and buying at a traditional auction sale. Chapter 25 enumerates the differences between traditional auctions and online auctions and discusses how to evaluate online auction descriptions, how to preview merchandise, how to evaluate photographs of merchandise on your computer screen, how to request additional information from sellers, and more.

CHAPTER 25

Buying Art at Internet Auctions

Internet auctions have forever changed the way fine art buyers and sellers do business, and they are, without a doubt, the wave of the future. In the old days, art dealers and collectors had to physically travel to galleries and auctions in order to see art for sale. Their other search tools included phones, faxes, trade publications, art dealer organizations, museum collector groups, and the like. People with art for sale had few options other than to sell to local galleries, consign to local auctions, or hold estate sales. Today, anybody can sell just about anything to anybody else assuming they have access to computers and understand the simple rules of buying and selling at online auctions.

The great majority of art buying at internet auctions is fun, easy, cost effective, and satisfying. Buyers can locate quality items for sale in far away places, and sellers can reach more buyers and occasionally sell for higher prices than ever before. The volume of internet auction transactions is steadily on the rise as people become increasingly comfortable with this new way of doing business.

If you're a beginner, though, buying art at online auctions is risky business even riskier than buying at traditional auctions like those discussed in the previous chapter. The nature of this risk, and the major difference between online auctions and traditional auctions is, without a doubt, that buyers cannot preview art for sale at online auctions in-person before bidding on it. If you'll recall from the last chapter, the most important part of the auction-buying process is attending the preview and seeing the art in person *before* you bid. Accurately assessing art from photographs on computer screens, as you're required to do at online auctions, is difficult even for seasoned professionals.

The Two Types of Online Auctions

The two basic types of online auctions are those that are vetted and those that are not vetted. A vetted auction is one where art specialists examine all works of art before they are placed up for sale in order to determine whether they are adequate in quality and are properly represented by the sellers who are usually established dealers, collectors, or traditional auction houses. Art that passes this critical inspection is deemed appropriate for auction and is placed up for sale in much the same way that meat or dairy products are inspected, graded, and deemed appropriate for sale at your local grocery store. (All art that you see for sale at better traditional auction houses has been vetted.)

Pretty much all traditional established auction houses (and many less-established ones), from major international companies to regional and local firms, host their own websites and conduct vetted online sales either on their own sites or through other websites, eBay in particular. eBay.com hosts what they term "eBay Live Auctions" at *liveauctions.ebay.com* where reputable, established international auction houses, pre-screened by eBay, conduct online sales, often in real time with actual auctions being held on their salesroom floors. Some of these auction houses have been in business hundreds of years and all fully stand behind their merchandise. eBay Live Auction sales are conducted according to the terms of eBay and are also subject to the terms of the individual auction houses conducting the sales.

If you're new to online auctions and would like to try your hand at bidding and buying, shopping at vetted sales either conducted by or under the auspices of established auction houses is the best way to start. These sales provide you with modest assurances and protections that, as you will soon see, are lacking at online auctions that are not vetted. At vetted sales, you can be reasonably sure that the art you are bidding on is authentic, properly represented, and accurately described.

Online auctions that are not vetted, eBay being pretty much the only game in town at this point, may be appropriately described as anarchistic, buy-sell, free-for-alls. In this arena, sellers need no art-related experience, references, resumes, or qualifications in order to place art up for sale. All they need to know is how to use a computer. For example, any seller can place any item up for sale, no matter what it happens to be and without any prior inspection by specialists, and call it "art." To complicate matters further, any seller can call herself a dealer and state that she has a gallery or a shop or has been buying, selling, or collecting art for decades. Online bidders who may live hundreds or thousands of miles away from these sellers cannot easily verify this information.

Although the overwhelming majority of online sellers are honest and do their best to properly represent their art, naive and inexperienced sellers routinely make mistakes in describing art, and novice buyers who believe that what these sellers state is correct overpay for those items. For example, prints are called paintings, reproductions are called originals, authorship is attributed without sufficient proof, an item made in the mid-1970's might be described as "old and rare," and that's only the beginning. At worst, sellers can make the most ordinary, everyday items sound like long lost treasures by peppering their descriptions with superlatives like "rare," "important," "fantastic," "exquisite," "beautiful," or "museum quality" without qualification or regard to accuracy. On December 30, 2006, for example, of the 336,331 works of art for sale on eBay, 37,914 contained the word "rare" in either their titles or descriptions. Now I don't mean to sound skeptical, but I have a hard time believing that over 11 percent of the art for sale on eBay, or anywhere else on the planet for that matter, is rare.

Another problem with online auctions that are not vetted is that a handful of unscrupulous sellers specializing in fakes, forgeries, and misrepresentations reach more unsuspecting buyers with greater ease and anonymity than ever before (learn how about their methods in Chapter 18). What's even more amazing is that they can cultivate respectable online presences for themselves through vehicles such as eBay's feedback system while, at the very same time, making spurious claims about their art and victimizing innocent buyers for anywhere from hundreds to tens of thousands of dollars. All a seller has to do to receive positive feedback and create a positive seller profile is to promptly answer inquiries from potential buyers, make sure that buyers believe that the art they're bidding on is authentic, pack the art securely when shipping it to winning bidders, ship it on time, and appropriately respond to all requests for information from potential bidders. For example, buyers who have no idea they've bought bogus art, assuming the transactions proceed smoothly, leave the sellers positive feedback.

To complicate matters, buyers who get burned by dishonest sellers are reluctant to leave negative feedback for fear those sellers will leave negative feedback for them in return, thereby compromising the buyers' user profiles even though they did nothing wrong. This practice, called leaving "retaliatory feedback," points up a major flaw in eBay's feedback system. Sadly (and amazingly), you can buy problem art from eBay sellers with 100 percent positive feedback. Just because a seller has perfect feedback is no guarantee that the art they sell is authentic or accurately represented.

Back in the good old days before the Internet, sellers almost always had to physically appear in person alongside the art that they had for sale. Regardless of the methods sellers chose to sell their art, buyers almost always knew who those sellers were, what they looked like, what their reputations were, where they lived, and how to contact them. Significant works of art rarely changed hands without being inspected and evaluated (or vetted) firsthand by experienced professionals like dealers, traditional auction house art specialists, or appraisers.

Dishonest sellers acquired reputations in their communities for trafficking in questionable works of art. When art dealers and collectors found out who these sellers were, they advised other dealers and collectors in the art community to avoid them. Traditional marketplace safeguards, such as those just mentioned, protected the great majority of art buyers and assured a reasonable level of quality control in the fine art marketplace. Online auctions that are not vetted, unfortunately, cannot provide these types of checks and balances.

Online auctions have a number of rules in place for warning less scrupulous sellers to be more careful about how they sell online. The worst offenders can be permanently banned from online auction sites. But banning sellers is not easy for online auction staff people, and even those sellers who do get banned can take on different identities or find confederates to continue selling their bogus merchandise for them, and be back in business without too much trouble.

To summarize, outside specialists are not required to inspect or evaluate any art that sellers place up for sale at non-vetted online auctions. The sellers alone, regardless of their credentials, decide how important their art is and how to describe it to potential buyers. Sellers are not required to support or qualify any subjective or descriptive claims, judgments, embellishments, representations, statements, or conclusions that they make about their art. Whatever the seller says, goes.

In spite of the downside, skilled and experienced buyers still find good-quality works of art at online auctions that are not vetted. Keep in mind that the key phrase in the above sentence is "skilled and experienced buyers." The best buyers know the art business, know art, are patient, professional, and buy only when they're sure that the art they're bidding on is right in every respect. They ask the right questions, qualify sellers, evaluate merchandise, request additional photos or computer scans when necessary, and assess accuracy of descriptions before ever placing bids. For the more adventurous among you who you feel like jumping into the non-vetted online auction fray, the following guidelines, custom tailored to online auctions and regularly followed by experienced online bidders, will help transform you into a skilled bidder, too. But please, newbies – be extremely careful.

- Read the COMPLETE description of any item on which you are interested in bidding. Some less scrupulous sellers hide disclaimers deep in their descriptions including that the art is being sold as-is, that they have no idea whether it's genuine or not, that all sales are final, and so on.

- *Beware of flowery language, subjective statements, or personal opinions about how rare, beautiful, special, or stunning art is when reading sellers' descriptions.* All you want are the facts like what kind of art it is, what its dimensions are, who the artist is, what its condition is, how old it is, and so on. If you have trouble separating out facts from sellers' personal opinions, study art auction catalogues from traditional auction houses, and see how professional auction specialists describe art.

- Long, detailed biographical information about an artist in an item description does not mean the art is genuine or even that it is by that artist. In fact, it is not unusual for an item description to ramble on and on about the life of an artist and proceed to state the art may not be by that artist or that the seller is not sure who it's by.

- *No claims that sellers make about either the value or authenticity of the art they are selling should be taken seriously* unless they either support those claims with proof or are nationally or internationally respected authorities on the art or artists they are selling.

- *Have sellers qualify all claims that they make about their art.* If a painting is described as rare, for example, find out who came to that conclusion, what they based it on, and what qualifications they have to make it.

- *Request to see all documentation that a seller says accompanies the art BEFORE you bid, and make sure that they are originals and not photocopies.* This includes appraisals, certificates of authenticity, bills of sale, and so on. Never bid on art when the seller refuses to show such documents, or says that it will be sent along with the art to the winning bidder only.

- Beware of art that is "attributed" to well-known artists. Sellers often use this word in their item descriptions when, in truth, they are not qualified to attribute art. Only known, respected experts on artists can make attributions, and even then, all "attributed" means is that they think the art could possibly be by the artist.

- *Get credentials and contact information from sellers as well as from any other individuals who sellers refer you to for additional information about art that's up for auction.* In order for someone's claims to be taken seriously, they should be known and respected experts in their fields. If they're not experts, consider what they say to be uninformed personal opinion and not much more.

- *Any seller can state that his or her art is a bargain.* Whenever such a claim is made, request concrete proof that this is so, like having them show you previous sales records for comparable works of art. Furthermore, much of the "bargain" art that's for sale at online auctions is problematic or compromised in one way or another.

- *When sellers state that art similar to the art that they're selling, or art by the same artists, sells for substantial sums of money at galleries or traditional auctions, request complete documentation on those sales including what sold (subject matter, size, condition, age, etc.), how much it sold for, and where, when, and under what circumstances it sold.* For example, someone auctioning a 12-inch tall sculpture online might state that the artist's sculptures sell at auction for as much as $100,000. The $100,000 sales, however, might turn out to be for sculptures that are 20 feet tall, not 12 inches tall, and 12-inch tall sculptures by that artist only auction for about $1,000 each. (Misleading descriptions like this are common at online auctions.)

- *When items are represented as coming from important estates, wealthy families, major collectors, or other exceptional circumstances, request physical proof including names, addresses, dates, receipts, auction records, or published news stories.* Never accept hearsay as fact, whether it's verbal or you're reading it on your computer screen, and never assume that all items that come from so-called wealthy estates are automatically high quality, authentic, or valuable.

- *When a previous owner is stated to be an important collector, find out what they collected, why they were considered important, where their collections were exhibited, and which experts or public records confirm that these statements are true.* You need verifiable names, addresses, dates, places, and events from reputable, established sources confirming the existence and significance of the collector. Accept nothing less.

- *Never assume that just because a work of art is signed or otherwise labeled by a particular artist that it is automatically a genuine work by that artist.* All other aspects of that art must also indicate that it is the work of the artist in question. Keep in mind that the signature or label is only one of many aspects that an expert examines when evaluating a work of fine art.

- *Request complete condition reports including locations and extent of all existing damage as well as previous repairs or restorations.* As you read in Chapter 17, condition problems can seriously devalue a work of art.

- *Never bid on or buy art that is only described, but not pictured online.*

- *Never buy art when the online pictures are fuzzy, too small to study detail, too dark, too light, show reflections, or are difficult to view in any other way.* Buying art based only on photographs is tough enough to do even when the photographs are good.

- *Never buy art from sellers who ONLY accept payment as forms of cash such as personal checks, money orders, or wire transfers.* If the art turns out to be problematic in some way, you have little or no recourse to get your money back. If paying by Paypal (*www.paypal.com*), make sure the seller has been active on Paypal for a significant period of time, has accepted many Paypal payments, is "Verified" by Paypal, and that the Paypal account contact information matches that of the auction seller.

- *In addition to pictures of the front of the art, also request scans of the back, top, bottom, sides, signature, and any other areas that may yield additional clues about the art.* By looking at the back of a painting, for instance, you can find out information like whether the age of the stretcher bars matches the age of the painting or whether the canvas has been damaged and repaired.

- *Ask for detail scans or pictures of any areas of works of art for which you have additional questions.*

- *Always check sellers' other online sales, both ongoing and completed.* Watch for repeated use of the same words or phrases in different descriptions. Works of art from different time periods and by different artists rarely share identical characteristics (unless they're part of a very specific collection), and repeated use of the same words can tip you off to potential problems with that art. For example, if a seller is auctioning 20 paintings and 10 of them are described as "rare" or "museum quality," either the seller has outstanding taste in art and is extremely fortunate to own so many top-quality examples, or he could be overstating the truth in his descriptions.

- *Be cautious when one seemingly important work of art is listed alongside ordinary everyday items.* For example, if a "Rare 16th Century Old Master Painting" is being offered along with lots consisting of kids toys, golf clubs, and car tires, this could be cause for concern.

- *Never assume that art is properly represented just because seller feedback profiles are positive.* As mentioned above, feedback profiles are not necessarily accurate indications of the sellers' integrity, so always perform complete independent research on art that interests you *before* bidding.

- *Get answers to all questions in writing (emails will do), especially relating to authenticity and condition,* before *you bid and not after.*

- *Make sure you have a money-back guarantee and adequate time to fully inspect (or have outside experts inspect) any art that you purchase.* You need at least one week from the day you receive a work of art to inspect it.

- *Make sure you have total freedom to select experts to evaluate your art.* Sellers should have no control over who you choose to examine it.

- *Save all email correspondences with sellers.* Also document all phone conversations, faxes, and other communications that you have with sellers as well as with their associates.

- *If you're at all unsure about a work of art, consult an independent expert **before** you bid, not after.*

- *If a work of art has few or no bids, but the description implies that it's supposed to be special in some way, get an outside expert opinion, and exercise caution before bidding.* Art that is genuinely exceptional tends to sell for higher prices and have multiple bids.

- *When a work of art's reserve or current high bid is substantially below what comparable works of art sell for on the open market, this could be cause for concern.* The art may be genuine, for instance, but may also be an inferior example of the artist's work. Quality items generally sell for higher prices no matter whether they're for sale at traditional venues or at online auctions.

- *To repeat, one of the essential ingredients of traditional auctions is being able to preview the art in person before you bid on it.* If art you see for sale at an online auction is offered by a seller in your area, make every attempt to inspect it in person (most sellers will allow you to do this). Not being able to physically inspect items first is a major drawback to online auction buying. Unless you're skilled at evaluating the art you're bidding on and can draw informed conclusions from computer scans, exercise caution.

- *Unless you're an experienced dealer or collector or you have access to proprietary information that few people have access to, never assume that you're the only one who spots an online art bargain.* Thousands of savvy and knowledgeable buyers from all over the world continuously monitor online auctions for all types of antiques, collectibles, and fine art.

Online Bidding Strategies

The key to successful online bidding is this: **Bid the highest amount of money that you're willing to pay for an item, bid that amount as close to the end of the auction as you possibly can, and keep your identity secret.** Maximizing your chances of making the winning bid at an online auction is that simple and no more complicated.

At traditional auctions, you bid incrementally on an item up to your predetermined limit (as you learned in the last chapter), you bid only as long as someone is bidding against you, and the bidding ends when you're the last bidder left standing no matter how long that takes. You then win the item and the next item in the catalogue comes up for auction.

At online auctions, the bidding paradigm is entirely different. An online auction lasts for a set time period, usually 7 to 10 days, and the winner is the last bidder who bids the highest amount *before* the close of the sale, that is, before the moment that the time limit for the sale expires. If you place a new high bid that reaches the auction site even a fraction of a second after the sale closes, that bid is not recorded, and you do not win the item.

The strategy of bidding high and bidding late is known in online auction parlance as "sniping" and is a successful strategy for several reasons. First of all, by bidding at or near the close of a sale, you don't give competing bidders time to perform additional research on the item up for sale or to reconsider, for any other reason, whether they should bid any higher than they already have. Second, sniping prevents "shill-bidding," or opportunities for sellers to notify friends or accomplices to fraudulently bid against you, not because they want to buy the item, but for the sole purpose of making you pay more for it.

Third, sniping minimizes unwanted competition from what online auction denizens call "stalkers." Stalkers are people who either already know or otherwise conclude that you're an experienced dealer or collector by reading your online auction feedback profile and studying the items that you've bid on and won. When they like what they see, they continually monitor your online activities in order to keep track of what you're bidding on. Even though stalkers may not know much about certain items that you're bidding on, they assume from your history that, whatever those items are, they're good quality, and you're getting them for reasonable prices.

Keeping your online identity secret not only minimizes sniping from stalkers, but also protects you from having to compete with others who might be inclined to bid against you on particular items just because they know who you are. For example, if you use the online nickname of "artdealer" and bid on art, competing bidders who buy art will assume that, since you're a dealer, any bid you make is at the wholesale level, and even if they outbid you, they'll still be getting good deals. Divulging information about who you are or what you buy, sell, or collect is fine as long as you wait until after an auction is over; when you're the high bidder. You should then reveal personal information only to the seller.

In order to help bidders place bids at the very close of auctions, several software companies have developed and sell sniping software. The majority of experienced online bidders still prefer to bid manually, however, without using sniping software. Sniping software works best when auctions end at odd hours or when bidders know they'll be away from their computers, such as in the middle of the night or on weekdays during working hours. Experienced bidders agree, though, that more and more experienced online sellers time their auctions so that they end when most bidders are at home, like on weekend afternoons or during the early evening hours at the beginning of the week. These sellers know how to make it as easy as possible for as many people as possible to bid on their items.

As an aside, online auctions also happen to be good places to do price research. Simply go to databases of completed auction items, type in the names of the artists you're researching as "keywords," and study the search results. You see not only what types of art by those artists collectors prize, but also what types don't sell well. Keep in mind that searching online auction databases is *never* an adequate substitute for complete art price research as outlined in Chapter 21.

The Future of Online Auctions

The online auction world is still pretty much of a free-for-all in a number of respects. The major auction sites continually seek feedback from experienced online buyers and sellers as well as from specialists in the traditional antiques, collectibles, and fine arts communities in attempts to minimize and, hopefully, one day, eliminate system abuses. The following modifications to online auction models are among those currently under consideration or already being incorporated onto auction websites.

- *Requiring all items with reserves or opening bids over a certain dollar amount (determined by the auction site) to be evaluated and approved of by neutral specialists.*

- *Requiring proof of authenticity for all items with reserves or opening bids over a certain dollar amount (determined by the auction site).*

- *Placing certain restrictions on the types of subjective claims and personal opinions that sellers are allowed to make about their merchandise.*

- *Requiring documentation for claims of rarity, scarcity, or other superlatives.* Documentation could include quotes from standard reference books (with appropriate bibliographic notations), appraisals by qualified specialists or appraisers (with contact information), opinions of qualified experts or authorities (with contact information), or other verifiable forms of concrete factual documentation.

- *Providing or contracting with expert consulting services to answer buyers' questions about auction items either by phone or by email.* Buyers would probably be required to pay modest fees for these services.

- *Having specialists or experts "police" sales of particular types of fine art, antiques, or collectibles where abuses of the online auction model are most prevalent.* This would be done in much the same way that law enforcement agencies patrol high-crime areas in major cities – crime is not necessarily eliminated, but it is substantially reduced. Sellers making questionable claims or placing questionable items up for sale would be contacted by experts and either queried, notified, or warned about the ways that they are representing their merchandise.

- *Archiving sales records of all items that sell for over a certain dollar amount (determined by the auction site) so that abusers can be more easily tracked once they're discovered.* When a seller is spotted selling a fake painting, for example, his or her selling history could be examined in order to assess the extent of his or her abuses. In serious cases, legal action could be taken and victims could be notified with greater ease than is now possible.

Example 1:

Unless you're an experienced dealer or collector, being able to preview art at auction in person before bidding on it is essential in order to make sure that it has the qualities that you're looking for. Suppose you're shopping for art at an online auction, and you see a Rocky Mountain landscape painting dating from the turn of the century that looks great on your computer screen. In the foreground are several small figures leading horses up a hillside trail. You do your artist research, ask the seller several questions about the condition of the painting, determine that the piece is properly represented, bid on it, and win.

It arrives at your home about a week later. You unpack it and hang it, with great anticipation, in a special place that you've prepared for it on your living room wall. You step back, take a look, and immediately notice something strange about one of the horses. You move closer and see that the horse's eye looks like it's crossed, and one hind leg is so poorly painted that it's in a totally unnatural position. Unfortunately, these problems were too small to be noticeable on your computer screen unless someone had tipped you off to them in the first place.

Since the painting was properly represented for sale and you had plenty of time to look at it and ask questions before buying it, you have no legal justification for returning it. So you leave it hanging on your wall, figuring that you might eventually be able to forget about the weird horse and focus instead on the skillfully painted mountains. The more you look at the picture, though, the more the weird horse bothers you. After a month of trying to ignore the animal, you take the painting off of your wall, drag it upstairs to your attic, set it in a nice dark corner, cover it with an old bed sheet, and chalk your online auction lesson up to experience.

Example 2:

A buyer who bought a painting at an online auction contacted me by email at my website, *www.artbusiness.com*. He explained that the painting was described as being attributed to a famous artist, and now that he owned it, he wanted it appraised. He sent me scans of the painting attached to an email; I took one look at them and immediately saw that the painting in no way resembled the style of the artist to whom the seller had attributed it. Below

245

are actual statements (in italics) made by the seller followed by facts about the painting, determined by myself and a nationally recognized authority on the artist, based on scans of the painting that were provided by the seller.

- *Important oil (on canvas) attributed to...* : First of all, this painting was so amateurishly executed that it wouldn't even be considered important at Bob's U-Name-It Thrift Shop. Second, when a traditional auction house describes a work of art as being attributed to an artist, this is a serious claim which normally means that, in the best judgment of the auction house specialists, the art may be by the artist either in whole or in part. In this online case, anyone familiar with the artist could instantly tell that the painting in no way resembled the style of the artist, which begs the question, "What expert made this attribution?"

- *The painting is on the original canvas*: What's that supposed to mean? Show me a painting that's not on its original canvas, and I'll show you a pile of paint flakes lying on the ground.

- *The painting is from an important estate*: No information about whose estate this was or why the estate was considered important was provided by the seller.

The buyer paid well over $10,000 for this painting. At best, the painting had a retail value of $500-$1,000. The happy ending is that, with support from *www.artbusiness.com* and the independent authority on the artist, the buyer contacted the seller, reported the results of the expert analysis, and was able to get his money back. He was one of the lucky ones.

A Look Ahead

So far, you've learned how to buy original works of art one at a time. This next and final chapter is about how build a collection or, in other words, how to relate those individual works of art to each other in such a way that they make a unified statement about your art-buying experiences.

CHAPTER 26

Building a Collection

Everyone collects something, and that includes you. Perhaps you clip coupons, keep a jar full of pennies, save rubber bands, have 30 paint cans in the garage, hold on to your children's report cards, have piles of old magazines in the basement, save ticket stubs from sporting events, and so on. Whether or not you're aware of it, anytime you accumulate a group of items that share a common characteristic, what you own is a collection, and what you are is a collector.

Your collection, whatever it happens to be, may be great, good, average, or awful. Unfortunately, most collections fall into the average-to-awful category for one simple reason – the people who assemble them are not conscious that what they are doing is collecting. They acquire randomly, haphazardly, arbitrarily, and with little purpose other than that they find the individual items that make up their collections in some way attractive at the moments they decide to keep them. Anyone who goes this route ends up with more of a jumble than a collection.

If you're like most people who buy art, you'll probably buy more than one or two pieces, which means that you should approach your buying as a collector, and follow certain principles in order to maximize the quality of your collection. Admitting to yourself that you are a collector is the first and most important step in either transforming a mediocre collection into a great one or creating a great collection from scratch. Understand at the outset that this in no way involves compromising your tastes; you still buy only what you like, but now you do it with an overall plan.

Building a quality collection has many benefits:

- The whole becomes greater than the sum of the parts.

- The resale values of the individual pieces are increased because of the "company" they keep.

- People are able to better understand and appreciate the art as a grouping than they are if they are looking only at arbitrary isolated pieces.

- You become the expert on what you collect, you learn the dollar values better than people who don't collect what you do, and you learn how to add the best pieces to your collection at the best prices.

- If you build a truly superior collection, you set standards and influence trends among other collectors.

These are goals that any art collector can achieve. Not that much effort is involved, and what's more, once you get a feel for the basics, collecting becomes fun, easy, and rewarding. What you're about to read is a recipe for successful collecting that you can take as far as you feel like taking it. Keep in mind that you don't have to become one of the world's great collectors or spend your every waking moment obsessing about details. You control your art collecting destiny.

Pose the Problem, and Map Out the Solution

A good art collection usually begins as little more than a curiosity about a particular artist or work of art. You see a piece of art you like or a type of art you like, and something about it strikes you favorably or you wonder who the artist is, and you decide that you want to know more. The key, at this early stage, is being able to generalize that curiosity and formulate it into a problem, the solution of which will be revealed through the art that you buy – through your collection.

For example, you go to an art show and see a painting of a coastal scene that you really like. On the one hand, you can find out the price, decide that you can afford it, do your research, buy it, take it home, hang it, and forget about it – this is the arbitrary, random, haphazard way to buy art. On the other hand, you can study the painting, reflect on how it affects you, and ask yourself questions such as the following:

- *What about this painting attracts me?*

- *Does it show a real or an imaginary coastline?*

- *Who is the artist, and what is she like?*

- *Why did the artist paint this picture?*

- *What is the artist trying to accomplish?*

- *How does this painting make me feel?*

- *Would I enjoy owning more paintings by this artist or would I rather own paintings that are similar in style, palette, setting, size, subject matter, or in other ways to this artist's coastal scene, but that are painted by other artists?*

Questions such as these help provide insight into what your preferences are, what attracts you to the art, and what collecting direction you might want to go in. On the basis of your answers, for example, you might consider collecting one of the following types of art:

- New England coastal scenes.

- Landscapes and coastal scenes that show either sunrises or sunsets.

- Paintings by the artist who painted the coastal scene that you like.

- Landscapes and coastal scenes by artists who seek to preserve undeveloped natural habitats or raise our consciousness about the environment.

- Coastal scenes with boats, people, buildings, animals, or specific water-related activities in them.

- Landscapes or coastal scenes that seem to transport you to imaginary, far-away places.

The more of the above types of paintings you see, the more refined the concept of your collection becomes. Thus begins the process of formulating and posing the specific problem that you will set out to answer, help solve, or elaborate on through the art that you buy. Refining the above examples one step further:

- *I want to own paintings that show how various artists paint sunrises over bodies of water.*

- *I love a particular artist's work, and I want my collection to show how his style develops and matures over time. I'll do this by buying one of his paintings per year.*

- *I love Cape Cod, and I want to own art that shows how various artists paint Cape Cod area landmarks.*

- *I want to own paintings by environmentalist artists who believe that we should be sensitive to our natural resources, who are able to convey those beliefs through their art, and whose paintings show endangered species and habitats.*

- *I want to buy seascapes that cost between $500 and $2,000 each.*

- *I want to buy seascapes that are no larger than 10 by 12 inches each.*

- *I want to own paintings that relax me and remind me of places that I've visited in my travels. I also want those paintings to relax my friends, relatives, and guests who visit me at my home.*

The more precisely you state your problem, the more focused you become in your collecting. You define what your art looks like, who creates it, where you buy it, how much you pay for it, what underlying ideas or philosophies it expresses, and so on. Once that's taken care of, the search is on.

Specialize

One of the keys to successful collecting is specialization. With all the millions and millions of artworks available, attempting to see and learn something about everything is a hopeless task. Stating your interests up front and precisely, as discussed above, is the first step in specializing; making a commitment to stay within those guidelines is the next step.

Many people hesitate to narrow their interests due to a concern that they'll be missing out on something. Not to worry. Keep in mind that you can change collecting directions at any time, and even with the most stringent set of constraints, the amount of art you'll have to choose from will amaze you. This may not seem true at first, but any experienced collector will tell you the more you explore and learn about your chosen field, the more you'll be inundated with art that matches your collecting criteria.

The way to miss out on good art is exactly the opposite – by not specializing. With no in-depth understanding of what you're looking at, you won't be able to make the qualitative judgments necessary to recognize the best examples for your collection. You'll also have difficulty evaluating prices, tracking the latest developments in your field, and getting to know the best resources for the art you want to own.

Research

Researching your collection is somewhat different from the standard art and artist research techniques that you learned about in Part III. Once you research a work of art and the artist who created it according to Part III guidelines, you then have to evaluate how well that work of art fits into your collection. You want to make sure that it relates well to the pieces that you already own and, hopefully, that it adds qualities that were previously missing from your collection.

Suppose, for example, that you collect paintings of San Francisco Bay from all time periods. An art dealer offers you a Bay scene painted by Murphy McMurphy in 1903. In addition to evaluating the painting on its own merits and researching Murphy McMurphy, you also have to ask yourself questions like the following:

- *Do I already have this particular view in my collection?*

- *Do I already own enough paintings by Murphy McMurphy?*

- *Is this painting better or more detailed than the McMurphy paintings I already own?*

- *Do I already have enough paintings dating from the turn of the century, or am I weak in this time period?*

- *Is McMurphy as good as or better than most of the artists in my collection?*

- *Was McMurphy known for his paintings of San Francisco Bay?*

- *What characteristics does this painting have that are currently lacking in my collection?*

- *Was McMurphy one of the first artists to paint this view, or did many other artists paint the same view before he did?*

- *Was McMurphy influential in teaching other artists how to paint San Francisco Bay the way that he did?*

Evaluating how well a painting fits into your collection is more informal and intuitive than Part III research is. You and fellow collectors who collect art like the type you collect are the ones who make the rules and establish the criteria by which individual pieces are to be judged. Once those criteria are established, however, you should stick with them and consider every potential purchase in those terms before adding it to your collection. By doing so, you stay focused on your goals, and every work of art you buy relates to all other works in your collection.

Get Involved

Do a good, comprehensive job researching and selecting art, and you'll find yourself immersed within your chosen area of collecting to a degree that few casual buyers ever experience. By getting involved, your collecting adventures can literally turn into a love affair with art. You learn more and more about the objects of your desire; each new experience provides you with a deeper and more profound connection to the art and to the artists who create it.

Investment considerations fade into the background. Fame of the artists and the art's trendiness take a back seat. What your boss or your friends think makes no difference. You are in the process of surrounding yourself with the things you really love, and that's what counts. All accomplished collectors will tell you that this is what happens to them as their collecting progresses. Below are some activities that dedicated, thorough, and involved collectors participate in.

- They try their own hands at creating art that looks like the art they collect.

- They become friends with the artists, experts, scholars, and other members of the art community who share similar collecting interests.

- They support charities, philosophies, organizations, and causes that the artists whose work they collect either support or are part of.

- They do community service work related to their collecting.

- They share their collections with local communities by either giving private tours or lending works of art to local museums, historical societies, or corporations.

- They visit the studios of their favorite artists, watch them create art, and learn how they create it.

- They offer financial support to artists whose work they believe in so that those artists can spend more time creating art and less time trying to make ends meet by working at unrelated jobs that don't allow them any contact with art.

When you find yourself doing these sorts of things, you can consider yourself a total collector. Owning fine art is far more than a money, status, fashion, or trend issue. It is allowing the greater good of the art world to become an essential part of your existence.

Be Complete

A superior collection addresses every aspect of the problem that the collector initially proposes. Not only is his curiosity satisfied, but so is the curiosity of others who come into contact with his collection. Every piece of art becomes like a piece of a puzzle that, when combined with all other art in the collection, forms a whole that illustrates or proves the point that the collector has set out to make.

Suppose, for example, that a collector decides to explore how various mentally, psychologically, and physically challenged individuals portray themselves in their art. He confines his selections to either artist self-portraits or works of art in which the artists place themselves within the compositions. Whenever possible, he also decides to accompany each piece with an explanation from the artist of what his or her portrayal within the art represents.

In order for this collection to be reasonably complete, the art must come from all segments of the mentally, physically, and psychologically challenged communities. If he purchases art from all but the visually impaired, for instance, he will have a gap in his collection. In other words, someone could inquire of the collector, "How do visually impaired individuals portray themselves in their art?" and the collector won't be able to answer by referencing specific pieces in his collection. The types of questions that serious collectors continually ask themselves as they build their collections are as follows.

- *Can anyone question any aspect of my collection?*

- *Do I adequately solve the problem that I've posed for myself?*

- *Is my collection missing anything?*

- *Am I weak in a certain area?*

- *Do I have too much of one thing and not enough of another?*

Keep considerations such as these in mind as you collect, and you'll maintain the evenness and balance characteristic of a quality collection. You may find yourself selling off certain pieces along the way or buying more in areas that you believed, at one point, were adequately represented. You might even modify your goals at various junctures along the way, but that's all part of the process. A collection is an ever-evolving entity.

Organize

Organizing your collection is important for several reasons. First, good organization helps others to understand what you're doing. Second, you can keep track of what you've purchased and fill any gaps with minimal effort. Third, good organization provides you with a better understanding of what your collection means and how it's evolving. No set rules for organizing exist; you decide how to present whatever you've collected.

Before you begin to organize, look around and get a feel for how other collections are organized. Visit museums and see how they present their permanent collections as well as how they arrange their temporary exhibits and traveling shows. The latter two types of collections are especially good to study because they usually don't contain that many pieces, and the text, explanations, and order of the individual pieces are easier to understand in relation to the whole. Historical societies, local museums, libraries, and corporations are also good places to see how collections are arranged. Some of the more common ways that collectors organize their collections are as follows.

- By date.
- By subject matter.
- By geographical region.
- By artist.
- By style.
- By nationality or ethnic group.

Ask yourself questions like those below in order to best organize what you collect.

- *What similarities or differences are apparent in my art?*

- *Can I arrange the pieces in a way that tells a story?*

- *Is any sort of evolutionary or growth process apparent in my art?*

- *What types of changes are consistently evident from one piece to the next?*

- *What arrangement best educates other people about either my values and philosophies or the goals of my collection?*

Experiment with different ways of looking at and organizing your art. Many times, the arrangement that you eventually settle on does not become apparent until you're well along in your collecting. Keeping organizational considerations at the forefront of your buying keeps you focused.

Believe in Yourself

Buy what you want to buy, and collect what you want to collect. Far too many people deny their own dreams, compromise their tastes, follow the crowd, and end up with dull, boring collections. One collection looks just like the next when unimaginative collectors try harder to be correct than they do to collect. This type of buying behavior is all too often based on fears of being rejected, ridiculed, of not doing what's "right," of wasting one's money, and so on.

In a way, fears like those mentioned above are justified. When you're true to yourself and you follow your own inner urges, you become vulnerable to harsh judgments by others who see art differently than you do. Your art tells outsiders revealing things about what you like, what you believe in, what your philosophies are, who you like, and how your mind works. And revealing yourself like this can be scary.

But the positive results of honest collecting far outweigh the negatives. For one thing, you end up owning art that you really love and not art that you feel lukewarm about just because someone else told you to buy it. You call the shots, you direct the show, you have total freedom and control over your actions, and, in the end, you experience a level of freedom that is not easy to come by in this day and age.

Example 1:

Not everyone has tons of discretionary capital to spend on art. Below are ideas for interesting and unusual collections that anyone can afford to make, regardless of their budgets.

- *Everyday objects that people have carved their initials into, made drawings on, painted on, or written words or messages on.* Examples could include pieces of old sidewalk, tree bark, discarded children's' toys, or old signs and advertisements with graffiti on them.

- *Your own art.* Maybe you've always had a secret desire to become an artist. Even if you've never created a single piece of art in your life and have no idea where to begin, give it a try. You could be surprised at the results.

- *Objects that look like art, but really aren't.* Perhaps you've seen an old bent piece of metal by the side of a road or a driftwood branch washed up on a beach that looked like an original sculpture. Put enough of these items together, and people will understand how you see art in the ordinary objects around you.

- *Artist rejects.* This collection would consist of artist mistakes, ideas that didn't work, art that got damaged, and so on. (The fun part about making this collection would be convincing the artists to give their mistakes to you rather than throw them out.)

- Art by people you know, but who aren't artists. Have your friends, co-workers, relatives, and anyone else who means something to you contribute their creative endeavors, whatever they may be, to your collection.

Conclusion

The ultimate secret to forming a gratifying and successful collection is this: Be true to yourself, and never be afraid. Now get out there, have some fun, make your mark, and become a master of the art of buying art!

APPENDIX I

Art Auction Records & Price Guides (Books & CD-ROMS)

1. *Artprice.com Art Price Annual CD-ROM:* Artprice.com, Saint-Romain-au-Mont-d'Or, France, 2006. Published annually. Current edition contains 4.5 million auction records of works of art by 342,000 artists at auctions held from 1991-2006.

2. *Davenport's Art Reference and Price Guide:* LTB Gordonsart, Inc., Phoenix, 2007 (2007/2008 Edition). Best quick artist price reference. This book can also be used as an art index. The current edition lists over 300,000 artists, includes brief biographical as well as price information about the artists, and, like an index, often refers you to other references where you can locate further information. Note that for some artists the price information is given in the form of price ranges instead of as specific auction sales results. Prices that are listed as ranges rather than as specific auction results tend to be subjective. Also available as a CD-ROM with advanced search features.

3. *Gordon's Photography Price Annual International:* LTB Gordonsart, Inc., Phoenix, 2007. Best reference for prices of vintage and collectible photographs. Published annually. Current edition contains over 18,000 auction results. CD-ROM version covers auctions from 1970-2006 and contains over 210,000 auction records.

4. *Gordon's Print Price Annual:* LTB Gordonsart, Inc., Phoenix, AZ, 2007. This auction record compendium is published annually and is the best reference for print auction records. Current edition contains almost 45,000 auction records. CD-ROM version contains auction records for nearly 900,000 prints by nearly 30,000 artists for sales taking place from 1985-2006.

5. *Hislop's Art Sales Index:* Art Sales Index, Ltd., Egham, England, 2006. The only major international art auction record compendium published in book form. Published annually. Current edition has auction results for over 156,000 works of art. Particularly strong on British artists. CD-ROM version has 2.7 million sales results of works of art by over nearly 250,000 artists at auctions held from 1981 through July of 2006.

6. *Hislop's Official International Price Guide To Fine Art, Second Edition:* Random House, New York, 2007. Published every five years. Current edition contains summarized prices for international fine art auctions from August 2005 through July 2006 with nearly

160,000 auction records for over 28,000 artists. Best summarized price guide for the auction market. Use price guides with care; in many cases, they provide only rough approximations of value.

7. *Hislop's Pocket Price Guide*: Art Sales Index, Ltd., Egham, England, 2007. Published Annually. Summarized prices for fine art auctions in the UK during 2006. Current edition contains over 31,000 auction records for nearly 11,000 artists. Best guide for summarized UK auction price results. Use price guides with care; in many cases, they provide only rough approximations of value.

8. *Lawrence's Dealer Print Prices International*: LTB Gordonsart, Inc., Phoenix, 2005. Best reference for retail dealer print prices. No longer published. Most recent edition contains 30,000 price records. CD-ROM version contains records of over 280,000 prints by over 15,000 artists taken from dealer catalogues from 1991-2004.

9. Morris, J. M. *Franklin & James Decade Review of American Artists at Auction, 5/91-5/01*: Franklin & James Publishing, Mansfield, OH, 2001. No longer published. Most recent edition contains nearly 100,000 auction prices. Good, quick comprehensive reference for auction records of American Artists, however increasingly out of date.

10. Rennert, Jack. *Poster Prices VIII*: Poster Auctions International, Inc., NY, 2005. Reference most recommended by poster dealers for auction records of vintage posters. Contains some illustrations. 21,000 sales records from 1985-2004.

11. Theran, Susan. *Leonard's Price Index of Latin American Art at Auction*: Auction Index, Inc., Newton, MA, 1999. 30 years and 30,000 auction records of mostly higher-end works of Latin American art. Also contains 1,100 biographies of Latin American artists. No longer published. Prices are increasingly out of date; bios are still helpful.

APPENDIX II

Internet Art Resources

Note: The following lists are by no means complete but will certainly get you acquainted with art on the internet. The internet is a rapidly changing place with websites coming and going daily, so don't be surprised if, during the course of your research, certain websites have substantially changed formats, services, and even ownership. The focus of these lists is on more established sites that have achieved some level of recognition within the art community.

Websites Offering Art at Fixed Prices

1. *www.absolutearts.com* All-purpose website features art from over 22,000 artists and art galleries, with art news, discussion forums, and more. This website is operated by the same company that operates Worldwide Arts Resources. absolutearts.com, 3678 Loudon Street, Granville, Ohio, 43023. 866.722.9927.
2. *www.guild.com* Juried site, established in 1985, subsequently expanded to the internet, fine and decorative art with a distinct decorative arts orientation. Mail order catalogues available. The Guild, 931 East Main St. Suite 9, Madison, WI 53703. 877.223.4600
3. *www.nextmonet.com* Emerging artists, established artists; art from dealers, galleries, and artists. NextMonet.com, 310 Center Street, Venice, FL 34285. 888.914.5050

All-Purpose Art Websites

1. *www.artcyclopedia.com* Provides basic biographical information about artists, art movements, links to museums, images of art, news, articles, information about major museum shows, and more. Artcyclopedia, 51 Tuscany Hills Terrace N.W., Calgary, Alberta, Canada T3L 2G7. 403.547.1506
2. *www.artinfo.com* Artinfo is the most comprehensive website for the world of art and culture. The site offers mini-sites for hundreds of galleries and museums, extensive global art venue directories, daily updated news and features, expert advice about collecting, editors picks of works for sale around the world, trend stories and exclusive interviews with artists, curators and collectors, the latest art gossip and events photos, video clips, educational

resources, art research tools, and so much more. LTB Media 111 8th Ave, suite 302, New York, NY 10011. 212-447-9555

3. *www.artnet.com* Artnet bills itself as "The Art World Online," and that pretty well sums up the site. Offerings include links and websites for the overwhelming majority of significant national and international art galleries, information about hundreds of thousands of works of art for sale at galleries worldwide, numerous artist websites, an art auction price database with images (fee-based), an auction notification service (fee-based), a superior online art magazine updated frequently, international art market and market trend reports, links to international auction houses, and much more. An excellent all around site. Artnet Worldwide, 61 Broadway, 23rd Floor, New York, NY 10006. 800.427.8638

4. *www.wwar.com* Worldwide Arts Resources offers a variety of art-related services, with numerous links to artists' portfolios, art articles, museums, online exhibitions, other art-related websites, appraisals, art history, art supply resources, and much more. The same company also operates *www.absolutearts.com*, the two sites sharing a large amount of the same content. World Wide Arts Resources, 3678 Loudon Street, Granville, OH 43023. 740.587.3326

Artist and Art Community Websites

1. *www.artscenecal.com* Guide to art galleries and museums in Southern California. Has an excellent calendar of art events plus articles, reviews, and maps to all gallery and museum locations. ArtScene, P.O. Box 2029, Thousand Oaks, CA 91358. 213.482.4357.

2. *www.artistsregister.com* Juried and non-juried sections of art for sale, purchases may be made directly from artists, database lists over 1,500 artists from 12 Western states, artist resources, art links. Operated by WESTAF (Western States Arts Federation) 1743 Wazee Street, Suite 300, Denver, CO 80202. 303.629.1166

3. *dks.thing.net* Best coverage of the New York City area art scene anywhere. Includes an excellent show calendar and information about museums, show reviews, links to art sections of major city newspapers, and much more.

4. *www.sculptor.org* Everything sculpture including links to individual sculptor websites, information on different mediums, technology and sculpture, sculptors classified by subject matters, supplies,

sculpture for sale, sculpture associations, educational section, articles, classifieds, history, events, discussion groups, more.

6. *www.wetcanvas.com* All-purpose arts and artist website including a resource directory of over 200,000 art-related websites, resources for artists, posts by members, online discussion groups, and much more.

Artist and Art Price Research Databases

1. *www.art-sales-index.com* The Art Sales Index database contains over 3.3 million sales records of works of art by over 255,000 artists sold at auctions from 1956 through the present. The site is continually updated as auctions around the world are completed and price results are made public. Semi-annual subscription options range from $225 to $450 for unlimited searches. Short-term subscriptions are also available. Within the near future, Art Sales Index will also include images for its auction records.

2. *www.artfact.com* The artfact.com database contains over 10 million auction results of works of fine art, decorative art, and collectibles at auctions held from 1986 through the present. Many results include images. Approximately 1.5 million records are for works of fine art. The site is continually updated as auctions around the world are completed and price results are made public. Subscription options range from $10 for a one-month partial database usage to $1995 for one-year of unlimited searches on the entire database.

3. *www.artnet.com* Artnet's art auction record database contains 2.9 million records of works of art – many that include images of the art – by 185,000 artists sold at auctions over the past ten years. The site is continually updated as auctions around the world are completed and price results are made public. Costs range from $14.95 per day or $99 per year for unlimited searches with no images (one search allows one user to view all auction records for one artist) to $2000 per year for a maximum of 900 searches with images.

4. *www.artprice.com* A pay-per-use auction record database with 4.5 million auction records of works of art by nearly 350,000 artists sold at auctions held from 1987 to the present. The site is continually updated as auctions around the world are completed and price results are made public. The site also offers databases of artist signature examples, artist biographies, notices of upcoming auctions, and more. User fees range from $1 per unit (one unit allows a user to view one auction record of one work of

art by one artist) when purchased in 20-unit blocks to $499 per year for complete unlimited access to all databases. Unlimited access to the art price database alone is available for $99 per year.

5. *www.artvalue.com* Art auction price database with both free and pay options, less than a year old. The free option allows you to read listings; the pay option includes images of the art that correspond with those listings. The database contains approximately 1.5 million auction records as of July 2007. The interface is a bit awkward, allowing only a maximum of 30 auction records per page, and the more established art price databases are superior, but the free option is a big plus. How long it will stay free is anybody's guess.

6. *www.askart.com* This website contains extensive information on over 52,000 American artists of all time periods including auction prices, images of their art when available, biographical and career data, reference books where additional information can be found, art dealer listings, and more. Subscription options for individual users range from $11.95 for a 24-hour period of access to $21.95 per month of access.

7. *www.findartinfo.com* Pay art auction price database with images, about a year old. You can see very abbreviated auction results at no charge (not much help, but better than nothing); to see complete details, you can pay by day, month, or 6-month periods. Contains only the past several years of auction records, though not necessarily complete depending on the artist . As of July 2007, contains nearly 1.2 million art prices. Reasonable resource for recent art prices, however at this point, the more comprehensive databases are superior in content.

8. *www.gordonsart.com* The LTB Gordonsart, Inc. website offers access to three different databases relating to fine art including prints, posters, illustrated books, Picasso ceramics, and photography with a combined total of approximately 1.5 million records from auction houses and dealers ranging from 1970 through present. The databases are continually updated (with entries often included for preview information before the auctions take place). Some results include images, and that number will increase dramatically in the near future. Semi-annual subscriptions include unlimited searches at any time. Subscription options range from under $70 for a one-month access to a single database to $350 for combined six-month access to *Gordon's Print Price Annual, Gordon's Photography Price International* and *Lawrence's Dealer Print Prices International.* Access to The Art Sales Index auction price

database (see below) is also available through the LTB Gordonsart website.

Online Auction Sites

The major online auction website (not including websites hosted by traditional auction houses such as those listed in Appendix III or mentioned in Chapter 25) is eBay, located at *www.ebay.com*. Numerous smaller online auction sites exist, but the overwhelming majority of items sold at online auctions are sold on *eBay*. (Review Chapter 25 for online auction buying basics.)

If you're a serious dealer or collector, an additional option for playing the online auction (and gallery) game to track specific art and artists through shopping websites that simultaneously search multiple online venues, the two most popular search engines being Froogle (*www.froogle.com*) and Yahoo (*www.yahoo.com*). They may save you the trouble of having to search individual sellers one-by-one, but until you're sure they help, the best procedure is to continue to search individual sites. Eventually, you'll find the overall search format that works best for you.

The Author's Website

Alan Bamberger's website, *www.artbusiness.com*, provides current articles, information, art reference book reviews, and regular updates on art business issues for dealers, collectors, and artists and offers a wide range of services including appraisals, seminars, consulting, collection development, expert witness testimony, and marketing and career consulting for artists. *www.artbusiness.com* is a consumer-oriented website with no conflicts of interest and prides itself on offering fair, honest, and straightforward advice, content, and opinions regarding current art world events and about how the art business works.

APPENDIX III

Art Periodicals

1. *The American Art Review*: P.O. Box 469116, Escondido, CA 92046.
   Phone: 760.738.1178
   Website: *www.amartrev.com*
   Excellent resource for period American art and artists, and contemporary artists who paint in traditional styles. Loads of dealer advertisements, excellent illustrated reviews of regional museum shows from around the country.
2. *Apollo*: 20 Theobald's Road, London WC1X 8PF, England.
   Phone: 44.020.7430.1900
   Website: *www.apollo-magazine.com*
   Articles and advertisements relate primarily to English and Continental fine and decorative arts.
3. *Art & Antiques*: CurtCo/AA, LLC. , 29160 Heathercliff Road, #200, Malibu, CA 90265.
   Phone: 310.589.7700
   Website: *www.artandantiques.net*
   Art articles and advertisements relate primarily to American and European period and contemporary art and also to antiques. Good content on the website.
4. *Art & Auction*: LTB Media, 111 8th Ave, #302, New York, NY 10011.
   Phone: 212.447.9555
   Website: *www.artandauction.com*
   The leading international authority on investing in fine art, antiques and other collectible objects and an independent source of knowledge and analysis. Written for the serious collector, the magazine provides the latest news and insider intelligence on the art market, investigates key trends and showcases the artists who drive the industry.
5. *Art In America*: Brant Publications, Inc., 575 Broadway, New York, NY 10012.
   Phone: 212.941.2800
   Website: *www.artinamericamagazine.com*
   Articles and advertisements relate to international contemporary art with the focus being on contemporary art in America.
6. *The Art Newspaper*: Umberto Allemandi & Co., 70 South Lambeth Road, London SW8 1RL, England.
   Phone: 212.343.0727 (USA)
   Website: *www.theartnewspaper.com*

Superior and scholarly art world news publication. Worldwide, in-depth coverage of galleries, museums, legal issues, collectors, personalities, and much more. A must-have publication for serious dealers, collectors, and scholars. Plenty of great content on the website, some available free, access to their entire article database available for a fee.

7. *Artforum*: Artforum International Magazine, Inc., 350 Seventh Ave., New York, NY 10001.
   Phone: 212.475.4000
   Website: *www.artforum.com*
   Articles and advertisements relate primarily to domestic and international contemporary and avant-garde art. Good online content includes international exhibition announcements.

8. *ARTnews*: Artnews Associates, 48 W. 38th St., New York, NY 10018.
   Phone: 212.398.1690
   Website: *www.artnews.com*
   Articles and advertisements relate primarily to international contemporary art. Good content on the website.

9. *Fine Arts Trader*: Sanbro, Inc., P.O. Box 1273, Randolph, MA 02368.
   Phone: 800.332.5055
   Website: *www.fineartstrader.com*
   Trade publication focusing primarily on American art, but also some European and Asian art. Mostly art gallery advertisements. Good resource for buying, selling, collecting secondary and less well-known artists.

10. *Gallery Guide:* LTB Media, 111 8th Ave, #302, New York, NY 10011.
    Phone: 212.447.9555
    Website: *www.galleryguide.com*
    The definitive monthly resource of information about gallery exhibitions in seven major regions across the United States: New York City, Chicago/Midwest, West Coast, Southeast, Philadelphia/Mid-Atlantic, Boston/New England, and international editions. The user friendly format and detailed maps make it easy for readers to find local galleries and venues.

11. *Journal of the Print World*: Journal of the Print World, Inc., P.O. Box 978, Meredith, NH 03253-0978.
    Phone: 603.279.6479
    Website: *www.journaloftheprintworld.com*
    Important resource for buying, selling, and collecting of prints, drawings, and photographs. Contains information about museum and library exhibitions, dealer catalogues, auction reviews, more.

12. *The Magazine Antiques*: TMA, 575 Broadway, New York, NY 10012.
    Phone: 212.941.2800

Website: *www.themagazineantiques.com*
Art articles and advertisements relate primarily to pre-1940 American art and artists. Good resource for advertisements of major American art dealers who specialize in period American art. Some European dealers also advertise.

13. *Modern Painters:* LTB Media, 111 8th Ave, #302, New York, NY 10011.

Phone: 212.447.9555

Website: *www.modernpainters.co.uk*

The definitive international source of commentary and analysis of contemporary art and culture. The magazine offers a direct and uncompromising approach to exploring art in every aspect along with photography, film, architecture, books, dance and design.

14. *Museums:* LTB Media, 111 8th Ave, #302, New York, NY 10011.

Phone: 212.447.9555

Website: *www.artinfo.com/museums*

Offering comprehensive information on exhibitions and events in the New York area. User-friendly editorial and knowledgeable recommendations, best source for a broad audience of affluent and highly educated readers who plan their leisure activities with local and worldwide exhibitions in mind.

Note: There are numerous additional local, regional, national, and international art-related periodicals, especially ones that focus exclusively on specific areas of collecting. Check with art dealers, collectors, art librarians, and curators to see which best suit your needs.

APPENDIX IV

Artist Indexes

1. *Art Index*: The H.W. Wilson Company, Bronx, NY. Published quarterly. This publication indexes articles and ads of over 450 art periodicals from around the world. It is extremely comprehensive and can be quite valuable in not only locating information about specific artists, but also in locating illustrations of works by those artists and names of dealers who deal in their art. All major art libraries subscribe to it and it is accessible online for a fee. Use it whenever you get the chance. *www.hwwilson.com*

2. *The Artists of the World: Bio-bibliographical index A-Z*: K.G. Saur, Munich, 2000. 10 Volume set indexes and provides basic biographical information on over 350,000 artists.

3. Busse, Joachim. *Internationales Handbuch Aller Maler und Bildhauer Des 19. Jahrhunderts*: Busse Kunst Dokumentation GmbH, Wiesbaden, 1977. This important and comprehensive index contains 89,000 entries of 19th century painters and sculptors and is particularly strong on European.

4. Caplan, H. H. and Creps, Bob. *Encyclopedia of Artist Signatures, Symbols, and Monograms*: Dealer's Choice Books, Land O' Lakes, FL, 1999. Over 25,000 cross-indexed signature examples of American, European, Australian, Latin American, Russian, and Canadian artists. Best signature index.

5. Castagno, John. *Artists as Illustrators: An International Directory With Signatures and Monograms, 1800-Present*: Scarecrow Press, Metuchen, NJ, 1989. If you collect illustration art, particularly by American illustrators, this book is for you. It's also good for European illustrators. Contains signature examples.

6. *Davenport's Art Reference and Price Guide*: LTB Gordonsart, Inc., Phoenix, AZ 2007 (2007/2008 Edition). Please see Appendix I (Art Auction Records & Price Guides - Books & CD-ROMS) for a full description. Also available on CD-ROM. *www.gordonsart.com*

7. Edwards, Gary. *International Guide to Nineteenth-Century Photographers and Their Works*. G.K. Hall & Co., Boston, 1988. Over 4,000 photographers of all nationalities. Much information taken from dealer and auction catalogues.

8. Havlice, P.P. *Index to Artistic Biography*: Scarecrow Press, Metuchen, NJ, 1973, 2 vols.; first supplement, 1981. Best for researching American artists, but also good for European.

Dealers and collectors will tell you that this is one of the more frequently consulted art reference indexes. Use it regularly.

9. Havlice, P.P. *World Painting Index*: Scarecrow Press, Metuchen, NJ, 1977, 2 vols.; first supplement, 2 vols., 1982. Use this reference whenever you want to locate publications that contain illustrations of art by whatever artists you happen to be researching.

10. Mallett, D.T. *Mallett's Index of Artists*: Peter Smith, New York, 1948, 2 vols. This index is a little out of date, but still worthwhile to check, especially if you are collecting art by artists who were active before 1950. Strong on American, adequate on European.

11. McNeil, Barbara. *Artist Biographies Master Index*: Gale Research Co., Detroit, MI, 1986. This index lists not only artists, but also photographers, craftspeople, illustrators, designers, graphic artists, and architects. Always an important index to check especially when you are researching less well-known artists. Strong on American, adequate on European.

12. Meyer, George H. *Folk Artists Biographical Index*: Gale Research Company, Detroit, MI, 1987. Essential to check if you collect American folk art. Lists artists who were active from the seventeenth century right on through to the present. Not necessary to check otherwise.

13. Palmquist, Peter E., editor. *Photographers, A Sourcebook for Historical Research*: Carl Mautz Publishing, Nevada City, CA, 2000. Includes a list of directories of photographers of all time periods and all nationalities, organized by country, and helpful articles and instructions on how to research photographers.

APPENDIX V

Artist Encyclopedias

1. Benezit, Emmanuel. *Dictionnaire critique et documentaire des peintres, sculpteurs, desinateurs et graveurs, de tous le temps et tous le pays:* Librarie Grund, Paris, 1999, 14 vols. Includes artists from around the world, particularly strong on European. Also available translated into English, published in 2006. *www.gordonsart.com*

2. Bihalji-Merin, Oto. *World Encyclopedia of Naive Art:* Scala/Philip Wilson, Yugoslavia, 1985. If you like to buy folk or naive art, this reference is for you. Contains numerous color illustrations.

3. Comanducci, A.M. *Dizionario illustrato del Pittori, Disegnatori e Incisori Italiani Moderni e Contemporanei:* Luigi Patuzzi Editore, Milan, 1970, 5 vols. Essential to check if you like to buy art by modern Italian artists. Contains numerous illustrations.

4. Creps, Bob. *Biographical Encyclopedia of American Painters, Sculptors & Engravers of the U.S., Colonial to 2002.* 2 volumes. Dealer's Choice Books, Land O' Lakes, FL, 2002. Recommended reference for American artists of all time periods. Contains numerous signature examples, many new, and updated artist biographical information culled from over 600 reference resources on American art and artists. Also includes data on nearly 5,000 living artists.

5. Gesualdo, Vincente. *Enciclopedia del Arte en America:* Bibliografica Omeba, Buenos Aires, 1968, 5 vols. This is the encyclopedia for you if you like to buy art by Latin American artists. Contains black and white illustrations.

6. Scheen, Pieter A. *Lexicon Nederlandse Beeldende Kunstenaars, 1750-1950:* Gravenhage, Netherlands, 1969, 2 vols. Lists artists who were active in the Netherlands between 1750 and 1950.

7. Thieme, Ulrich and Becker, Felix. *Allgemeines Lexikon der Bildenden Kunstler:* Seemann, Leipzig, 1908-1950, 37 vols. This is the best and most comprehensive artist encyclopedia. It lists artists from around the world who were active from the earliest times up through 1950, but is particularly strong on Europeans. Many times you will find an artist listed here who is listed nowhere else. Currently being revised and enlarged by *www.saur.de*.

8. Various Authors. *The Artists of the World. Biobibliographical Index, A-Z:* K.G. Saur, Munich, 1999-2000. Ten Volumes.. Contains information on over 350,000 artists. *www.saur.de*

9. Various Authors. *Grove Dictionary of Art*: Grove's Dictionaries, Inc.,
    NY, 1999. Encyclopedia of 45,000 articles covering art and
    artists worldwide. Covers all forms of the visual arts: painting,
    sculpture, architecture, graphic and decorative arts, and
    photography, from prehistory to the present. *www.groveart.com*
10. Vollmer, Hans. *Allgemeines Lexicon der Bildenden Kunstler des 20.
    Jahrhunderts*: E.A. Seamann, Germany, 1996-1997. Check this
    reference if you collect art by twentieth century artists. Includes
    artists from around the world, but is particularly strong on
    Europeans. 6 Volumes. *www.saur.de*

APPENDIX VI

Artist Dictionaries

1. Cederholm, Theresa D. *Afro-American Artists, A Bio-bibliographical Directory*: Boston Public Library, Boston, 1973. Major African-American artist reference.

2. Cummings, Paul. *Dictionary of Contemporary American Artists*: St. Martins Press, Inc., New York, 1994. Good for researching American artists who began their careers after 1950.

3. Falk, Peter H. *Who Was Who in American Art*: Sound View Press, Madison, CT, 1999. 3 Volumes. This is a superior single reference for researching American artists who were active at any time from the last quarter of the nineteenth century through 1975. It is primarily a condensation of artist listings from a series of books published between those years called *American Art Annuals* and the first four volumes of another series called *Who's Who in American Art*, but numerous other references on American art and artists were consulted. Contains a few signature examples.

4. Groce, George C. and Wallace, David H. *The New York Historical Society's Dictionary of Artists in America, 1564-1860*: Yale University Press, New Haven, 1957. This is the best single reference for researching American artists who were active at any time before 1860.

5. Johnson, J. and Greutzner, A. *The Dictionary of British Artists, 1880-1940:* Antique Collectors' Club, England, 1984. The title of this book is self-explanatory.

6. Krantz, Les. *American Artists, an illustrated survey of leading contemporary Americans*: Facts on File Publications, New York, 1985. Best for researching American artists who began their careers after 1950. Each listing contains descriptive statements about the artist's art in addition to the usual biographical data. The book is also illustrated.

7. Lester, Patrick D. *Biographical Directory of Native American Painters*: Sir Publications, Tulsa, OK, 1995. Best reference for American Indian artists.

8. Mackay, James. *Dictionary of Sculptors in Bronze*: Antique Collectors' Club, Suffolk, England, 1977. Biographical information on 8,500 sculptors primarily from the 18th through early 20th centuries.

9. Milner, John. *A Dictionary of Russian and Soviet Artists, 1420-1970*. Antique Collectors Club, England, 1993. Best quick reference on the subject. Contains illustrations.

10. Naylor, Colin. *Contemporary Artists*: St. James Press, Chicago, 1989. This dictionary is recommended for researching contemporary artists from around the world. Most useful when researching artists who began their careers after 1950.

11. Opitz, Glenn B. *Dictionary of American Sculptors, 18th Century to the Present*: Apollo Book, Poughkeepsie, NY, 1984. If you collect American sculpture, this book is an absolute necessity. Has illustrations at the rear of the book.

12. Opitz, Glenn B. *Mantle Fielding's Dictionary of American Painters, Sculptors & Engravers*: Apollo Book, Poughkeepsie, NY, 1986. This book was once a standard art business reference, but has since been superceded by more specialized and comprehensive references. Still good to check, though. Primarily covers American artists who were active before 1940.

13. Petteys, Chris. *Dictionary of Women Artists*: G.K. Hall, Boston, 1985. This extremely well-researched dictionary contains information about women artists from around the world who were active before 1900. It also has a great bibliography.

14. Wood, Christopher. *The Dictionary of Victorian Painters*: Antique Collectors' Club, England, 1981. Lists British artists who were active between 1837 and 1901. Contains about 500 illustrations that cover the full scope of Victorian painting. Excellent reference.

15. Zellman, Michael D. *300 Years of American Art*: Wellfleet Press, Secaucus, NJ, 1987, 2 vols. This dictionary lists over 800 American painters and covers the time period from the late seventeenth through the mid twentieth centuries. Artist listings are comprehensive. Each contains at least one color illustration, many also contain market information which, unfortunately, is already well outdated. This is one of the best and most unique American art reference books ever published.

APPENDIX VII

Art Annuals and Directories

1. *American Art Annual*: American Federation of Arts, Washington, DC, 1898-1936, 33 vols. This is an excellent source of information about American artists who were active during this time period. Any major art library has the entire set of AAA's in their reference section.

2. *Art in America Annual Guide to Galleries, Museums, Artists*: Special issue of "Art in America" magazine published every August by Brant Publications, New York, NY. Contains thousands of listings of art galleries, museums, artists, private dealers, print dealers, and so on. Focus is on contemporary American artists, but also includes information about a number of resources for period American art collectors. *www.artinamericamagazine.com*

3. *International Auction House Directory*: Gordon's Art Reference, Phoenix, AZ, 2001. Good source for auction house locations and contact information, listing over 5,000 national and international. In addition to normal contact information, you will find specialty departments and representatives (including phone and fax). It also contains three great indices for locating an auction house by region or specialty or region and specialty. This directory is no longer in print, and contact information for certain auction houses may be somewhat out of date. *www.gordonsart.com*

4. *International Directory of Arts*: K. G. Saur, Munich, 2006. The 2007 edition is 3 Volumes, and contains more than 142,000 addresses including phone, fax, and website information. This reference is extremely comprehensive and lists tens of thousands of museums, universities, artists, art galleries, auctions, book publishers, periodicals, booksellers, art restorers, and more. The closest thing to an almanac of the art world. *www.saur.de*

5. *Official Museum Directory*: National Register Publishing, New Providence, NJ, 2007. Best annual directory of American museums, historical sites, and similar institutions. Current edition contains basic information on over 9,400 total museums. Listings include collections, specialties, personnel, exhibitions, contact information, and more. *www.nationalregisterpublishing.com*

6. *Who's Who in American Art*: Marquis Who's Who, New Providence, NJ, published since 1936, currently in its 27th edition for the years 2007-2008. Published every two years, this is the best

Alan Bamberger

source of basic information about American artists who have been active at any time between 1936 and the present. The more recent editions also list art curators, art scholars, art librarians, art writers, art critics, art collectors, and other art-related personalities. *www.marquiswhoswho.com*

APPENDIX VIII

Significant American Auction Houses

1. *Altermann Galleries* 225 Canyon Road, Santa Fe, NM 87501. 505.983.1590. *www.altermann.com*

2. *Bonhams and Butterfields* 220 San Bruno Ave., San Francisco, CA 94103. 415.861.7500. *www.bonhams.com/us/*

3. *Christie's* 20 Rockefeller Plaza, New York, New York 10020. 212.636.2000. *www.christies.com*

4. *William Doyle Galleries* 175 East 87th St., New York, NY 10128. 212.427.2730. *www.doylenewyork.com*

5. *Du Mouchelles* 409 East Jefferson Ave., Detroit, MI 48226. 313.963.6255. *www.dumouchelles.com*

6. *Eldred's Auctioneers.* 1483 Route 6A, Box 796, East Dennis, MA 02641. 508.385.3116. *www.eldreds.com*

7. *Samuel T. Freeman and Company* 1808 Chestnut St., Philadelphia, PA 19103. 215.563.9275. *www.freemansauction.com*

8. *Leslie Hindman Auctioneers* 122 North Aberdeen Street, Chicago, IL 60607. 312.280.1212. *www.lesliehindman.com*

9. *James D. Julia Auctioneer* Route 203, Skowhegan Road, ME 04937. 207.453.7125. *www.juliaauctions.com*

10. *John Moran Auctioneers* 735 West Woodbury Rd., Altadena, CA 91001. 626.793-.1833. *www.johnmoran.com*

11. *Neal Auction Company.* 4038 Magazine St., New Orleans, LA 70115. 800.467.5329. *www.nealauction.com*

12. *Phillips, de Pury & Company* 450 West 15th Street, New York NY 10011. 212.940.1200. *www.phillipsdepury.com*

13. *Schrager Auction Galleries, Ltd.* 2915 North Sherman, Milwaukee, WI 53210. 414.873.3738. *www.schragerauction.com*

14. *Skinner Inc.* 63 Park Plaza, Boston, MA 02116. 617.350.5400. *www.skinnerinc.com*

15. *Sotheby's* 1334 York Ave., New York, NY 10021. 212.606.7000. *www.sothebys.com*

16. *Swann Galleries* 104 East 25th St., New York, NY 10010. 212.254.4710. *www.swanngalleries.com*

17. *Adam A. Weschler and Son, Inc.* 909 E St. NW, Washington, DC 20004. 800.331.1430 or 202.628.1281. *www.weschlers.com*

For more detailed information about domestic and international auction houses, consult the *International Auction House Directory* published by Gordon's Art Reference (see Appendix XI, Art Reference Booksellers). This reference, published in 2001 and now out of print, contains names and contact information for over 5,000 international auction houses (some contact information may be out of date). You can also search for auction companies online, particularly at some of the major art price database websites listed in Appendix II.

APPENDIX IX

American Appraiser Associations

1. *American Society of Appraisers*
   555 Herndon Parkway, Suite 125
   Herndon, VA 20170
   Phone: 703.478.2228
   Fax: 703.742.8471
   www.appraisers.org

2. *Appraisers Association of America*
   386 Park Avenue South, Suite 2000
   New York, NY 10016
   Phone: 212.889.5404
   Fax: 212.889.5503
   www.appraisersassoc.org

3. *Association of Online Appraisers, Inc.*
   P.O. Box 2049
   Frederick, MD 21702-1049
   Phone: 301-228-2279
   Fax: 301-695-6491
   www.aoaonline.org

4. *International Fine Art Appraisers*
   478 West Broadway
   New York, NY 10012
   Phone: 212.475.0622
   Fax: 212.475.5709
   www.ifaacertified.com

5. *International Society of Appraisers*
   1131 SW 7th St. Suite 105
   Renton, WA 98057-1215
   Phone: 206.241.0359
   Fax: 206.241.0436
   www.isa-appraisers.org

When choosing appraisers, the most important questions to ask are whether they specialize in appraising art – particularly the kinds that you own – and how long they've been appraising it, not which associations they belong to or how long they've belonged. In some instances, independent appraisers with no organizational affiliations (including associations of independent appraisers) may be the most qualified individuals for appraising certain types of art.

APPENDIX X

Art Dealer Associations

1. *Art and Antique Dealers League of America, Inc.*
   1040 Madison Ave.
   New York, NY 10021
   Phone: 212.879.7558
   www.artandantiquedealersleague.org

2. *Art Dealers Association of America*
   575 Madison Ave.
   New York, NY 10022
   Phone: 212.940.8590
   www.artdealers.org

3. *Association of International Photography Art Dealers*
   1767 P Street, NW, Suite 200
   Washington, DC 20036
   Phone: 202.986.0105
   www.aipad.com

4. *Fine Art Dealers Association*
   Phone: 800.656.9278
   www.fada.com

5. *International Fine Print Dealers Association*
   15 Gramercy Park South, Suite 7A
   New York, NY 10003
   Phone: 212.674.6095
   www.printdealers.com

6. *National Antique and Art Dealers Association of America*
   220 East 57th Street
   New York, NY 10022
   Phone: 212.826.9707
   www.naadaa.org

7. *Private Art Dealers Association*
   P.O. Box 872
   Lenox Hill Station
   New York, NY 10021
   Phone: 212.572.0772
   www.pada.net

APPENDIX XI

Art Reference Booksellers

1. *Antique Collector's Club Ltd., Eastworks*
   116 Pleasant St.
   Easthampton, MA 01027
   Phone: 800.252.5231 (413.529.0862)
   www.antique-acc.com

2. *Hennessey + Ingalls*
   214 Wilshire Blvd.
   Santa Monica, CA 90401
   310.458.9074
   www.hennesseyingalls.com

3. *LTB Gordonsart, Inc.*
   13201 N. 35th Avenue, Suite B-20
   Phoenix, AZ 85209
   Phone: 800.892.4622 (602.253.6948)
   www.gordonsart.com

4. *Ursus Books Ltd.*
   981 Madison Ave.
   New York, NY 10021
   Phone: 212.772.8787
   www.ursusbooks.com

Note: For out-of-print, hard-to-find, and rare art book titles, visit the Antiquarian Booksellers Association of America website (*www.abaa.org*) and search their membership directory for booksellers specializing in the types of art that you like to buy. If you know the title and/or author of the book you're looking for, you can also search international online databases of new, used, rare, and out-of-print books by going to *www.addall.com*, *www.bookfinder.com*, *www.abebooks.com*, or *www.alibris.com*.